D1212043

STUDIES IN INTERDISCIPLINARY HISTORY

Hunger and History

Hunger and History

The Impact of Changing Food Production and Consumption Patterns on Society

Edited by ROBERT I. ROTBERG and THEODORE K. RABB

Contributors:

Ester Boserup
Ann G. Carmichael
Philip D. Curtin
Roderick C. Floud
Robert W. Fogel
Olwen Hufton
Massimo Livi-Bacci
Michelle B. McAlpin
Thomas McKeown
Gretel H. Pelto and Pertti J. Pelto

Robert I. Rotberg
Roger Schofield
Nevin S. Scrimshaw
Julian L. Simon
Santhebachahalli G. Srikantia
Carl E. Taylor
Joan Thirsk
Louise A. Tilly
Etienne van de Walle
Susan Cotts Watkins

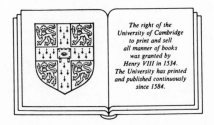

The right of the
University of Cambridge
to print and sell
all manner of books
was granted by
Henry VIII in 1534.
The University has printed
and published continuously
since 1584.

CAMBRIDGE UNIVERSITY PRESS

CAMBRIDGE

LONDON   NEW YORK   NEW ROCHELLE

MELBOURNE   SYDNEY

Published by the Press Syndicate of the University of Cambridge
The Pitt Building, Trumpington Street, Cambridge CB2 1 RP
32 East 57th Street, New York, NY 10022, USA
10 Stamford Road, Oakleigh, Melbourne 3166, Australia

© 1983 by the Massachusetts Institute of Technology and the editors of *The Journal of Interdisciplinary History*

First published by Cambridge University Press 1985
Reprinted 1986
Printed in the United States of America

Library of Congress Cataloging in Publication Data

Main entry under title:

Hunger and history.

Originally published as The Journal of interdisciplinary history, v. XIV, no. 2, Autumn 1983.

1. Food supply—History—Addresses, essays, lectures. 2. Food consumption—History—Addresses, essays, lectures. 3. Nutrition—History—Addresses, essays, lectures. 4. Poverty—History—Addresses, essays, lectures. 5. Malnutrition—History—Addresses, essays, lectures. I. Rabb, Theodore K. II. Rotberg, Robert I. III. Boserup, Ester.

HD9000.5.H83   1985   363.8'09   84-21423

ISBN 0 521 30438 5 hard covers

ISBN 0 521 31505 0 paperback

Contents

Hunger and History

Robert I. Rotberg

Nutrition and History Nourishment is fundamental. The story of human history, reduced to essentials, revolves around the basic requirements for life. In prehistoric times people survived by adapting to the available resources; initially they gathered, scavenged, and hunted. Their successors gained a greater control over food supplies when they invented settled agriculture and animal husbandry. Later still, communities competed for control over granaries or for the riches with which to assure themselves fuller lives. Throughout, and into the contemporary period, humankind has been differentially endowed according to terrestrial geography, as a result of cycles of climatic fortune and misfortune, and as a consequence of genetically or randomly induced susceptibilities to infection or disease. Man has had to adapt and sustain himself by varying or expanding the basic kinds or forms of his nutritional staples, by migration, or by employing remarkable ingenuities to alter his environment.

Pestilence, flood, drought, volcanic eruptions, war, and other disasters have occasioned episodes of seasonal hunger, endemic undernutrition, or widespread starvation. The vicissitudes of human survival are many, obvious, and underchronicled, as are the ways in which whole populations have or have not coped.

Despite the importance of food in human history, we have few reliable records on which to base a sensible analysis of nutrition and malnutrition in the past. Yet, what is striking is the extent to which many modern scientists who have written on the diets or food insufficiencies of the past have misinterpreted the historical record. Their apocalyptic conclusions have often been founded on anecdotal or impressionistic evidence which, when reanalyzed according to the canons of contemporary demographic and historical scholarship, prove insufficient or inconclusive. Likewise, historians and historical demographers have for generations assumed commonsensical correlations between food intake, disease, and the mechanisms which push or pull populations

Robert I. Rotberg is Professor of Political Science and History at The Massachusetts Institute of Technology and is co-editor of *The Journal of Interdisciplinary History*. He is the editor of *Imperialism, Colonialism, and Hunger: East and Central Africa* (Lexington, Mass., 1983).

and affect their stability. Those correlations, however, are belied by contemporary scientific and medical experience and experimentation. Hence, the gathering of historians, demographers, economists, food scientists, and nutritionists at the Villa Serbelloni, Bellagio, Italy, in 1982 proved unusually productive of interdisciplinary ferment and insight. (The meeting was made possible through the generosity of the Humanities Division of the Rockefeller Foundation.) The conference participants focused on the role of food in history and the real or false impact of its sufficiency or insufficiency on variables such as fertility, morbidity, and mortality. They examined the meaning of those nutrition-linked factors for the more macroscopic movements that usually comprise the meat of history.

In an interdisciplinary setting it was to be expected that historians, social scientists, and food scientists would quickly appreciate how much each branch of learning could contribute to our overall understanding of the definition, as well as the resolution, of important questions. One central conclusion of this interaction was an agreement on the vast inadequacy of nearly all existing understandings of the influence of nutrition in past human societies. Following the Bellagio conference, the results of which were originally published as an entire issue of the *Journal of Interdisciplinary History*, XIV (Autumn, 1983), and are now included in their entirety and without alteration in this first volume of a series of books based on issues of the *Journal*, those who study the past will have to revise their general and specific conceptualizations of the food-history chain, and of each of its crucial links. Roger Schofield, Ann Carmichael, Joan Thirsk, and Philip Curtin make that point in different ways for different periods and cultures in their contributions to this volume. Because of the lack of direct data on food intake and nutrition, Robert Fogel and his colleagues present an elaborate and ingenious justification for using stature as a proxy, much as wine yields have been used as proxies for otherwise nonexistent data about the climates of past times.[1]

---

1 Christian Pfister, "The Little Ice Age: Thermal and Wetness Indices for Central Europe," *Journal of Interdisciplinary History*, X (1980), 665–696; Emmanuel Le Roy Ladurie and Micheline Baulant, "Grape Harvests from the Fifteenth through the Nineteenth Centuries," *ibid.*, 839–849.

The diverse essays of this volume reveal how much of the past can be better understood if the distinctions which are obvious to clinicians and nutritionists, although obscure to traditionally trained historians, are assimilated by those who devote their efforts to unravelling the social and political contours of the past. Likewise, this volume challenges assumptions about the mechanisms of population growth and decline, as well as theories of how populations react or adapt to constraints on their resource endowments.

This is a volume that directs attention to crucial underresearched questions concerning the relationship between food and modern history. With Malthusian paradigms very much a matter of contention, it explores limits to growth in theory and history, with diametrically opposed positions represented in the provocative articles by Ester Boserup, Julian Simon, Susan Watkins and Etienne van de Walle, and Schofield. There is the basis of a debate between Thomas McKeown and Carmichael over the impact in past times of nutrition on infection and disease and the impact of morbidity on population size. Those authors, and others, examine the influence of fertility and mortality on population size, and the relationship of nutrition and malnutrition to those basic variables. The nature of food shortages and famines, their impact on the ebb and flow of populations over time, and the relevance of such phenomena to political and social history are examined comparatively by Olwen Hufton and Louise Tilly (for Europe), and Michelle McAlpin and Santhebachahalli G. Srikantia (for India).

Another theme which most of the articles explore is the extent to which research on contemporary issues of fertility, morbidity, and mortality by food scientists and nutritionists is relevant for earlier periods. To what extent is our knowledge of the links between today's levels of nutrition and disease applicable to earlier centuries, different cultures, and distinctive associations with foodstuffs? Nevin Scrimshaw addresses those questions explicitly in the concluding essay of this volume.

Synergy—in this case the combined impact on each other of one or more of the variables of human well-being—was much discussed at Bellagio. It is explained in the report on contemporary nutritional practice by Carl Taylor and in the review by Carmichael of our understanding of the past. It also is a central aspect of the diagrams and charts which formed the basis of a special session of the Bellagio meeting. This session enhanced the interdisciplinary understanding of the participants and gave them a heightened appreciation of the assumptions, as well as the fundamental intellectual constructions, of the diverse disciplines represented there.

Although the prose which now accompanies the charts cannot fully convey the intellectual struggle and excitement of the chart session, the charts themselves are meant to suggest how historians, scientists, and social scientists jointly ought to conceptualize nutrition, malnutrition, and the synergistic links between nutrition, infection, and disease. Utilizing this new conceptual underpinning, as well as the findings and research strategies which are both explicit and implicit in the articles that follow, historians and colleagues from other disciplines will be better equipped to quantify and qualify their conclusions about the extent to which historical events have been influenced by nutritionally related or induced realities.

The articles in the volume raise as many new questions as they provide answers. Future research on nutrition and history will reexamine the findings of these articles and also challenge the conclusions of one or another of the population growth models which are developed by the contributors to the volume. It is clear from the articles and discussions at Bellagio that 1) nutritionists need to decide what constitutes adequate data on food sufficiency in the various conditions of the present, so that historians can use the same criteria to investigate the different circumstances of the past; 2) historians and food scientists need to evaluate proxy data (like stature) for nutrition in the past and to seek out and fashion additional kinds of proxies for the otherwise unavailable data about nutrition in earlier times; 3) historians and historical demographers need to develop retrospective methods of measuring adult nutrition and adult output since most of our data for the past are heavily dependent upon figures for the early childhood years; 4) those who work on the past will want to define performance—should it be based on cognition, stature, mortality, longevity, productivity, or the stability of society? 5) historians will want to seek a measure for the impact of nutrition on societal creativity; and 6) historians will need to assess the effect of deficiency diseases or hidden malnutrition on political or social developments.

A reading of the essays in this volume makes the relevance and the importance of these tasks more comprehensible. The essays establish the existing parameters of the state of our knowledge of the contribution of nutrition to history, place the Malthusian questions at the center of a continuing debate among different disciplines, and reflect at least some of the exciting intellectual understanding and clarification which was generated during the conference at Bellagio.

Susan Cotts Watkins and Etienne van de Walle

Nutrition, Mortality, and Population Size: Malthus' Court of Last Resort

The notion of an equilibrium between population and resources is pervasive and persuasive. Historians have drawn on Malthus to explain periods of population growth as well as population stagnation. A notable example is Le Roy Ladurie's argument that between the thirteenth and eighteenth centuries the population size of France tended toward the carrying capacity of the land. The Malthusian logic which insists that food supplies ultimately constrain population growth is compelling. The relevance of the Malthusian equilibrium between resources and population is, however, often exaggerated, and even when the Malthus scissors appear to be closing, the mechanisms linking fertility and mortality to food supplies require empirical support which is not yet, as we show, convincing.[1]

Malthus, who was fond of aquatic metaphors, said that a population can grow freely to fill the economic space, as water fills a pool, but the maximum level of the pool is fixed by the point of overflow. In other words, there is an upper bound to the ratio of population and resources. A logical corollary is that at this upper bound there must also be an equilibrium between the rate of entry into the population and the rate of exit. At any given level of resources, then, assuming unchanging technology with which to exploit and transport these resources and unchanging social arrangements which determine their distribution, there is a maximum population size at which the net rate of population growth must be zero.

Susan Cotts Watkins is Assistant Professor of Sociology at the University of Pennsylvania. Etienne van de Walle is Professor of Demography at the University of Pennsylvania. He is the author of *The Female Population of France in the Nineteenth Century* (Princeton, 1974).

1   Emmanuel Le Roy Ladurie, *Les paysans de Languedoc* (Paris, 1966).

There are thus two equilibria: that between birth rates and death rates, and that between population size and resources. Some have proposed that the two are linked by homeostatic adjustment mechanisms which, viewed literally, implies that populations are systems responding to logical rules, and that the forces that determine the level of vital rates are largely endogenous to that system. Thus, Wrigley and Schofield have proposed that in pre-industrial England the relation between population and resources was characteristically dominated by negative feedback. In a typical sequence a rise in real income would lead to an earlier age at marriage in the population. This would result in higher overall fertility and a larger population size, hence pressure on food supplies and eventually either a fall in nuptiality and therefore in overall fertility or a rise in mortality.[2]

Finely tuned homeostatic mechanisms permit a comfortable balance between prudent populations and their resources, a low-pressure equilibrium in which per capita resources are above, and perhaps well above, the minimum necessary for survival. Cruder versions of the story rely more heavily upon mortality to bring feckless populations back into line: they depict a high-pressure equilibrium in which per capita resources are close to the minimum necessary for survival, and in which the threat of starvation is ever present.

In the system of homeostatic adjustment mechanisms, it is only if neither impediments to the stream of births nor death rates from causes unrelated to resources are sufficient to maintain the necessary balances that appeal will be made to what is in effect Malthus' court of last resort: deaths from famine, or chronic mortality related to chronic scarcity. Malnutrition, then, is the logical ultimate constraint in the system of homeostatic mechanisms which has been postulated to keep a population within the bounds of its resources.

This logic is depicted in the classical graphical presentation of the Malthusian equilibrium. For a certain maximum population size, the average product, which is also the average consumption,

2 E. Anthony Wrigley and Roger S. Schofield, *The Population History of England 1541–1871: A Reconstruction* (Cambridge, Mass., 1981), 33–65. See also Jacques Dupâquier, "De l'animal à l'homme: le mécanisme autorégulateur des populations traditionelles," *Revue de l'Institut de Sociologie* (Brussels), II (1972), 177–211.

intersects the subsistence level, and returns diminish as the population grows beyond the point of intersection. Eventually there must exist a point at which real income per head reaches a level below which mortality will prevent further population growth.

This type of graphical presentation is, however, too schematic to indicate the mechanisms involved; additional refinements must be introduced. We wish to call attention to three of these. First, real income per head is an average notion; very few people actually consume at the average level. Second, it is difficult to determine a recognizable minimum of subsistence. Third, there is a need to distinguish between endogenous and exogenous mortality.

First, although it is customary to use an average real income per head as a measure of the balance between population and resources, some modern analysts of populations living close to the margin of subsistence insist on the role of distribution in designating who is going to die, or even whether people are going to die. Because of the dramatic changes in transportation, which have permitted easier movement of food from surplus to deficit areas, questions of distribution have often been seen as involving transportation technology or infrastructure that make the physical transfer of resources possible. Others, however, have stressed the importance of considering distribution more broadly, emphasizing exchange entitlement, or access to resources rather than food production and supply.[3]

Second, the minimum level of subsistence has often been defined with reference to other needs as well as those that ensure continuance of life itself. There is, however, an imaginable minimum level of subsistence below which one dies, although this may not be the same for all individuals or for all populations. Malthus himself believed that the Chinese were subsisting on a diet that would have meant starvation for Europeans. Populations can be "forced," he said; they can grow accustomed to living on the smallest possible quantity of food, a view compatible with modern concepts of adaptation through genetic or systemic

---

3 John D. Post, "Famine, Mortality, and Epidemic Disease in the Process of Modernization," *Economic History Review*, XXIX (1976), 14–37; Amartya Sen, *Poverty and Famines: An Essay on Entitlement and Deprivation* (Oxford, 1982); Louise A. Tilly, "Food Entitlement, Famine, and Conflict," in this issue.

change. Even this "smallest possible quantity" appears to vary among individuals: persons who remain in good health, maintain body weight, and perform activities that require the same energy expenditure have been found to have energy intakes that vary over a wide range; it is likely that the energy intakes needed to maintain life also vary. In addition, in currently developing countries modern medical technologies such as anti-malarial drugs and oral rehydration have surely reduced the number of calories required for subsistence, by reducing the demands on the body to fight infections and their consequences. Although diversity in the smallest possible quantity may complicate the task of precise description, nevertheless the concept of a minimum level of subsistence remains a useful one when considering the constraints that resources place on population size.[4]

Third is the critical distinction between endogenous and exogenous mortality. Most pre-industrial economies were particularly vulnerable to crises. But how much was that vulnerability the result of population pressure, and how much was it linked to modes of production that accumulated few surpluses, were not very diversified, and were not covered by systems of insurance and solidarity as have been developed by the modern state? In reference to those forced populations identified by Malthus, where population had managed to grow at the costs of decreased levels of subsistence, Wrigley wrote: "A large proportion of the population in these circumstances is very close to the Malthusian precipice and may be pushed over it in large numbers by even a moderately poor harvest. There is almost no cushion against disaster . . ."[5]

In the logic of the Malthusian system, a cushion against disaster could be provided only by the rise in standards of living that would attend the resort to prudential restraint, the preventive check allowing lower fertility. By the same logic, it is a population's density that triggers the positive checks. Famines, for example, are one of the most obvious of the system's ways of getting rid of a population surplus. The immediate cause of a famine,

4 T. N. Srinivasan, "Malnutrition: Some Measurement and Policy Issues," *Journal of Development Economics,* VIII (1981), 3–19.
5 Wrigley, *Population and History* (New York, 1969), 35.

such as a drought, a bad crop, a disease in the food crop, or a breakdown of transportation, is then interpreted as a mere agent in the general economy of the principle of population.

How far can we stretch the notion of endogeneity? Grigg concludes a general review of the symptoms of overpopulation in Europe without ambiguity: "Crisis mortality has not for the most part been related to population pressure." It could be argued that, in the case of the potato famine, the Irish made themselves overly dependent on a single crop, and that disaster was inevitable and inherent in the particular economy. But how does one account for bad winters, rotten summers, and wars that disrupted transportation? The area of the Basse Meuse studied by Gutmann was repeatedly devastated by war between 1620 and 1750 because it lay along the path taken by armies in transit. Just as deaths followed the armies in the Basse Meuse, so the geographical diffusion of the plague seems to have followed—in England at least—the routes etched by commercial exchange. Even exceptionally high endemic mortality may mirror the geographical distribution of swampy and malarial areas and may only be tenuously tied to the resources available to the populations living in those areas.[6]

In Europe, most crises can be attributed to infectious diseases, but the conclusion that an overpopulated community will be more vulnerable to climatic accidents or infectious disease need not follow. Consider European epidemics of plague, smallpox, and cholera. Although there clearly were socioeconomic factors associated with these diseases, *prima facie* they had an exogenous character, at least initially: they came from outside and were diffused by vectors external to the population. Or they were new factors to which people had developed neither an immunity nor what might be called institutional lines of defense.

In fact, society was doing its best to find ways of overcoming the new mortalities. Quarantines, for example, may have played a role in the disappearance of plague. The cholera crises of the nineteenth century led to frantic research that resulted eventually

6 David B. Grigg, *Population Growth and Agrarian Change: An Historical Perspective* (Cambridge, 1980), 47; Myron P. Gutmann, *War and Rural Life in the Early Modern Low Countries* (Princeton, 1980); Wrigley and Schofield, *Population History*, 670–676; Nevin S. Scrimshaw, "The Value of Contemporary Food and Nutrition Studies for Historians," in this issue.

in a germ theory of disease which proved of fairly general applicability to the removal of positive checks. The solutions to many mortality crises were not endogenous—that is, they were not brought about by change in the societal conditions that are said to have caused them—and their causes were not unambiguously endogenous either.

The graphical presentation usually employed to summarize the equilibrium between population and resources is too schematic to indicate the mechanisms involved. It fails to depict either the inequalities in entitlement or the possible diversity in what is needed for survival. Malthus himself does not clearly distinguish between those sources of mortality which are only tenuously, if at all, linked to resources and those in which the relationship is apparent. If, then, the notion of an equilibrium is flawed, what remains of the necessary relationship which Malthus postulated between population and resources? Assuming a closed population in which individuals are equal in entitlement and in requirements for survival, we examine the endogenous aspects of the Malthusian equation, specifically the way in which resources are linked to the stream of births and deaths which jointly determine population size.

FERTILITY   Fertility may play a role in the homeostatic adjustment. Total fertility, or the average number of children born to a group of women by the end of their childbearing years, has commonly been thought to be necessarily high in pre-industrial populations in order to balance typically high death rates. A recent examination by Coale of total fertility rates in pre-industrial societies, however, shows that the total fertility rates for several European populations in the eighteenth century, for rural China around 1930, and for India during the period 1901 to 1911, was moderate, ranging from about 4.1 to 6.2. This is well below either the biological maximum estimated by Bongaarts as fifteen births or the number of children that would have been born had the highest reliably recorded marital fertility rates (for the Hutterites) been combined with the early and universal marriage of traditional China. Since overall fertility is determined both by the proportion of the female population living in a sexual union and by the rate at which these women bear children, if there were a mechanism by which societies linked resources with the stream of births, it could be expected to affect either the former or the latter.[7]

In many historical societies, births were more or less confined to married women. Thus, an important determinant of the yearly number of births was the proportion of women of childbearing age who were married. For England between 1541 and 1871, Wrigley and Schofield found a clear relationship between resources, as measured by a real wage index, and crude marriage rates. This relationship figures importantly in their interpretation of England's relatively high standard of living.[8]

There is an *a priori* reason to expect that a similar relationship may be found in other populations characterized by the Western European marriage pattern; once marriage was separated from menarche, and neither its timing nor its incidence was a function of biology, it was free to fluctuate with changes in the economic environment. In Western Europe marriage appears to have been linked to household formation, and specifically to a preference for nuclear family households. This connection plausibly links marriage to resources through the ability to form an independent household, although what was considered necessary to establish a proper household varied among groups in the population.[9]

In many non-European societies, marriage was closely linked to menarche. In such circumstances, the relationship between resources and the age at marriage has been made through nutrition, since the age of menarche responds to changes in nutrition. Under some assumptions, a substantial decline in the age of menarche could have a considerable effect on overall fertility.[10]

7   Ansley J. Coale, "The Decline of Fertility in Europe Since the Eighteenth Century as a Chapter in Demographic History," in *idem* and Watkins (eds.), *The Decline of Fertility in Europe,* forthcoming; John Bongaarts, "A Framework for Analyzing the Proximate Determinants of Fertility," *Population and Development Review,* IV (1978), 105–132.
8   Wrigley and Schofield, *Population History,* 402–453.
9   A preliminary analysis by Weir shows that the crude birth rate was responsive to fluctuations in real wages in France between 1740 and 1789. David Weir, "Life Under Pressure," a revised version of a paper presented at the Conference on British Historical Demography (1982).
10   More precisely, the consumation of marriage was determined by menarche, since the marriage may have been contracted previously. Jane Menken, James Trussell, and Watkins, "The Nutrition Fertility Link: An Evaluation of the Evidence," *Journal of Interdisciplinary History,* XI (1981), 425–441.

In at least some non-European populations in which marriage is both early and universal, marital fertility is puzzlingly low. Nomadic populations of Central Asia in 1926 and the Chinese farmers of the early 1930s experienced levels of fertility about half that of the Hutterites. Fertility levels were almost that low in early twentieth-century Taiwan and Korea. As a result of low marital fertility, there is greater similarity in crude birth rates between Western European populations and those Asian populations than a comparison of either their marriage patterns or their levels of marital fertility would suggest. Since there is reason to believe that the Western European marriage pattern provides a potentially flexible link between resources and overall fertility, it is reasonable to ask whether there may be a functionally equivalent link in non-European societies between resources and marital fertility.[11]

The study of the Chinese farmers indicates that the low level of marital fertility was not due to parity-specific family limitation, nor is it believable that the nomads of Central Asia were practicing family limitation. Their low recorded fertility must then be due to factors which affect the length of the birth interval, or to infanticide.

Infanticide is not, strictly speaking, a factor affecting fertility, but it is obviously a flexible and timely way of relating the number of children to the family's resources: if a birth occurs at a time when resources are relatively abundant, a child may be permitted to survive, and if not, not. An evaluation of the demographic impact of infanticide depends on the extent to which it was practiced. Sophisticated scholars of premodern Chinese society and many anthropologists take multiple references to infanticide as a sign that it was a relatively prevalent practice. However, societies in which infanticide is thought to have been practiced are also societies in which demographic events were poorly recorded. Thus, an accurate evaluation of the demographic importance of infanticide is not yet possible.

11 Coale, Barbara A. Anderson, and Erna Härm, *Human Fertility in Russia Since the Nineteenth Century* (Princeton, 1979); George W. Barclay, Coale, Michael Stoto, and Trussell, "A Reassessment of the Demography of Traditional Rural China," *Population Index*, XLII (1976), 606–634.

Alternatively, resources could affect the length of time from one live birth to another, either through the duration of post-partum amenorrhea (the period following the birth of a child until ovulation resumes) or through the waiting period (the length of time between the resumption of ovulation and the conception that leads to the birth of the next live child) or through the duration of gestation. The most obvious path is through nutrition. (Evidence linking fertility and nutrition has been reviewed thoroughly elsewhere.)[12]

In our view, the evidence that ovulation ceases when nutritional deprivation is extreme is convincing, although such periods are also likely to be times in which ordinary family life is atypical in other ways. Short of extreme deprivation, however, the available evidence suggests that neither the period of post-partum amenorrhea nor the length of the waiting period vary substantially among women of different nutritional statuses. That the waiting period does not seem to be affected by nutrition also suggests that under conditions of chronic malnutrition (rather than starvation) foetal loss is not substantially increased.

Nutrition is not, however, the only factor to be considered. Coital frequency may be reduced when times are bad, either because couples act with deliberate restraint, or because they are separated, or perhaps because the demands associated with a particularly difficult economic situation make intercourse less attractive. Long average periods of post-partum amenorrhea have been found in societies which practice prolonged breastfeeding. The effect of nursing on the average length of birth intervals is enhanced in populations where suckling is frequent and in populations where custom proscribes sexual intercourse while the mother is nursing.[13] It is not clear whether customs regulating nursing are associated with resources, but it may be that populations in which these customs took hold were better able to cope with a chronic insufficiency of resources than were those in which births normally followed one another with great rapidity. There

12 Rose E. Frisch, "Population, Food Intake and Fertility," *Science,* CXCIX (1978), 22–30; Bongaarts, "Does Malnutrition Affect Fecundity? A Summary of the Evidence," *Science,* CCVIII (1980), 564–569; Menken, Trussell, and Watkins, "The Nutrition Fertility Link."
13 Melvin Konner and Carol Worthman, "Nursing Frequency, Gonadal Function, and Birth Spacing among the !Kung Hunter-Gatherers," *Science,* CCVII (1980), 788–791.

is far too little evidence to treat these possible connections between births and resources as more than speculative. Western European populations clearly had available to them, through nuptiality, a way in which fertility could respond flexibly to changes in the economy, a way which permitted the maintenance of a standard of living well above subsistence level. The links between resources and births in populations with early and virtually universal marriage are less obvious, but the possibility that such links existed should be taken into account.

MORTALITY: STARVATION   If population size is not kept in balance with resources through variation in the stream of births, then the only alternative is variation in the stream of deaths. If the balance of births and deaths over the long run is such that the ratio of population to resources falls below a minimum determined by the necessities of life, then mortality will increase to right that balance.

There are two possible mechanisms that could be responsible for the balance between births and deaths through the agency of endogenous positive checks. On the one hand, the normal level of mortality could be balanced with fertility, either through widespread starvation or through an increased susceptibility to infectious disease among the malnourished. On the other hand, there could be mortality crises due to a sudden scarcity of resources which accounted for exceptional losses: such crises might even affect fertility at the same time as they affected mortality.

Excluding periods of crisis mortality, neither the high death rates of the past nor the comparatively high death rates of some contemporary countries can confidently be attributed to widespread starvation. For example, parish priests in England sometimes noted the death of a "poor hungerstarved beggar child," but often made no such comment. Graunt, studying the burial records of London over a twenty-year period, wrote in 1662 that "of 229,250 which have died, we find not above fifty-one to have been starved, excepting helpless infants at nurse . . ." In some contemporary countries with high infant and child mortality rates, marasmus and kwashiorkor are prevalent, but they are more often the result of infection and unbalanced diet than of food shortage.[14]

14   Peter Laslett, *The World We Have Lost* (New York, 1975), 121, 117.

If starvation does not seem to account for the high levels of mortality that prevailed in the absence of crises, what about periods of crisis when there is evidence that these coincided with an abrupt drop in resources? How frequent were famines in the past, and how important were they in maintaining an equilibrium between births and deaths?

As Meuvret and many others have pointed out, even if many of the deaths in a famine period were due rather to disease than to outright starvation, nevertheless the sudden rise in death rates was sometimes associated with an abrupt fall in the availability of food to some, whatever the causes of this scarcity. Where it is possible to compare parallel series of staple prices or real income and deaths, the peaks in both sometimes coincide. When neither series is available, it is still possible at times to know whether there was a famine. Crises of short duration may not have been recorded by contemporary chroniclers, but they are likely to have made and noted the connection between widespread suffering and death and a time of dearth.[15]

Dupâquier estimated the frequency of mortality crises in Western Europe by examining series of deaths for the rural parishes of Nantais (1576–1600) and the Parisian Basin (1681–1720), for ten French regions (1750–1792), and national statistics (1732–1799). Less than one quarter of the years observed in any of the aggregates were years of crisis. Since Dupâquier does not distinguish between crises due to famine and those from other sources, it can be assumed that famine accounted for fewer than the total number of crises. A list of "natural calamities" compiled by local authorities of Hupei province in China between 1664 and 1911 distinguishes among crises due to famines, droughts, floods, epidemics, and locusts and pests. In many years no county in Hupei was affected by any calamity, and the majority of calamities were not due to famine. Although presumably all of these calamities may have affected the production and/or the distribution of food, the Chinese state traditionally assumed as its responsibility the redistribution of grain in times of severe shortage. Thus, it is likely that only when it was unsuccessful in doing so were famines

15 Jean Meuvret, "Demographic Crisis in France from the Sixteenth to the Eighteenth Century," in David V. Glass and David E. C. Eversley (eds.), *Population in History* (London, 1965), 507–522.

recorded. Hanley and Yamamura conclude that "famine was not responsible for the low or zero rates of population growth in the province of Bizen for the 125 years from 1721 to 1846." Despite the glaring lacunae in the evidence, famines may have been sufficiently infrequent and sufficiently local that we may want to reevaluate them as major restraints on population growth in the past.[16]

One approach to estimating the importance of famines in maintaining a balance between a population and its resources is to consider the demographic effects of famine. If a population is pressed against the limits by its resources, according to the Malthusian view, a stream of deaths will temporarily relieve the population pressure. But how long will the respite provided by a period of temporarily heightened mortality last? The number of years needed to regain pre-crisis population size depends on the magnitude and duration of the crisis, as well as the mortality and fertility patterns that normally prevail. In a closed population, in which birth rates and death rates are equal both before and after a crisis, the net loss (deaths minus the temporary increase in births that sometimes follows a crisis) is permanent. Populations with mortality and fertility schedules that normally permitted growth could make up for the losses; however, the speed of recovery will depend on the age patterns of deaths during the crisis and on normal rates of natural increase. Estimating the demographic effects of famine on the basis of historical records is difficult to do with precision, since the records rarely give a population base or age specific mortality and fertility rates, but it can be done mathematically or by computer simulation.[17]

16 Dupâquier, "L'analyse statistique des crises de mortalité," in Hubert Charbonneau and Andre Larose (eds.), *The Great Mortalities: Methodological Studies of Demographic Crises in the Past* (Liège, n.d.), 83–112; Ping-ti Ho, *Studies on the Population of China* (Cambridge, Mass., 1959), 292–300; Lillian M. Li, "Food, Famine, and the Chinese State," *Journal of Asian Studies,* XLI (1981), 687–707. Ho notes that the frequency with which a county was accorded disaster status depended in part on the effectiveness of its representation with the Emperor, so that the list probably does not represent the distribution of calamities with complete accuracy. Susan B. Hanley and Kozo Yamamura, *Economic and Demographic Change in Preindustrial Japan, 1600–1868* (Princeton, 1977). For a different view on the quantitative impact of famine, see Michelle B. McAlpin, "Famines, Epidemics, and Population Growth: The Case of India," in this issue.
17 Hervé Le Bras, "Retour d'une population à l'état stable après une 'catastrophe'," *Population,* XXIV (1969), 861–896; Watkins and Menken, "A Quantitative Perspective on Famine and Population Growth," unpub. ms. (1983).

Simulations by Watkins and Menken considered the impact of famine in a closed population in which the entire population was at risk of death and there was no migration. The famines simulated were quite severe, ranging from those in which crude rates increased by about 110 percent for two years, to those in which crude death rates increased by about 150 percent for five years. Famines of such magnitude and duration appear to be outside well-documented experience in Western Europe: for example, in England the median length of a crisis was under two months. The most severe crisis simulated (a 150 percent increase in crude death rates for five years) seems to be outside the range for China and India as well as Western Europe. The age pattern of deaths was taken from that recorded in the Bangladesh famine of 1974/75, where death rates rose disproportionately in the youngest and oldest ages; reasonable alternative specifications of the age pattern of famine mortality did not, however, significantly affect the results.[18]

In the simulations, it was assumed that age specific mortality and fertility rates returned to pre-famine levels once the crisis was over. Three assumptions about the normal rate of natural increase were made: that it was zero, .5 percent per year, and 1 percent a year. Although we know that over the very long run population growth rates approximated zero, we do not know that such was the case in the short run, where rates even higher than 1 percent are conceivable. The range chosen, however, brackets the majority of values found by Wrigley and Schofield for England between 1541 and 1871, and seems reasonable for other large past populations.

Populations growing at .5 percent a year recovered their pre-crisis size seventeen years after a "mild" famine (a 110 percent increase in crude death rates for two years), and forty-three years after a "severe" famine (a 150 percent increase in crude death rates for five years). Populations growing at 1 percent a year recovered even more quickly: in twelve years after the lesser of these famines, and in twenty-three years after the more severe. Hence, in order for famine to be the mechanism by which populations were kept in balance with their resources, they would have had to have

---

18 Wrigley and Schofield, *Population History*, Appendix 10.

occurred at regular intervals, the length of the interval being the time until recuperation.

Records such as those compiled by Dupâquier and Ho, however, suggest that famines were not so frequent. In addition, the simulations considered entire and closed populations; when one takes into account the local nature of famines, and the fact that out-migration could increase the apparent losses during the famine and in-migration could hasten the time to recovery, the effect of famines may have been even more fleeting than the simulations describe. Moreover, the simulations were based on the assumption that mortality and fertility schedules after the famine were the same as those that prevailed before the famine. If the gap between them in fact increased, recovery from the effects of the crisis would have been even more rapid. If resources constrained population growth in the past by elevating mortality, then it would appear that famines did not play a major role in this drama, both because they seem to have been rather infrequent and local, and because their effects on the demography of a population could be erased quickly in all but a population with normally identical birth and death rates. The effects of famine on the other aspects of society, however, could be much more enduring.[19]

MORTALITY: MALNUTRITION   The typically high death rates of the past were due primarily to disease rather than to starvation alone. Yet mortality may be tied to the availability of food at levels of undernourishment that fall short of starvation—that is, to chronic insufficiency rather than to extreme deprivation. If chronic malnutrition is to be an explanation for historical population changes, then we must know not only that there is a relation between malnutrition and disease, but also the degree to which lack of food increases the susceptibility to, and lethality of, disease.

That individuals who are malnourished are more likely to die from infectious diseases than individuals who are well nourished is widely believed. Much of the evidence to support this belief comes from clinical studies of physiological susceptibility

---

19 If the out-migration were measured, it would inflate the effect of the crisis by reducing the denominator.

and resistence or from animal experiments. For human populations in which infectious diseases are normally a primary cause of death, as they were in historical populations, and in which a substantial proportion of the population is chronically malnourished, the evidence linking malnutrition and mortality is surprisingly sparse and inadequate.[20]

The best evidence linking malnutrition and mortality is drawn from studies of contemporary populations in several relatively poor countries. These studies have been of two types: those which examined the improvement in mortality following programs of nutritional supplementation, and those which classified a population by nutritional status and compared subsequent death rates for these groups over time. As in historical populations, deaths of infants and children from disease are a large proportion of all deaths in such populations.

In studies conducted in eastern Guatemala and in the town of Narangwal in the Punjab, India, groups which received nutritional supplements were compared to groups that did not. There was a greater fall in infant mortality in the former than in the latter; in addition, there was a greater fall in mortality among those who received more supplementation than among those who received less. The evidence however, is ambiguous. Often the groups were rather small, making statistically significant estimates of the effect difficult. And even when the experimental and control groups were roughly matched, differences remained in other characteristics which are thought to affect mortality, such as the level of the mother's education.[21]

More precise estimates of the link between nutritional status and death rates are available from micro-level studies in Matlab

20   Ancel Keys, Josef Brožek, Austin Henschel, Olaf Mickelsen, and Henry Longstreet Taylor, *The Biology of Human Starvation* (Minneapolis, 1950).
21   Carl E. Taylor, "The Narangwal Experiment on Interaction of Nutrition and Infections: I," *Indian Journal of Medical Research,* LVIII (1978), 1–20; *idem,* "Synergy among Mass Infections, Famines, and Poverty," in this issue; Aaron Lechtig, Hernan Delgado, Reynaldo Martorell, Douglas Richardson, Charles Yarborough, and Robert E. Klein, "Effect of Maternal Nutrition on Infant Mortality," in W. Henry Mosley (ed.), *Nutrition and Human Reproduction* (New York, 1978); Juan M. Baertl, Enrique Morales, Gustavo Verstaegui, and George Graham, "Diet Supplementation for Entire Communities: Growth and Mortality of Infants and Children," *American Journal of Clinical Nutrition,* XXIII (1970), 705–715; Davidson R. Gwatkin, Janet R. Wilcox, and Joe D. Wray, *Can Health and Nutrition Interventions Make a Difference?* (Washington, D.C., 1980).

thana, Bangladesh, and Narangwal, where the nutritional status of infants and children was measured using height-for-age to summarize the individual's nutritional history, weight-for-height to reflect recent diet, and other anthropometric measures.[22]

Infants and children who were severely malnourished were several times more likely to die than were children who were well-nourished or moderately malnourished. In one study in Bangladesh, children aged one to nine years who were classified as severely malnourished were 3.4 times more likely to die in the subsequent eighteen months than were those who were well-nourished. The differentials were more marked among one- to four-year-olds than at other ages, and tended to diminish over time. Another study in Bangladesh followed children aged thirteen to twenty-eight months for two years, and found that severely malnourished children were twice as likely to die over the subsequent twelve months as were the normally nourished or the mildly or the moderately malnourished children; during the second year of the follow up, those who had been initially classified as severely malnourished were at an even greater disadvantage, and experienced a four-fold greater mortality risk than their better nourished counterparts. Children who were severely malnourished on both the height-for-age (stunting) and weight-for-height (wasting) scales were at particularly great risk of dying.[23]

It is interesting that in Matlab thana there seemed to be a threshold level of malnutrition. There was not much difference in death rates among mildly malnourished and well-nourished children; only among the severely malnourished did the risk of death rise sharply. At Narangwal, however, there was an ap-

22 Other anthropometric measures have been found to correlate well with these measures. Lincoln Chen, A.K.N. Alauddin Chowdhury, and Sandra Huffman, "Anthropometric Assessment of Energy-Protein Malnutrition and Subsequent Risk of Mortality Among Preschool Aged Children," *American Journal of Clinical Nutrition*, XXXIII (1980), 1836–1845. If the link between nutrition and infectious disease is thought to work through immunological responses, then a more direct measure would require observation of immunological changes; as far as we know, this has not yet been done for a population.

23 Alfred Sommer and Matthew S. Loewenstein, "Nutritional Status and Mortality: A Prospective Validation of the QUAC Stick," *American Journal of Clinical Nutrition*, XXVIII (1975), 289. (Some of the discrepancy in the results is due to differences in the way that the studies were conducted, especially in the definition of severely malnourished, in the age of the children at the time that the measurements were taken, and in the length of time that the children were observed.) Chen et al., "Anthropometric Assessment," 1843.

proximate doubling of mortality rates with each 10 percent deterioration in nutritional status. That there may be a threshold level of malnutrition, below which differences in nutritional status have little impact, may explain the finding by Lee that in England between 1541 and 1871 there was only a weak relationship between mortality levels and wheat prices. Early modern England may have had a sufficiently high standard of living that variations in grain prices led to painfully tighter belts, but not to substantially higher mortality. Whether or not there is a threshold level of malnutrition, however, the raising or lowering of the overall mortality of a population in response to changes in resources as reflected in nutritional status will depend on the distribution of the population by levels of malnutrition.[24]

The effect of changes in nutritional status on overall death rates will also depend on the distribution of the population by age, since age and nutritional status interact. Kielmann and McCord found that among the severely malnourished, children aged six to twelve months were at greater risk of dying than either infants under six months or children between the ages of one and three. Sommer and Lowenstein, comparing severely malnourished with well-nourished children, found that by far the highest relative risk was for three-year-olds. The relative risk for infants under one was 3.9 and for children five to nine it was 2.0, whereas three-year-olds who were severely malnourished had 17.7 times as great a likelihood of dying as did children of the same age who were well nourished. Since virtually all children under one in these populations are breastfed, and since breast-feeding is thought to confer immunities, it is likely that breast-feeding explains the relatively low risk of infants. The particularly high relative risk found in the second half of the first year by Kielmann and McCord, and in the third year by Sommer and Lowenstein, may reflect the timing of weaning.[25]

---

24 *Ibid.*; Sommer and Loewenstein, "Nutritional Status and Mortality"; Arnfried A. Kielmann and Colin McCord, "Weight for Age as an Index of Risk of Death in Children," *The Lancet* (June 10, 1978), 1249; Ronald Lee, "Short-term Variation: Vital Rates, Prices, and Weather," in Wrigley and Schofield, *Population History*, 399.

25 Kielmann and McCord, "Weight-for-Age"; the approximate doubling of mortality rates with each 10% deterioration in nutritional status occurred only for children below 80% of the Harvard weight median, a commonly used scale. Sommer and Loewenstein, "Nutritional Status and Mortality," 289.

It is reasonable to expect that the mortality risks to children, especially to children under one, are related to the nutritional status of the mother. There is evidence, both from the studies cited previously and from other work, much of it reviewed in Siegel and Morris and in Chen, that maternal nutritional status affects neonatal mortality, especially through greater prematurity, a greater likelihood of difficult labor, and lower birth weight, all of which are associated with a greater likelihood of death in the period immediately after the birth. The effects of a mother's nutritional status appear to diminish over time: among malnourished children, those with malnourished mothers were significantly more likely to die, but maternal nutritional status made no difference for normal children.[26]

Although it is also reasonable to expect that the nutritional status of the mother is relevant for nurslings who are deriving all or most of their nutrition from their mother's milk, the evidence is contradictory. Some studies have found no effect of maternal supplementation on either milk production or infant weight, while others show that a poorly nourished woman will produce less milk and that the milk will be deficient in fats and vitamins.[27]

In summary, these studies provide evidence that nutrition and mortality are linked in populations in which malnourishment is chronic. Although, on the one hand, the studies are about children rather than adults, it is the deaths of infants and children that account for most of the deaths when death rates are high, and it was the decline in infant and childhood mortality that was responsible for the great secular increase in the expectation of life at birth. On the other hand, the evidence on which to base estimates of the magnitude of the effect of malnutrition on death rates is not as unambiguous as would be desirable both for those interested in the sources of the relatively high death rates in some contemporary countries or for those whose curiosity is about the

---

26 Earl Siegel and Naomi Morris, "The Epidemiology of Human Reproductive Casualties, with Emphasis on the Role of Nutrition," in *Maternal Nutrition and the Course of Pregnancy* (Washington, D.C., 1970), 5–39; Chen, "Child Survival: Levels, Trends, and Determinants," in Ronald Lee, Paula Hollerbach, and Bongaarts (eds.), *Determinants of Fertility Change in Developing Countries,* forthcoming; Chen et al., "Anthropometric Assessment," 1842.

27 Population Information Program, *Breastfeeding, Fertility, and Family Planning, Population Reports* (Baltimore, 1981).

ways in which resources constrained population growth in the past.

Studies in contemporary populations have the advantage of permitting a more direct observation of the mechanisms linking resources with population than is possible using the limited information that survives from historical societies. Because one can measure weight, height, and age, and can observe accurately subsequent mortality rates by age, it is possible to show that those who are severely malnourished by these anthropometric measures are more likely to die than those who are well nourished.

Yet, although the anthropometric measures speak to variations in nutrition more openly than do grain prices, they are still an imprecise measure of nutritional status. Height and weight reflect past and current diet, but they also reflect past and current disease, since some infectious diseases are known to affect the ability of the body to absorb and utilize nutrients. Thus it is not certain that the anthropometric measures used in these studies are accurately measuring the degree to which an insufficient diet is related to the risk of death. Rather, they may measure the effect of past illness on nutritional status. If this is the case, they do not answer the question of the relationship of resources (in the form of diet) to the risk of death.[28]

Even if the anthropometric measures did adequately measure the sufficiency of the diet, the studies themselves do not adequately disentangle the effects of nutrition from other characteristics of the environment in which the population lives, such as income and education. Reviewing studies of this sort, Preston has concluded: "The demographic returns from these studies have been disappointing . . . None has provided a rich description of the main factors that seem to differentiate high mortality from low mortality groups and families . . . it is appropriate only to say that much of the promise of these studies for demographic research on mortality has yet to be realized."[29]

---

28 Carl E. Taylor and John E. Gordon, *Interactions of Nutrition and Infection* (Geneva, 1968).
29 Samuel H. Preston, "Research Developments Needed for Improvements in Policy Formulation on Mortality," paper presented at the IRG Workshop on Research Priorities for Population Policy (1978).

Studies in contemporary developing countries are of considerable value to historians, since they permit a more direct observation of nutritional status and death rates than is possible for past populations. That they are still inadequate for exposing the precise mechanisms by which nutrition is related to death, however, suggests caution in using this relationship to interpret population changes in the past.[30]

There are other problems in carrying the present into the past. Much in the environment changed between then and now, and changed in ways that are likely to matter for our interpretation of the demographic importance of malnutrition in the past. When it becomes possible to translate family income into improved access to health care, and to translate mother's education into greater knowledge of how to keep children alive, then education and income can dampen the effect of nutrition on mortality. The link may have been simpler in the past, when income could not buy medical care as well as food, and when education did not bring knowledge of nutrition and disease.

There is a general consensus that deliberate interventions such as improvements in water supply, public sanitation, and medical therapies were not significant before the early nineteenth century. In earlier times one advantage that wealth would have conferred against the ravages of mortality would have been the ability to buy a better diet, particularly with respect to quantity (although not necessarily with respect to quality). Although wealth could also have bought larger and perhaps more isolated housing, and thus have reduced the exposure to infectious diseases, the aristocracy could be presumed to have drunk from the same lakes and streams and to have been exposed to whatever diseases afflicted those with whom they came into frequent contact (such as servants). Wealth may also have permitted its holders to flee an epidemic and take refuge in healthier locations.

For those who emphasize the importance of nutrition for the susceptibility to disease and death, it is significant that before the seventeenth or mid-eighteenth centuries the expectation of life among the aristocracy was low. Hollingsworth's estimates of expectation of life among the aristocracy of England between

---

30 But cf. Scrimshaw, "Value of Food and Nutrition Studies."

1550 and 1750 fall between 30.0 and 38.8 for males and 33.7 and 38.3 for females: Wrigley and Schofield estimate cohort life expectancy (e_0) for both sexes in the same period as falling between 30.7 and 39.7[31]

In a summary of mortality levels for other aristocratic groups, Livi-Bacci found that among the European ruling families, the Genevan bourgeoisie, and the dukes and peers of France, e_0 did not rise above thirty-five years. He further notes that the mortality of Italian Jesuits admitted to the order between 1540 and 1565 was high (an expectation of life at age twenty compatible with an e_0 below thirty years), even though they could have been expected to enjoy better than average environmental and nutritional conditions, and in addition were selected for their health and constitution. If we believe that the aristocracy and the Jesuits did not go to bed hungry at night, it would appear that their full bellies were no protection against death from disease.[32]

Equally important in the consideration of environmental differences between present and past is the fact that those diseases currently prevalent in contemporary developing countries may be different from those endemic in the past. On the basis of clinical evidence, some diseases are classified as relatively independent of nutrition, such as plague and typhoid, and some others as only slightly related to nutrition, such as typhus, smallpox, and syphilis. Some infectious diseases have been much reduced in incidence even in a country like Bangladesh where, for example, the last case of smallpox was recorded in 1975. Because we have as yet no better basis for linking resources and mortality in the past than the contemporary studies of nutritional status and mortality rates, it is necessary to consider them carefully. Because the environment in which people lived and died is considerably different now from what it was then, it is necessary to use extreme caution in transporting the baggage of the present to the past.[33]

The slow rate of population growth in the past, in the context of a world in which the ability to expand production changed only

---

31 Thomas H. Hollingsworth, "Mortality in the British Peerage Families since 1600," *Population*, XXXII (1977), 325–352; Wrigley and Schofield, *Population History*, 530.
32 Massimo Livi-Bacci, "The Nutrition-Mortality Link in Past Times," in this issue.
33 Cf. Scrimshaw, "Value of Food and Nutrition Studies."

slowly, has tempted historians to interpret this long-run immo-
bility as the result of constraints imposed by a necessary equilibrium between population and resources. Although the balance
between births and deaths was local and unstable, permitting
periods of growth and periods of decline, the size of the population could not exceed bounds set by resources and by the arrangements that determined the distribution of those resources. In this
schema, once population grew to fill the economic space, any
excess of births over deaths was necessarily erased by deaths from
insufficiency.

Dramatic mortality from famine, however, appears to have
been relatively rare, and, because populations could recuperate
rather rapidly from a crisis, it appears that famine was not a major
mechanism by which the balance between population and resources was maintained in the past. Studies in contemporary populations suggest a connection between malnutrition and death,
but the evidence is far from adequate, even for the present. In
order to evaluate the role of this link in the past we need not only
to know more about the way in which nutrition and mortality
were related, but also to know more about the populations of the
past, for example the proportion of the population that could be
considered malnourished, the degree of malnourishment, and the
distribution of specific diseases.

Those populations in which the balance between births and
deaths permitted a comfortable margin between population and
resources had the capacity to avoid famine and malnutrition, at
least most of the time; those populations in which mortality was
high for reasons unrelated to resources could also avoid the ultimate positive check. The evidence for this link between nutrition
and mortality is still sufficiently scant to inspire skepticism about
the role that this link in fact played. Although an insufficiency of
resources was indeed the court of last resort, as Malthus knew,
for most populations an appeal to that court may have been less
frequent than hitherto thought.

Food, Infection, and Population   Where complex issues are concerned, it is easier to state the conclusions than to analyze our reasons for accepting them. I therefore outline in simple terms an interpretation of the relation between food and population growth before attempting the more difficult task of presenting the grounds on which it is based. The conclusions are as follows: the slow growth of the human population before the eighteenth century was due mainly to lack of food, and the rapid increase from that time resulted largely from improved nutrition. The influence of food on population size in the historical period was determined essentially by the relation between nutritional state and response to infectious disease.

Although I now believe that these conclusions rest on positive grounds—on a reading of the determinants of health and of the major influences which have modified it in the past—I came to them first through rejection of other explanations for the modern increase in population size, on the principle enunciated by Sherlock Holmes: when we have eliminated the impossible, whatever remains, however improbable, must be the truth. I concluded that: (a) personal medical measures (immunization and therapy) had an insignificant effect on mortality before the twentieth century; (b) fortuitous variation in the character of infectious diseases is an inadequate explanation for the major changes in man's experience of them; (c) the expansion and aggregation of populations which followed industrialization initially increased exposure to the infections; and (d) the measures by which it is suggested that fertility was restricted before the nineteenth century were relatively ineffective.

Stating these conclusions, I am aware that one is at risk of being thought to overstate them. In suggesting that immunization

Thomas McKeown is Professor Emeritus of Social Medicine at the University of Birmingham. He is the author of *The Role of Medicine: Dream, Mirage, or Nemesis?* (Princeton, 1979).

and therapy had a negligible effect on the death rate before the twentieth century I do not underestimate the contribution made by medical science at an earlier date through understanding of the nature and mode of transmission of infectious diseases. Although variation in the character of the diseases does not account for the different experience of the infections in the hunter-gatherer, agricultural, and industrial periods, I recognize that man's relation to micro-organisms is constantly changing. The belief that exposure to infectious diseases initially increased with industrialization is consistent with recognition that hygienic measures later reduced the risk, particularly from water- and food-borne diseases. And the conclusion that deliberate attempts to restrict fertility were relatively ineffective does not overlook the importance of unconscious restraints from malnutrition and disease, or of postnatal measures which limit numbers, particularly infanticide. Because these influences on population growth are still debated it will be desirable to present the reasons for rejecting them.

PERSONAL MEDICAL MEASURES   It is historians, rather than medical people, who find it difficult to accept that immunization and therapy achieved little before the twentieth century. Clinicians are well aware of our inability to reverse the course of many established diseases even in the present day, and there are doctors still in practice who recall from personal experience the ineffectiveness of the treatment of infectious diseases before the sulphonamides became available. We still lack remedies for viral infections. It is hardly surprising that most physicians readily accept that medical intervention was not effective before 1900, and are unconvinced by the assertion that eighteenth-century hospitals cured or relieved nearly all of their patients, a claim that could not be substantiated for any present day hospital.[1]

Clinical experience is supported by investigations of the reasons for the decline of deaths from individual infectious diseases. In England and Wales it is possible to follow the trend of mortality by cause from 1838, with some reservations concerning the reliability of certification and classification of causes of death. Except

---

1   E. Sigsworth, "A Provincial Hospital in the Eighteenth and Early Nineteenth Centuries," *Yorkshire Faculty Journal*, XVI (1966), 24.

in the case of vaccination against smallpox, which was associated with only 1.6 percent of the decline of the death rate to 1971, it is unlikely that immunization and therapy had a significant effect on deaths from infectious diseases before the twentieth century. Between 1900 and 1935 these measures contributed in some diseases: antitoxin in diphtheria; surgery in appendicitis, peritonitis, and ear infections; salvarsan in syphilis; intravenous therapy in diarrheal diseases; passive immunization against tetanus; and improved obstetric care in prevention of puerpural fever.[2]

But even if these measures were responsible for the whole decline of mortality from these conditions after 1900—which clearly they were not—they would account for only a small part of the reduction of deaths which occurred before 1935. From that time the first powerful chemotherapeutic agents—sulphonamides and, later, antibiotics—came into use, and they were supplemented by improved vaccines. However, they were certainly not the only influences which led to the continued fall of mortality. I conclude that immunization and treatment contributed little to the decrease of deaths from infectious diseases before 1935; over the whole period since cause of death was first registered they were less important than other influences.

It would be surprising if personal medical measures were more effective in the century that preceded registration of cause of death than in the one that followed. However, because the suggestion is still taken seriously that inoculation against smallpox was an important influence on the decline of mortality and the growth of population, I will briefly state the reasons for rejecting it.[3]

First, although I accept that many people were inoculated or vaccinated, I do not believe that the level of immunity in the general population was sufficient to have so profound an effect on mortality from smallpox, particularly before vaccination was made compulsory (in 1852 in England and Wales). In reaching this conclusion I am particularly impressed by recent experience in countries such as India, where smallpox continued to be endemic in spite of claims that 80 percent of the population had

2   McKeown, *The Modern Rise of Population* (London, 1976), 108.
3   Peter E. Razzell, "Population Change in Eighteenth-Century England: a Reinterpretation," *Economic History Review*, XVIII (1965), 312.

been vaccinated, a level far higher than that reached in England and Wales before the mid-nineteenth century. Eradication of the disease was finally achieved by surveillance and vaccination of contacts.

Second, inoculation undoubtedly saved lives; it also caused deaths and contributed to the spread of the disease. Since experts are not agreed about the balance of gains and losses from whooping cough immunization, introduced as recently as 1952, it is clearly impossible to assess accurately the results of inoculation in the eighteenth century. My own guess, which I believe would be that of most virologists and epidemiologists, is that the disadvantages probably outweighed the advantages.

Third, even if the benefits of inoculation were as great as has been suggested, I do not think that any single disease could account for the reduction of mortality from all causes which occurred before 1838. Tuberculosis, which was so common in the nineteenth century, was responsible for less than one fifth of the decrease in the number of deaths between 1848–51 and 1971; and from the time of registration, or soon after, the reduction was not limited to one or a few conditions, but was spread across the whole range of infectious diseases. It therefore seems unlikely that the fall of the death rate during the previous century was due essentially to the decline of a single disease.

Although effective clinical measures were not available before the twentieth century, medical science did contribute earlier in other ways.

> The modern improvement in health was initiated and carried quite a long way with little contribution from science and technology, except for the epidemiological investigations of environmental conditions in the eighteenth and nineteenth centuries. This was true of the increase in food production, the beginning of hygienic measures and the control of numbers. These advances resulted from simple but fundamental observations on everyday life: conservation of fertility increased agricultural output; sanitary measures prevented infectious diseases; and limiting the number of births improved the conditions of life for parents and their children. From the second half of the nineteenth century, however, the original steps were extended by scientific developments of a non-personal kind. Some of these (for example, improved transport, chemical fertilizers and mechanization in agriculture, technology in distribution of water

and disposal of sewage, and refrigeration of food) owed little to medical science and would have been introduced if no health interests were involved. But for extension and refinement of methods of preventing the spread of infectious diseases we are indebted to medical science, and particularly to laboratory research.[4]

CHANGES IN THE CHARACTER OF INFECTIOUS DISEASES   Perhaps from despair of finding any other explanation, some have concluded that changes in the character of the infections, determined by variation in the host-parasite relationship, were responsible for major changes in the experience of infectious disease. It is an interpretation that has obvious attractions. The relationship between micro-organisms and man is constantly changing as a result of the operation of natural selection on host and parasite, and there is no infection of which it can be said that there has been no change over a considerable period. There is, moreover, one disease, scarlet fever, in which this seems the best explanation for the variation in mortality observed in the nineteenth and twentieth centuries. Hence there is no difficulty in accepting that at any time some infections might increase in virulence, others decrease, and still others remain relatively constant.[5]

But this explanation—variation in the character of the diseases, essentially independent of both medical intervention and environmental change—does not explain the major shifts which have occurred in the past: the predominance of infectious diseases (particularly the human infections) as causes of sickness and death, which followed the transition to an agricultural way of life; and their decline, which coincided with industrialization. Moreover, if we were to accept this explanation for the reduction of infectious deaths, the transformation of health, and the growth of population in the past three centuries, we should have to explain why the improvement was confined to developed countries. If we are satisfied that the advance was not due to immunization and therapy, we must seek an explanation in the vast changes in conditions of life associated with industrialization.

4 McKeown, *Role of Medicine*, 161–162.
5 Jonathan C. Chambers, *Population, Economy and Society in Pre-Industrial England* (Oxford, 1972), 12, 22.

EXPOSURE TO INFECTION   The feasibility of controlling the transmission of micro-organisms is largely determined by the ways in which they are spread. In developed countries it is relatively easy to prevent exposure to water-borne diseases; it is more difficult to control those spread by food, personal contact, and animal vectors; it is usually impossible to prevent transmission of airborne infections.

There are no grounds for thinking that the reduction of mortality from airborne diseases such as measles and scarlet fever owed anything to reduced exposure. In others (such as tuberculosis, whooping cough, diphtheria, and smallpox) less frequent contact contributed to the decline of the death rates; but it came about as a secondary consequence of the lowered prevalence of the diseases in the community, rather than through control of the means of their spread.

The contribution of reduced exposure as a primary influence was mainly in water- and food-borne diseases. The improvement in water supplies and sewage disposal in the later years of the nineteenth century was largely responsible for the fall at that time in mortality from enteric and diarrheal diseases. The provision of a safe milk supply was the main reason for the reduction of deaths from gastroenteritis and contributed substantially to the fall in infant mortality from 1900. The improvement of milk, together with the elimination of tuberculous cattle, also led to a decrease in deaths from the bovine types of non-respiratory tuberculosis. Personal hygiene, particularly bathing, may have contributed to the decline of typhus but could have had no significant effect on water-borne diseases. The only successful personal measures— boiling or chemical treatment of water—were unknown at that time.[6]

In summary, reduction of exposure to infection was important mainly in the case of diseases spread by water and food, and the basic measures were introduced progressively from the later years of the nineteenth century. In relation to the general interpretation of the determinants of health and population growth the important conclusion is that exposure to infection increased in the

6 McKeown, *Rise of Population*, 126–127; M. W. Beaver, "Population, Infant Mortality and Milk," *Population Studies*, XXVII (1973), 243.

early period of industrialization when mortality from infectious diseases was falling. Again, we must look elsewhere for the main explanation of the reduction in deaths.

CONTROL OF FERTILITY   It has been suggested that for both early and modern man deliberate restriction of fertility played an important part in preserving health and limiting population growth. I find such a notion unconvincing.

First, that human fertility was effectively restricted is thought to find support in the suggestion that other animals, in their natural habitats, maintain their "numbers at about the level at which food resources are utilized to the fullest extent possible without depletion." This regulation of numbers by behavior is thought to have evolved from group selection, it being to the advantage of the group not to expand beyond its food suplies. The thesis has been criticized by many biologists, who have argued that natural selection acts by favoring some individuals rather than others (and not some populations rather than others). Lack provided a forceful account of the objections to the concept of group selection based on restriction of fertility.[7]

Second, the effectiveness of the methods that restrict human fertility has been overestimated. There is no convincing evidence that the growth of any population has been limited substantially by restraints on the frequency of intercourse. Prolonged lactation is not an effective measure: 30 percent of a group of postpartum women became pregnant within a year after delivery; two fifths of them were still lactating at the time of conception and one tenth conceived without having menstruated. In another study, the cycle reappeared within five months of birth in 40 percent of women whose children were wholly breast fed. It was concluded that in women, as in experimental animals, the cycle is fairly effectively suppressed during the early period of lactation; it reappears in an increasing proportion as lactation continues and returns more rapidly if the child is partially weaned. Moreover, the ability of the breast to secrete enough milk to feed a child diminishes after the early months and children kept at the breast for the

7 V. C. Wynne-Edwards, *Animal Dispersion in Relation to Social Behaviour* (Edinburgh, 1972), 9, 11; David Lack, *Population Studies of Birds* (Oxford, 1966), 280.

prolonged periods quoted for primitive people must be receiving their food largely from other sources. Under such conditions the stimulus of suckling is reduced and the effect on fertility small.[8]

The other possible influences on conception are contraceptive measures of the kinds that are common today. There is little evidence of the practice of birth control in the English demographic literature of the century preceding the Industrial Revolution and, although individuals and groups have undoubtedly avoided pregnancy by coitus interruptus and other methods, the earliest evidence that they did so on a scale which affected national fertility trends is the decline in the French birth rate from the end of the eighteenth century.[9]

Another influence on fertility is the termination of an established pregnancy by abortion. As recent experience shows (for example in Japan), there is no doubt about the feasibility of this procedure, and the only question is whether it was effective with the techniques available before the twentieth century. There is no reason to think so. In spite of the extensive lore about the effect of drugs, violence, and psychological stress, it is difficult to interrupt a normal pregnancy by any means other than direct interference with the contents of the uterus. This intervention can be undertaken with reasonable success and safety by an experienced physician operating under appropriate conditions. In any other circumstances the procedure is both unreliable and dangerous and often results in the septic abortions which were common before the grounds for abortion were liberalized. It is unlikely that abortion could have provided for early man what it has not until recently provided for modern man—an effective means of restricting fertility.

There is little doubt about the use and effectiveness of the other method of limiting population size often discussed in this context, namely the deliberate killing of infants and children after birth. However, this is an aspect of mortality and should properly

8 C. G. Peckham, "An Investigation of Some Effects of Pregnancy Noted Six Weeks and One Year After Delivery," *Johns Hopkins Hospital Bulletin*, LIV (1934), 186; McKeown and J. R. Gibson, "A Note on Menstruation and Conception During Lactation," *Journal of Obstetrics and Gynaecology of the British Empire*, LXI (1954), 824.
9 R. R. Kuczynski, "British Demographers' Opinions on Fertility, 1600–1760," in Lancelot Hogben (ed.), *Political Arithmetic* (London, 1938), 283.

be considered with other causes of postnatal death rather than as a means of reducing fertility.

Third, in developing countries today there is little evidence that fertility is effectively controlled by the restraints that are practiced (for example, by avoidance of intercourse in the period after birth, in association with polygyny). It is difficult to believe that the invaluable capacity to limit numbers, deeply rooted in instinctive behavior, was available to primitive people and lost only in the last few centuries.

Fourth, the evidence for successful control of fertility before the nineteenth century, based largely on family reconstitution studies, is unconvincing. It has led to conclusions (for example, on infant mortality) in the sixteenth century which are quite inconsistent with current knowledge. It has also suggested that an increase in the number of births, due to removal of restraints of fertility, was an important influence on the growth of population in the last three centuries. It can readily be shown that if mortality had not fallen in this period, any increase in population size which resulted from a rising birth rate in the eighteenth century would have been offset by its later fall. Moreover, the idea that restraints on fertility kept numbers and resources in balance in the early eighteenth century, so that the Malthusian adjustment of high mortality was unnecessary, is inconsistent with the vital statistics of that time, when the death rate was about thirty per 1,000 and life expectancy at birth nearer thirty than forty years. The vastly different figures for countries such as Sweden today give us some idea of the level of mortality at which numbers and resources can be said to be in balance.[10]

However, if prenatal control of fertility was ineffective, there is no reason to doubt that numbers were restricted by the neglect or killing of infants and children. It may therefore be asked whether there is any need to distinguish between abortion and infanticide, since both are methods of eliminating unwanted births.

There is of course an elementary distinction to be made between control of numbers by limiting births and by postnatal

10 McKeown, "Fertility, Mortality and Causes of Death," *Population Studies,* XXXII (1978), 537.

killing; in the present context, however, it is less important than the distinction between deaths (whether before or after birth) for which man was responsible and deaths due to the environment. Although it is not possible to assess the balance between the two, what is hardly in doubt is that, as deaths due to deliberate killing were mainly random, for natural selection to have operated, a considerable proportion of the deaths must have been due to the environment. In relation to health and population growth the problem is to determine the nature of the adverse influences.

DETERMINANTS OF HEALTH   From the conclusion that fertility was not effectively controlled, it follows that the slow growth in population before the eighteenth century was due to high mortality, and that the expansion since that time resulted from less frequent deaths. And if we exclude medical intervention, changes in the character of infectious diseases, and reduction of exposure as the major influences on the decline of the infections, we are left with the possibility that response to the diseases was modified by improved nutrition.

This conclusion is consistent with the fact that there was a large increase in food supplies from advances in agriculture and transportation in the period when the population expanded. It is supported by extensive recent experience in developing countries, which leaves no doubt that although malnutrition has not the same effects on every disease (it is marked in diarrhea, measles, and tuberculosis, but is less significant in whooping cough), in general it is a major determinant of infection rates and of the outcome of infections. The World Health Organization concluded that "one half to three quarters of all statistically recorded deaths of infants and young children are attributed to a combination of malnutrition and infection" and "an adequate diet is the most effective vaccine against most of the diarrheal, respiratory and other common infections."[11]

When interpreting the experience of infections I do not think it is safe to confine attention to one or a few diseases, or to a short period such as the eighteenth century. The evidence before

11   World Health Organization, "Better Food for a Healthier World," *Features*, 19 (1973); Moises Behar, "A Deadly Combination," *World Health* (Feb./Mar., 1974), 26.

cause of death was registered—and some would say even after—
is so treacherous that an ingenuous writer can find support from
the literature for almost any hypothesis that he cares to elaborate.
It is therefore essential to consider infections in the hunter-gatherer, agricultural, and industrial periods, and to try to account for
the profound changes in experience of the diseases which occurred
from one period to another. For this purpose it is desirable to
have a concept of the determinants of health upon which to base
conclusions.

1. Until the last 300 years man, like other living things, was
exposed to rigorous natural selection, the large majority of individuals conceived having died before or, more often, after birth
without reproducing. Man is therefore well adapted to the environment in which he evolved.

2. Only a small part of the burden of disease is determined
irreversibly at fertilization by abnormalities of genes and chromosomes. Most diseases are due to adverse environmental influences on people whose genes make disease more or less likely but
not inevitable.

3. Under the conditions of evolution the adverse influences
were of two kinds: deficiencies and hazards. Of the four essentials
for life—food, water, oxygen, and heat—only food has been
seriously deficient. (It is interesting, if not unexpected, that the
length of time man can survive without the essentials is inversely
related to their availability: oxygen/minutes; heat/hours; water/
days; food/weeks). The common hazards were from other living
things competing for existence—parasites (viruses, bacteria, pro-
tozoans, helminths, and arthropods) and predators, particularly
human predators. The basic requirements for health were the
provision of food and protection from the hazards presented by
other living things.

4. Changes in the environment from the conditions under
which man evolved create new hazards from exposure to influences to which the genes were not adapted.

Against the background of this analysis disease may be said
to arise in the following ways:

Diseases determined before birth   The diseases in this class
comprise those determined at fertilization—mainly single gene

disorders, chromosomal aberrations, and certain disabilities associated with aging—as well as congenital abnormalities not so determined (such as most types of mental subnormality and malformations), in which environmental influences are prenatal.

The conditions determined prenatally are relatively intractable, but I am not suggesting that they offer no scope for prevention and treatment. The prevention of rhesus hemolytic disease is a remarkable example of an advance made possible by a combination of genetic and clinical knowledge. The identification and abortion of a fetus affected by Down's syndrome is another solution to an apparently intractable problem. Equally impressive in a quite different way is the immense technical accomplishment which restores a child with patent ductus arteriosus or atrial septal defect to a life of normal duration and quality.

With the possible exception of some determined in the uterus, the diseases in this class are unlikely to be controlled by modification of their origins, and must be tackled through knowledge of their mechanisms. This is indeed the field which uniquely requires the traditional laboratory and clinical approach, and the more successful postnatal measures are in dealing with preventable conditions, the more important the residual congenital problems will be seen to be.

Diseases due to deficiencies and hazards   Where man is well adapted to his environment, as he was for most of his existence, diseases (excluding those determined before birth) arise mainly from a deficiency in essential requirements, or from hazards of life resulting from competition for resources. Food was by far the most important of the essentials, and the hazards were from both parasites and predators. The present day differences in health indices (such as death rates and expectations of life) between continents, between countries, and between social classes within the same countries, indicate that the deficiencies and hazards associated with poverty are still the predominant causes of ill-health in the world as a whole.

Diseases due to maladaptation   Large and rapid changes in the conditions of life may lead to disease by exposing a population to influences to which it is not adapted. Adaptation may of course occur if mortality is increased or fertility reduced by disease. But, in view of the slow rate of human reproduction, the time required is long, and it is lengthened by measures which improve the survival or fertility of those affected.

In developed countries the predominant health problems are no longer mainly attributable to food deficiency or hazards from other living things; they are due to profound changes in the conditions of life under which man evolved. Many of these changes are the result of behavior facilitated by affluence—smoking, consumption of excessive or refined food, lack of exercise, and the like. Although the effect of such influences cannot be measured exactly, during the past century one of them (smoking) appears to have halved the increase in life-expectancy of adult males who smoke.

I conclude that diseases can be broadly divided into two categories according to the possibility of their prevention by manipulation of environmental (i.e. non-genetic) influences. Those in the first category cannot be controlled in this way, either because they are due to abnormalities of genes or chromosomes, or, if they are not, because the influences which lead to them are prenatal and likely to be inaccessible. Most of these conditions result in spontaneous abortions or are present at birth, although some are not recognized until later and others are not manifested until later in life. Diseases of this type can be thought of as the price to be paid for the advantages which accrue from the intricate exchange of genes at fertilization, or from the protected environment provided by a period of intrauterine life. These disease problems are relatively little affected even by profound changes in the conditions of life. Their solution depends on prevention of the conception or birth of those affected, or on treatment, as in the case of cardiac malformations or, in late life, of arthritic hips.

By definition all other diseases are due to postnatal influences which in principle might be controlled. However a distinction must be made between (a) those occurring in an environment to which the population is well adapted and where the main requirements for health are provision of food and protection from hazards, and (b) diseases resulting from exposure to influences to which the genes are not adapted, for which a solution must be sought in removal of such influences or in treatment.

It is against the background of these conclusions that I consider man's health and population growth in the past. There are various ways in which history might be divided for this purpose, but probably the most instructive division is into three periods— hunter-gatherer, agricultural, and industrial—identified by ways of life and the character of the predominant health problems.

THE HUNTER-GATHERER PERIOD   Conditions of life varied so greatly in the long hunter-gatherer period that it is scarcely surprising that there are wide differences of opinion about the effects of food on disease and population growth. The only point that is beyond dispute is that the human population increased very slowly, although it seems also to be agreed that mortality was high and expectation of life at birth was short. I have given reasons for doubting that fertility was effectively controlled and, if this conclusion is accepted, it is the high level of mortality that must be explained.

In wild animals the causes of death are malnutrition, disease, predation (including human destruction), and parasitism, and I suggest that the same causes were responsible for the high death rates of early man. Although they are often discussed separately, it is well recognized that these causes interact and, in the light of the determinants of human health, I suggest that most of the deaths were due directly or indirectly to food shortage.

In a population which is well adapted to its environment by natural selection, deaths from malnutrition and disease are largely due to inadequate food intake; deaths from predation and parasitism result from the search for food by other living things, and those from homicide in its multiple forms (infanticide, cannibalism, tribal wars, etc.) are also attributable to competition for resources, of which food was by far the most critical. Indeed, to the extent that deliberate restraints on fertility occurred, they too must be attributed to immediate or prospective food deficiency. We can hardly believe that parents refrained from intercourse, aborted, or killed their children without reason.

This discussion leaves open, necessarily, the relative importance of the different causes of death, apart from the conclusions that (a) the various causes were all associated, directly or indirectly with insufficient food, and (b) for natural selection to operate, a large proportion of the deaths must have been due to selective environmental conditions rather than to random checks through restriction of fertility or deliberate killing. But in view of the great importance of infectious diseases in historical times, something should be said about their significance in the hunter-gatherer period.

In an illuminating discussion of the effects of changing social organization on the infectious diseases of man, Fenner wrote:

> In contrast to other types of disease (genetic, traumatic, degenerative, neoplastic), the infectious diseases are dependent upon contact, either directly or indirectly through vectors or fomites, between individuals of the same species or, in the zoonoses, individuals of different species. For this reason social organization, particularly community size and the degree and frequency of contact between individuals of the same and different communities, has played a significant part in determining the nature and prevalence of the infectious diseases of man.[12]

As early man lived in small bands with infrequent contact with other closed bands, many agents—especially viruses—now regarded as universal could not have existed. The only human infections that could have survived under these conditions were those characterized by latency and recurrent infection. Herpes simplex and chicken pox are examples of viruses which exhibit these features. But "most viral diseases were not originally 'human' diseases and were caused by viruses of some other animal which 'accidentally' infected man." The same is true of most bacterial and protozoal diseases, although again there are exceptions (such as staphylococcal and streptococcal infections of wounds, tuberculosis, leprosy, and trypanosomiasis) which, because of latency and chronicity, could have survived in small isolated communities.[13]

But although numbers were not large enough to maintain directly transmitted microparasitic diseases, living mainly in tropical areas (it was only after cereals were planted and stored that man could move readily into temperate zones), early man was plagued by debilitating tropical infections from parasites which complete their life cycles by passing from one human host to

12   Frank Fenner, "The Effect of Changing Social Organization on the Infectious Diseases of Man," in S. W. Boyden (ed.), *The Impact of Civilization on the Biology of Man* (Toronto, 1970), 48.
13   *Ibid.*

another via one or more intermediate species. (The statement that some of the few surviving hunter-gatherers appear to be healthy is based on the observation that they do not have diseases such as hypertension, diabetes, heart disease, and cancer. Of course they do not, since these conditions have only become predominant since industrialization.)

It may never be possible to assess with any confidence the relative importance of infections and other causes of sickness and death in the hunter-gatherer period; but what is hardly in doubt is that nutritional state had a considerable bearing on the frequency and severity of many infections. In a recent review of the population biology of infectious diseases, May and Anderson concluded:

> Of special importance are the effects that can arise from the now widely recognized fact that the impact of an infection is often related to the nutritional state of the host. Broadly speaking, malnourished hosts have lowered immunological competence, and are less able to withstand the onslaught of infection. The effective pathogenicity of a parasite therefore tends to increase as host density arises to the level where competition for resources is severe.[14]

THE AGRICULTURAL PERIOD   There have been two major changes from the conditions of life of early man and both had profound effects on health and population growth. The first occurred with the transition to a settled way of life; the second was associated with the agricultural and industrial developments of the last three centuries.

The first agricultural revolution brought an increase in food supplies which led to a decline in mortality and an increase in numbers. Why then, after an initial spurt, did the world's population rise so slowly that it was not until 1830 that it reached 1 billion? The answer must be sought in the effect of the change in ways of life on the experience of infectious diseases.

The expansion and aggregation of populations led to the predominance of infections as causes of sickness and death. Community size had reached the level needed to maintain diseases such

---

14   Robert M. May and Roy M. Anderson, "Population Biology of Infectious Diseases: Part II," *Nature,* CCLXXX (1979), 460.

as smallpox, measles, and rubella, and a large closely knit society living in poor hygienic conditions permitted the spread of fecal-oral and respiratory organisms. It seems probable that most of the infections were acquired from other animals. These infections probably included: measles from dog distemper virus; mumps, smallpox, and influenza from related viruses in domestic animals and birds; the common cold from rhinoviruses of horses; syphilis from treponematosis of monkeys; tuberculosis from disease of cattle; and diphtheria from cows.[15]

In the light of these conclusions it is not difficult to interpret the reasons for the predominance of infectious diseases during the past 10,000 and particularly during the last 6,000 years. The increase in food supplies from agriculture led to the growth of populations to the size and density needed for the propogation and transmission of micro-organisms. But since fertility was not effectively controlled, populations expanded to the size at which food resources again became marginal, so that the relation between man and micro-organisms evolved over a period in which man was, in general, poorly nourished. The relationship was unstable and finely balanced according to the physiological state of host and parasite; improvement in nutrition would have tipped the balance in favor of the one and deterioration in favor of the other. Under these conditions an increase in food supplies became a necessary condition for a substantial reduction in mortality from infectious diseases, and limitation of numbers would have had to follow for the advance to be maintained. These changes, together with hygienic improvements, were the critical advances made in the last three centuries.

THE INDUSTRIAL PERIOD   Since the eighteenth century there has been a vast improvement in health, most clearly reflected in increased life expectancy at birth, which has coincided with the modern rise in population. The interpretation of these events and of their relationship is fundamental to an understanding of the influence of food on health and population growth.

---

15 Aidan Cockburn, "Where Did Our Infectious Diseases Come From? The Evolution of Infectious Disease," *CIBA Foundation Symposium 49* (London 1977), 103; Richard N. Fiennes, *Zoonoses and the Origins and Ecology of Human Disease* (London, 1978), 18–29.

These events have a common explanation, for the rise in population was due to the decline in mortality which led to the increase of life expectancy. Mortality declined essentially because of a reduction in deaths from infectious diseases. With the possible exceptions of starvation and infanticide, a decline in non-communicable causes of death made no substantial contribution to the improvement in health before the twentieth century. The central problem in interpreting the modern changes in health and population size is the explanation for the decline of deaths due to infectious disease.

The earliest and most important reason for the decline in infectious diseases was an improvement in nutrition which resulted from advances in agriculture and transportation. The advance was due initially to the introduction of new crops, such as the potato and maize, and to the more effective application of traditional methods of agriculture—increased land use, manuring, winter feeding, and rotation of crops—rather than to mechanical or chemical methods associated with industrialization. In the beginning, therefore, the Industrial Revolution did not create its own labor force, since the decline in mortality and growth in population preceded it and were for some time independent of it. From the second half of the nineteenth century, however, agricultural productivity was greatly increased by the introduction of mechanization and the use of chemical fertilizers and pesticides.

Second only to nutritional influences over time, and probably in importance, were the improvements in hygiene introduced progressively from the second half of the nineteenth century. They were the main reasons for the decline in water- and food-borne diseases, which accounted for about a fifth of the reduction in mortality in England and Wales from all causes between the mid-nineteenth century and the present day. In the nineteenth century there were no great improvements in working and living conditions, and the main advances were in the purification of water and in sewage disposal (which coincided with the decrease in deaths from intestinal infections). From about 1900 these measures were greatly extended by food hygiene, affecting most critically the quality of milk. Before that time it was not possible to protect milk from micro-organisms, and the rapid fall in the number of deaths from gastroenteritis, which contributed sub-

stantially to the decline in infant mortality, was due to the introduction of sterilization, bottling, and safe transportation of milk.
Environmental measures have been extended in the present century by improvements in working and living conditions. The
latter include advances (such as control of atmospheric pollution)
in the community at large as well as in domestic circumstances.[16]

The conclusions concerning the influence of immunization
and therapy have been discussed earlier in this article. In summary, they contributed little to the reduction in deaths from
infectious diseases before 1935, and over the whole period since
cause of death was first registered (1838 in England and Wales)
they were less important than the other influences.

The other reason for the modern transformation in health
was the change in reproductive behavior which led to a decline
in the birth rate. The significance of this change can hardly be
exaggerated. In England and Wales, if the birth rate had continued
at its early nineteenth-century level, the population today would
be about 140 million rather than 50 million, with effects on health
and welfare that can be imagined. Hence, although the initial
progress was due to other influences, the reduction in the birth
rate was the essential complement without which the advances,
like those associated with the first agricultural revolution, would
soon have been reversed.

Moreover, the restraint on reproduction probably had a direct effect on mortality. If infanticide was as significant as has
been suggested, the elimination of unwanted pregnancies may
have made the largest contribution to the decline in non-infective
causes of death.

It would be unwise to estimate numerically the contribution
that different influences have made to the decline in mortality and
population growth. Nevertheless, it is possible to draw some
general conclusions concerning the main influences during the
past three centuries.

First, an improvement in nutrition exerted the earliest and,
over the whole period since about 1700, the most important
influence. Second, hygienic measures were probably responsible

16 McKeown, *Role of Medicine,* 75–78.

for at least a fifth of the reduction in the death rate between the mid-nineteenth century and the present day. This is the proportion of the decline which was associated with water- and food-borne diseases. Third, with the exception of vaccination against smallpox, the contribution of which was small, the influence of immunization and therapy was delayed until the twentieth century and had little effect on national mortality trends before the introduction of the sulphonamides in 1935. Since that time immunization and therapy have not been the only nor even the most important influences. Fourth, the change in reproductive practices which led to a decline in the birth rate was very important, since it ensured that the improvement in health brought about by other means was not reversed by rising numbers.

The high level of mortality and the slow rate of population growth until recently indicates that, for almost the whole of his existence, man's control of his environment was insufficient to enable him to advance his health significantly beyond that of other living things. But since the number of those born was greatly in excess of the number that survived, through natural selection he was well adapted to the conditions under which he evolved. It was lack of food, which could not be offset by genetic adaptation, that was chiefly responsible for the high death rate and the slow growth in population.

The domestication of plants and animals, and the transition to a settled way of life marked the beginning of a degree of control of the environment unique to man, and they led to a decline in mortality and an increase in numbers. However, the failure to limit reproduction again made food supplies marginal; but, with expanded populations and defective hygiene, infectious diseases became the predominant cause of sickness and death.

The agricultural and industrial developments of the past three centuries brought still greater control of the environment, an increase in food supplies from advances in agriculture, and protection from hazards, particularly from infectious organisms. This time, however, the advances were not lost, as they had been 10,000 years earlier, by an increase in numbers, because agricultural and hygienic improvements were followed by a fundamental change in behavior—the control of reproduction which led to a decline in the birth rate. For the first time it could be said that numbers and resources were in reasonable balance, so that the Malthusian adjustment through high mortality no longer operated. However, industrial and economic developments have brought new threats to health by creating an environment for which man's genes are not adapted.

Ann G. Carmichael

Infection, Hidden Hunger, and History   The links between undernutrition and infection among the poor of today's Third World are socially and demographically significant. From birth to an early grave the victims of hidden hunger endure episodes of illness which wealthier nations and individuals do not suffer. Biochemists contend that undernutrition does not make the human body prone to more severe or more frequent infection, but biochemical models do not address the social circumstances which allow widespread undernutrition. An impoverished environment enhances morbidity and mortality. To what extent has this differential morbidity been an important part of the history of infectious diseases? Are the modern Third World populations even comparable to societies or groups within societies living before the last century?[1]

In now classic studies of morbidity and mortality in Guatemala and India, Scrimshaw, Gordon, and Taylor argued that malnutrition progressively enhances infection in an individual, and that infection often causes further malnutrition. An ill person does not eat well, even though his metabolic needs are greater. Similarly, poorly nourished individuals rapidly exhaust protein and caloric reserves in the process of fighting infection. This "synergistic package," as Taylor has called it, is reflected in the staggering statistics of death and illness in Third World nations. "Synergism" in this context means that the "behavior of most diseases is shaped by the nutritional state of the affected host."[2]

Ann G. Carmichael is Assistant Professor of History and Philosophy of Science at Indiana University, Bloomington.

The author wishes to thank George Alter, Saul Benison, Frank Fenner, Jeanne Peterson, and Eugene Weinberg for their helpful suggestions.

1   See Michael C. Latham, "Nutrition and Infection in National Development," *Science,* CCLXXXVIII (1975), 561–565; Sidney L. Kark, *Epidemiology and Community Medicine* (New York, 1974), 249–255.
2   Articles useful on the synergistic model include Carl E. Taylor, "Synergy among Mass Infections, Famines, and Poverty," in this issue; Nevin Scrimshaw, John Gordon, and

Such a model raises at least two objections. First, the physiological and microbiological aspects of synergism have not been demonstrated in controlled laboratory studies. Second, the commonplace "first famine than fever" will not bear close historical scrutiny. Famines and epidemics are not invariably linked in historical records. These objections, however, often dismiss inquiry into the socioeconomic dimensions of morbidity and mortality. Poverty now and in the past is a "hidden hunger," an added environmental burden creating the circumstances for repeated and multiple infections.

This study cannot address all of the issues linking or failing to link malnutrition and infection in historical records. In particular, it omits discussion of the contributions of modern medicine, public health, and improving nutrition to the disappearance of many lethal infectious diseases. It contends that exposure to infection was unequal among individuals living before the sanitary awakenings of the modern world, just as unequal as the distance between the twentieth and seventeenth centuries in general exposure to infection. In the social circumstances which link hidden hunger and infection in today's Third World there is a vicious synergism which helps our understanding of the past.

OBJECTIONS TO SYNERGISM   From the biologists' perspective one of the most serious reservations concerning the synergistic package is that a microorganism requires many of the same nutrients that are essential to the host's well-being. A robust host, in theory, offers more to sustain the growth of a pathogen. For the synergistic model to work at the cellular level, the malnourished host must be unable to invoke the complex cellular and humoral immune systems that govern the ingestion and destruction of parasites, and that produce antibodies to inactivate would-be invaders. Failure of the immune system occurs only in severe levels of

---

Taylor, *Interactions of Nutrition and Infection* (Geneva, 1968); Ranjit K. Chandra, "Nutritional Deficiency and Susceptibility to Infection," *Bulletin of the World Health Organization*, LVII (1979), 167–177; Leonardo Mata, "Malnutrition and Concurrent Infections: Comparison of Two Populations with Different Infection Rates," in John S. Mackenzie (ed.), *Viral Diseases in South-East Asia and the Western Pacific* (New York, 1982), 56–76; Gordon, "Epidemiological Insights on Malnutrition: Some Resurrected, Others Restructured, A Few Retired," *American Journal of Clinical Nutrition*, XXXI (1978), 2341.

malnutrition. Starvation, rather than chronic undernutrition, pre-cipitates the fatal interaction between infection and undernutri-tion, and then only in the final stages of illness.[3]

Nutritional immunity has come to refer to the ability of vertebrates to withhold substances crucial to a microorganism's growth. A malnourished host may even have a slight advantage in forestalling clinical infection.

The example of iron and infection well documents this phe-nomenon. Humans manufacture a circulating protein that binds iron, and complex biochemical strategies determine the levels to which this molecule is saturated with free iron. In response to infection, the iron necessary for both human and microbial cell growth is made unavailable to the microbe by increased produc-tion of the protein and by saturation of the existing molecules. Further defense strategies by the host include decreased absorption of dietary iron and increased storage of iron in the liver and other tissues. A severely malnourished individual will be unable to synthesize enough of the iron-binding protein to withstand lethal parasitism, just as he will be unable to manufacture antibodies. But a moderately malnourished host will have less free iron to store or bind than the well-nourished one, whose better diet may even contribute to the microorganism's survival. Research over the last decade with iron and infection suggests that it may be detrimental to "feed a fever." Many mechanisms similar to the iron model may exist to protect an undernourished host from "increased susceptibility" to infection.[4]

Virulence in an organism is generally understood as its ability to overcome host defenses. In defeating nutritional immunity, a virulent organism succeeds because of its ability to steal iron from the binding protein, or because its growth liberates iron by dam-aging storage tissue. Hepatitis, yellow fever, and malaria are ex-amples of the latter category.

3 Ancel Keys et al., *The Biology of Human Starvation* (Minneapolis, 1950), 2v.; John and Anne Murray, "Suppression of Infection by Famine and its Activation by Refeeding—a Paradox?" *Perspectives in Biology and Medicine,* XX (1977), 471–483; Michael Katz, "Malaria and Malnutrition," *Reviews in Infectious Diseases,* IV (1982), 805.
4 See Eugene D. Weinberg, "Iron and Infection," *Microbiological Reviews,* XLII (1978), 45–66; Barrett Sugarman, "Zinc and Infection," *Reviews of Infectious Diseases,* V (1983), 137–147.

In cellular and humoral immunity, a virulent organism withstands host attempts to ingest infected cells and to block the replication of the organism, or it replicates itself rapidly, outrunning the production of antibodies. A viral infection, for example, may take over in host cells, reproducing itself many times and breaking out to infect neighboring cells, all with a rapidity that seriously challenges the normal immune system.[5]

From a historian's perspective, the repeated, unpredictable appearance of virulent infectious diseases distinguishes pre-modern mortality and morbidity. The ordinary infections of the past resemble those of developing nations today, but the extraordinary, demographically significant mortality of past times depended little on synergism with malnutrition. If some pathogens appear among human communities independent of the existence of malnourished persons, this premise also would constitute a limitation to the usefulness of the malnutrition/infection model.[6]

Virulent epidemic diseases can produce supramortality without preying on the malnourished. Influenza pandemics in the last 100 years have reminded us that human communities are vulnerable to sudden, devastating epidemic mortality of a type and magnitude not affected by the nutritional status of nations or individuals. Furthermore, influenza epidemics are not created or sustained by the existence of malnourished individuals in a society. Although the disease has been a major killer only since rapid transportation made the world a global community, epidemics of influenza may have had important local effects throughout the history of civilization.[7]

Recent studies have shown that humans are exposed to novel strains of influenza by the recombination of human and animal strains of the virus, or even by the recombination of mammalian and avian influenza viruses. The sudden appearance of a mutant

---

5 Frank Fenner and David O. White, *Medical Virology* (New York, 1976; 2nd ed.).
6 See John D. Post, "Famine, Mortality, and Epidemic Disease in the Process of Modernization," *Economic History Review*, XXIX (1976), 14–37.
7 For popular accounts of the influenza pandemic, see Alfred W. Crosby, *Epidemic and Peace* (Westport, Conn., 1976); Richard Collier, *The Plague of the Spanish Lady* (New York, 1974). Migratory birds can transmit unfamiliar strains of influenza, so any densely settled civilization may have experienced significant population losses due to myxoviruses.

strain can leave vast numbers of people vulnerable to an infection for which no one has prior immunological protection.[8]

Influenza is, however, an atypical example among past and present killing infections. Human influenza is unique in its ability to produce varying recombinant antigenic strains. But in the circumstances of its transmission lies an important generalization: domestic animals commonly furnish novel human infections. Often a microorganism well adapted to one species may prove virulent to a different animal host, or even lethal to a distant cousin of the original host.[9]

One could argue that other zoonoses, the diseases transmitted from animals to man, become virulent infections because of man's purposeful influence on environmental conditions. Human poverty often encourages zoonotic infections by placing animals and man in close association. Explaining the decline of malaria in Europe, Bruce-Chwatt and de Zulueta argued that malaria "is related to less developed agriculture and poorer animal husbandry. When larger groups of human populations are insufficiently protected from exposure to mosquitoes by stabled domestic animals situated close to large anopheline breeding places, epidemics of malaria may occur in years when heavy rainfall coincides with hot summers." Clearly human infection is not strictly exogenous to human events.[10]

In the search for killing infections which have nothing to do with the existence of malnourished individuals within a society, mutations within the microbial world, taking first the special case of microbial infections, are important. Both streptococcal organisms (those that cause scarlet fever, for example) and diphtheria

---

8   Martin M. Kaplan and Robert G. Webster, "The Epidemiology of Influenza," *Scientific American*, CCXXXVII (1977), 88–104; William I. B. Beveridge, *Influenza: The Last Great Plague* (London, 1977); Richard Fiennes, *Zoonoses and the Origins and Ecology of Human Disease* (New York, 1978), 37–45; Edwin D. Kilbourne, "Epidemiology of Influenza," in *idem* (ed.), *The Influenza Viruses and Influenza* (New York, 1975), 483–538.

9   Cedric Mims, "The Emergence of New Infectious Diseases," in Neville F. Stanley and R. A. Joske (eds.), *Changing Disease Patterns and Human Behavior* (New York, 1980), 231–250; Andre Nahmias and Darryl Reanney, "The Evolution of Viruses," *Annual Review of Ecology and Systematics*, VIII (1977), 29–49; Fenner and F. N. Ratcliffe, *Myxomatosis* (Cambridge, 1965); Fiennes, *Zoonoses and Human Disease*.

10   Leonard Bruce-Chwatt and Julian de Zulueta, *The Rise and Fall of Malaria in Europe: A Historico-Epidemiological Study* (New York, 1980), 4–5.

are bacteria that are susceptible to infection by bacteriophages which increase the virulence of the organism.[11]

The New England throat distemper of 1735 to 1740 has been the subject of medico-historical studies which use the unpredictable circumstance of a virus infecting a bacterium to explain variations in the way humans experience disease and their impact on historical events. The state of nutrition of individual hosts does not determine these changes in virulence due to a phage virus, nor are specific human actions responsible for the microbial infection—that is, the infection of one microorganism by another. The "tox+" gene that is introduced by the virus would be as lethal to a well-nourished child or adult who had no immunological experience with diphtheria as it would to a malnourished person. Variation in the virulence of a microorganism need not depend upon infection by a bacteriophage or the addition of genetic information by a plasmid.[12]

There is some evidence to suggest that plague, historically one of the most important infections, varies in virulence even during an epidemic, and that this change is largely independent of differences in human hosts. An increase in virulence is presumably not to the microorganism's long-term advantage. Mutations only rarely produce an infective, virulent organism. The familiar acute community infections (measles, chickenpox, diphtheria, whoop-

---

11 On phage viruses generally see Alwin M. Poppenheimer, Jr., "The Evolution of Infectious Disease of Man," in Jacques Monod and Ernest Borek (eds.), Of Microbes and Life (New York, 1971), 174–188; on tox+ gene see Lane Berksdale, "The Gene tox+ of Corynebacterium diphtheriae," in ibid., 215–232.

12 Ernest Caulfield, The Throat Distemper of 1735–1740 (New Haven, 1939), argued that a mixture of scarlet fever and diphtheria caused the complex epidemic pattern; W. Barry Wood, Jr., From Miasmas to Molecules (New York, 1961), reviews the epidemic in light of research with tox+ gene. See also the reservations of Mary K. Matossian, "The Throat Distemper Reappraised," Bulletin of the History of Medicine, XIV (1980), 529–539, who argues that mycotoxicoses are a better explanation of the throat distemper episodes.

On the formation of new microorganisms see 9n. above and Arthur Koch, "Evolution of Antibiotic Resistance Gene Function," Microbiological Reviews, XLV (1981), 355–378. See also Maxwell Finland, "Emergence of Antibiotic Resistance in Hospitals, 1935–1975," Reviews of Infectious Diseases, I (1979), 4–21. It is in the interest of both host and parasite that virulent infections are infrequent events. "Tox+" gene is more properly known as a beta phage and, when diphtheria is lysogenized (the phage is attached to the bacterial DNA), toxin can be produced. Without phage the diphtheria organisms are avirulent. High levels of iron restrict toxin production; low concentrations of iron favor toxin production.

ing cough, mumps), for example, are very stable microorganisms which would not mutate readily.[13]

Historians, nevertheless, are intrigued with the possibility that lethal mutations might explain some major epidemics. Small-pox, for example, did not become a lethal epidemic in Europe before the mid-sixteenth century, yet historians have long attributed the destruction of the Aztec empire to *Variola major,* introduced by the Spaniards between 1519 and 1521. A non-lethal strain of smallpox may well have been common in Europe before the conquest of the Western Hemisphere. Among European epidemics around 1500 one looks in vain for the lethal *Variola major* strain of smallpox so familiar to seventeenth- and eighteenth-century Europeans. The massive replication of the *variola* organism among so many non-immunized persons may have increased the chances of the successful mutant, *Variola major.*[14]

Mutations, plasmids, phage viruses, recombinant strains of a virus, and infections derived from animal diseases illustrate mechanisms whereby an especially virulent infection appears without any synergism with human malnutrition. Another accidental circumstance can lead to exaggerated mortality: infections in "virgin soil" populations. The most dramatic cases have been drawn from Amerindians, a genetically similar group of peoples

13 See esp. James E. Williams et al., "Atypical Plague Bacilli Isolated from Rodents, Fleas, and Man," *American Journal of Public Health,* LXVIII (1978), 262–264; Jack D. Poland and Allan M. Barnes, "Plague," in James H. Steele (ed.), *Bacterial, Rickettsial, and Mycotic Diseases* (Boca Raton, Fla, 1981), I, 595.

14 "New" diseases abound in sixteenth- and seventeenth-century Europe. See Lloyd Stevenson, "New Diseases in the Seventeenth Century," *Bulletin of the History of Medicine,* XXXIX (1966), 1–21; Erwin Ackerknecht, *The History and Geography of the Most Important Diseases* (New York, 1965), 33–35, 117–127. Crucial environmental changes may have been responsible: see William McNeill, *Plagues and Peoples* (New York, 1976); Emmanuel Le Roy Ladurie, "A Concept: The Unification of the Globe by Disease (Fourteenth to Seventeenth Centuries)," in (trans. Siân and Ben Reynolds), *The Mind and Method of the Historian* (Chicago, 1981), 28–83.

Only one fifteenth-century smallpox epidemic seems to have claimed many lives: that in Paris, 1444. See Janet Shirley (ed. and trans.), *A Parisian Journal* (Oxford, 1968), 359. Mention of smallpox is rare in chronicles, diaries, and legislative records of Spain and Italy before 1540. See Alfonso Corradi, *Annali delle epidemie occorse in Italia* (1856–1891; repr. Bologna, 1974), 5v; Joaquin Villalba, *Epidemiología Española o Historia Cronólogica de las Pestes, Contagios, Epidemias y Epizootias* (Madrid, 1803). The portage of smallpox to the Aztecs was blamed on an African slave, but the disease may well have been measles or relatively non-virulent smallpox.

who had no effective contact with other civilizations for thousands of years. Their migrations to the Western Hemisphere, presumably when the last Ice Age provided a land bridge across the Bering Straits, could not have occurred in populations large enough to sustain any of the major acute community infections.[15]

At present there is no firm support for the hypothesis that the Amerindians' long-term unfamiliarity with many viral infections was coupled with genetic deficiencies in their immune responses. Rather, supramortality was due to massive community infection within a brief period. Virgin soil infections usually claim many lives because provisions cannot be made for all of the ill. This breakdown in social services often leads to heavy loss of life because secondary infections overwhelm those suffering from the primary disease.[16]

Secondary infections could also account for many of the influenza victims. Mere unfamiliarity with influenza was not responsible for all of the deaths in this pandemic, which claimed an estimated 15 to 20 million persons worldwide. In industrialized nations a major contributing cause of mortality was secondary bacterial pneumonia. Research with the influenza virus has suggested that bacterial pneumonias occur independently of the state of host nutrition, because the organism suppresses normal immune defenses which would ward off secondary infection. The important synergistic effect, if one exists in this case, is of infection with infection.[17]

15 Alfred W. Crosby, "Virgin Soil Epidemics as a Factor in Aboriginal Depopulation in America," *William and Mary Quarterly,* XXXIII (1976), 289–299.

16 See the review of James V. Neel, "Infectious Disease among Amerindians," *Medical Anthropology,* VI (1982), 47–55. Genetic differences are possible, however. See Francis Black, "Measles," in Alfred S. Evans (ed.), *Viral Infections of Humans: Epidemiology and Control* (New York, 1976), 297–315.

17 It is unclear whether influenza alone is capable of undermining host defenses. Secondary bacterial pneumonias may be caused by pathogens normally inhabiting the upper respiratory tract, because mucous is not cleared from the lower respiratory tract and thus forms a culture medium, or because moderate to severe influenza suppresses immune responses. Some individuals exposed to influenza may be made less resistant to bacterial infection by mechanisms which do not depend upon secondary malnutrition. See Robert B. Couch, "The Effects of Influenza on Host Defenses," *Journal of Infectious Diseases,* CXLIV (1978), 284–291; Philip A. Mackowiak, "Microbial Synergism in Human Infection," *New England Journal of Medicine,* CCXCVII (1978), 21–26, 83–87.

THE HISTORICAL IMPORTANCE OF THE SYNERGISTIC PACKAGE   One may question whether synergism between malnutrition and infection has any important historical meaning. Many lethal diseases have not depended on the presence of large numbers of malnourished persons to gain entry into or to multiply within a society. Moreover, famines and epidemics do not coincide neatly in historical records. Many historians are concerned, however, with more than mortality statistics, just as many physicians perceive a clinical and social dimension to undernutrition that does not respond to laboratory rebuttal.[18]

The measles virus provides an ideal case study because malnutrition appears to enhance the severity, duration, sequellae, and mortality associated with the infection, and because measles is one of the infections involved in virgin soil epidemics. Nutritional immunity does not seem to play an important role in measles infection, so that objection to synergism may be set aside. Measles in severely malnourished children is frequently fatal, but here we need only concentrate on the incidence of measles among populations not subjected to starvation. In a territory where no member of the population has previously been exposed to the virus, mortality from measles rises dramatically. Some populations, however, suffer much more than others.[19]

Squire argued as early as 1877 that the severe epidemic of measles in the Fiji was not due to heightened biological susceptibility. He understood that both the failure to obtain nursing care

18   On the historically questionable links between famines and epidemics, see Paul Slack, "Mortality Crises and Epidemics, 1485–1610," in Charles Webster (ed.), *Health, Medicine, and Mortality in the Sixteenth Century* (New York, 1979), 9–60; Andrew Appleby, "Nutrition and Disease: The Case of London, 1550–1750," *Journal of Interdisciplinary History*, VI (1975), 1–22.

19   Saul Krugman, Robert Ward, and Samuel Katz, *Infectious Diseases of Children* (St. Louis, 1977), 132–148; David Morley, "Measles and Whooping Cough," in Robert Cruickshank (ed.), *Epidemiology and Community Health in Warm Climate Countries* (New York, 1976), 63–76.

A classic study was done by Peter Ludwig Panum, and is translated "Observations Made During the Epidemic of Measles on the Faroe Islands, 1846," in *Medical Classics*, III (1939), 803–886. Neel et al., "Notes on the Effect of Measles and Measles Vaccine in a Virgin Soil Population of South American Indians," *American Journal of Epidemiology*, XCI (1970), 418–429. On severe cases of measles see Morley, "The Severe Measles of West Africa," *British Medical Journal*, I (1969), 297–300, 363–365.

and the occurrence of secondary infection accounted for supramortality in the Fiji epidemic. During the past century epidemics of measles among virgin soil populations have demonstrated that the provision of nursing care reduces mortality among adequately nourished populations to less than 5 percent of the cases, even without the addition of antibiotics. In 1846, measles in the remote Faroe Islands showed that aggressive nursing care and the fact of very small, dispersed communities helped to hold mortality to under 2 percent. Such mortality rates were as good as the experience of Greenlanders with virgin soil measles in 1952, when antibiotics were available.[20]

Panum's description of the Faroe Islands' epidemic of measles alluded to a recent occurrence of influenza as well. The timing of the two epidemics was close, but the earlier influenza epidemic did not contribute to losses from measles. Other instances where measles and influenza epidemics coincided were not so mild. Measles was associated with influenza in the devastating Fiji epidemic of 1877, in the Canadian Arctic in 1952, and recently among isolated South American Indians. The "Great Sickness" among Eskimos in 1900 illustrates the usual pattern of measles in a virgin soil.[21]

Eskimo deaths during the summer of 1900 were tragically visible to the traders and gold-seeking Caucasians who had recently penetrated the Alaskan interior. The whites did not suffer from the great mortality, which began with an epidemic of measles. The immediate cause of death during July was frequently dysentery, and educated observers noted that tuberculosis also

---

20 William Squire quoted in Neel, "Notes on the Effect of Measles," 418. Over 20,000 deaths were related to this epidemic. See Bolton Glanville Corney, "The Behaviour of Certain Epidemic Diseases in Natives of Polynesia, with Especial Reference to the Fiji Islands," *Transactions of the Epidemiological Society*, III (1884), 76–95; *idem*, "A Note on an Epidemic of Measles at Rotumá, 1911," *Proceedings of the Royal Society of Medicine*, VI (1913), 138–142.

In the Faroes, 13 per 1,000 died. In the Greenland epidemic, the death rate was 18 per 1,000; 45 percent of the cases had secondary complications, usually viral or bacterial pneumonia. See Polv E. Christensen et al., "An Epidemic of Measles in Southern Greenland, 1951; I: Measles in Virgin Soil," *Acta Medica Scandinavica*, CXIV (1952), 313–317.

21 Panum, "Measles on the Faroe Islands," 869; Corney, "Behaviour of Certain Epidemic Diseases," 86–90; Arthur F. W. Peart and F. P. Nagler, "Measles in the Canadian Arctic, 1952," *Canadian Journal of Public Health*, XLV (1954), 146–156; Robert J. Wolfe, "Alaska's Great Sickness, 1900: An Epidemic of Measles and Influenza in a Virgin Soil Population," *American Philosophical Society Proceedings*, CXXVI (1982), 91–121.

reappeared among the Indians. Late in the summer, as a final tragedy, an epidemic of influenza swept through the debilitated population. The killing infections of measles and influenza in a virgin soil were punctuated by reminders that chronic diseases (here tuberculosis) and chronic disease-contributing environments (accentuating summer dysentery) added to the losses. Most of the deaths occurred in the context of social and economic poverty.[22]

An astute missionary in South America noted, similarly, that 16 percent of Indians dying from measles were a group heavily infested with tapeworms and malaria. The metabolic requirements and immune strategies needed to defeat several microbial invaders may exhaust even a reasonably well-nourished individual. Fluid losses, from high fever and low fluid intake, from secondary diarrhea, or even from living in the tropics, could explain many additional deaths. But the fact that secondary infections figure significantly in mortality and morbidity is important in understanding the historical importance of the synergism between hidden hunger and infection.[23]

But so narrowly have we understood the usual case fatality rates of killing diseases like influenza, plague, and smallpox, that we have ignored the presence of many infections simultaneously besetting a population. Not everyone in a complex society may be equally exposed to infection; not everyone will be equally, much less equitably well fed. Rather than explore and explain the differential mortality in the pestilences of the past, historical accounts try to understand why a given infectious disease claimed so many lives. Phrases like "less resistant" and "more susceptible" often overlook obvious instances of human hunger.

At least two influences of the "synergistic package" in historical change are dealt with in detail elsewhere in this volume: the demographic impact of differential morbidity and mortality, and the potential decline in labor productivity. Two further examples are offered here to suggest that we have just begun to explore the historical usefulness of a full understanding of the common association between malnutrition and infection.[24]

22 *Ibid.*, 105–108.
23 See Neel et al., "Notes on the Effects of Measles," 418–429.
24 Susan Cotts Watkins and Etienne van de Walle, "Nutrition, Mortality, and Population Size: Malthus' Court of Last Resort," and Robert W. Fogel et al., "Secular Changes in American and British Stature and Nutrition," both in this issue.

First, bioanthropologists and paleopathologists have suggested that overpopulation in Paleolithic times led to the transition to the farming and settled communities of the Neolithic revolution. This population pressure advanced at a modest rate of 0.03 persons per year or less, until around 10,000 B.C., but growth accelerated after settlement. Studies of modern hunter-gatherers suggest that the allocation of food resources during scarcity differed in these communities from the practices of agricultural societies. All of the members of a tribe suffered the pressure of extra mouths in a hunter-gatherer society. In an agricultural society hunger was not shared by all. In general the bony evidence for malnutrition and/or infection increased at the times of population increase, so that late paleolithic and early neolithic communities both show "hunger lines" or "Harris lines" on long bones. But the striking feature of settled communities is that the distribution of Harris lines is unequal. In the first all-important revolution, undernutrition in some individuals became a tolerated social response to population increase. Differential nutrition and differential mortality may be linked this far into the past.[25]

Second, within recorded time the association of documented famines and food crises with individual epidemic diseases has not been uniform. Most human communities would have had little unambiguous experiental data on which to base their responses

25 Mark N. Cohen, *The Food Crisis in Prehistory* (New Haven, 1977); for this reference and many that follow in this section I am grateful to Della C. Cook, Department of Anthropology, Indiana University.

"Harris lines" are linear radiographic densities representing the temporary arrest of bone growth due to infection or to moderate malnutrition occurring acutely. It is interesting that in this parameter, at least, the body's reaction to infection and to malnutrition is the same. See Cook, "Subsistence Base and Health in Prehistoric Illinois Valley: Evidence from the Human Skeleton," *Medical Anthropology*, III (1979), 109–124; Jane E. Buikstra and Cook, "Paleopathology: An American Account," *Annual Reviews in Anthropology*, IX (1980), 433–470. Cohen, "Speculations on the Evolution of Density Measurement and Population Regulation in *Homosapiens*," in Cohen, Roy Malpass, and Harold Klein (eds.), *Biosocial Mechanisms of Population Regulation* (New Haven, 1980), 275–303; Black, "Infectious Diseases in Primitive Societies," *Science*, CLXXXVI (1975), 515–520; Frederick L. Dunn, "Epidemiological Factors: Health and Disease in Hunter-Gatherers," in Richard Lee and Irvin DeVore (eds.), *Man the Hunter* (Chicago, 1968), 221–228; Don E. Drumond, "The Limitation of Human Population: A Natural History," *Science*, CLXXXVI (1975), 713–721; Diana Shard, "The Neolithic Revolution: An Analogical Overview," *Journal of Social History*, VII (1973), 165–170.

to virulent infection, and so perceptions about the causes of community misfortune often motivated defenses that exaggerated differential morbidity and mortality. For example, northern Italians first devised medical and social defenses against recurrent plague which were not dominated by the precepts of Galenic physiology, but they did so only after a century and some eleven plagues had passed. The lazaretto and later the health boards were instituted with the increasing conviction that plague was contagious and that it was a disease of the poor. The first medical treatise on contagion emphasized both of these links, yet plague is a disease that is not usually spread by human contact nor is it exquisitely a disease of poverty.[26]

The association between socioeconomic poverty and threats of epidemic had a profound effect on determining bureaucratic responses to the problems of poverty and plague. Moreover, the association between poverty and the threat of plague was enhanced with the development of institutions that segregated poor from rich during crisis times. Typhus was first noticed and described in the early sixteenth century, and it was then seen as "new." Urbanization and urban poverty may have made typhus visible and threatening; elites may have been exposed to typhus only as adults, worsening their chances of recovery. The perception of differential mortality led to responses which aggravated deaths among part of the population, thereby reinforcing the elites' perceptions that the poor were dangerous.[27]

For historians, part of the task of hunger studies is to encompass the complexity and variations of the phenomena of poverty and hunger, both socially loaded terms which refer, only indirectly, to the narrower nexus of individual human malnutrition and infection.[28]

---

26 See Carmichael, "Plague Legislation in the Italian Renaissance," *Bulletin of the History of Medicine,* forthcoming.

27 The earliest medical account of typhus dates from the civil wars in Granada, 1490. See Villalba, *Epidemiología Española,* 69; Hans Zinsser, *Rats, Lice, and History* (Boston, 1965), 183–200; Corradi, *Annali delle epidemie,* I, 368–376; II, 273–280.

28 Larger issues not addressed here surely include the links between social stresses of all kinds and infection, and the links between undernutrition and dysfunctional behaviors. E.g., see the review of James L. Smart, "Undernutrition and Aggression," in Paul F. Brain and David Benton (eds.), *Multidisciplinary Approaches to Aggression Research* (Elsevier, 1981), 179–190; John Fernstrom and Loy Lytle, "Corn Malnutrition, Brain Serotonin, and Behavior," *Nutrition Reviews,* XXXIV (1976), 257–262.

THE USES OF HISTORICAL EPIDEMIOLOGY   Identifying the diseases of past civilizations adds another dimension to the historical study of human hunger. Even when we ignore the shared problem of whether the samples are sufficiently large or representative, historians and bioanthropologists will not have quantifiably equal data. If heights are to be an index of nutrition, paleopathologists are better served by the bones that they use than are historians with measured adult heights. Long bones, and even teeth, give more objective evidence of childhood stresses which were severe enough to halt growth. Measurements of the strontium content in bones can give details about the relative contributions of animal and vegetable food sources in the overall diet of individuals. Osteoporotic bone loss in meat-based diets and dental caries in people who consumed large amounts of carbohydrates are additional useful measures for bioanthropologists. Bioanthropologists seem to know more about the nutritional status of pleistocene and early neolithic communities than we do about populations in our own culture during the last millennium. But historians have better data from which to multiply the number and variety of indices which permit an evaluation of nutritional states of all individuals in a culture. They are able to provide a richer assessment of diseases and deficiencies.[29]

Too often students of past epidemics have written as though they believed in Sydenham's model of "epidemic constitutions." Sydenham thought that the humoral responses of individuals in times of epidemic became so homogenized that all specific diseases took on the appearance of the dominant infection. Conversely, he also argued that specific seasonal parameters and specific chemical excresences in the air could cause the same epidemic infection in everyone. In this case humoral responses varied, but the cause of pestilence was the same, so that all the sick and dying were victims of the same disease.[30]

It is little wonder that historians insist on the autonomous behavior of many infections: most of their best studies have been written with that assumption. Few of the studies of specific

---

29   See Cook, "Subsistence Base and Health."

30   Thomas Sydenham, "On Acute Diseases: Preface to the Third Edition (1681), in (trans. R. G. Latham), *The Works of Thomas Sydenham, M.D.* (London, 1848), I, 11–27.

plagues or illnesses do more than admit that other microorganisms exist. Occasionally, the microbes of malnutrition are called upon to explain supramortality among the poor, or among children, or among women of childbearing ages, or in the wake of a virgin soil epidemic. Data outside the target area that explain an epidemic are used to enhance understanding of why a particular microorganism caused, or failed to cause, so much destruction.

Biraben, in his *Les hommes et la peste,* has been justly congratulated for sifting through thousands of local histories of plague, spanning over 400 years. Most scholars never attempt to write, much less digest, so much. But Biraben was not concerned with any other epidemic infection that appeared or disappeared during the plague years, let alone those which intersected or filled in spaces between plagues. Nowhere does he devote attention to other infections that were common to early modern Europeans. This is not to berate Biraben, but to illustrate that a more useful index of human nutrition is to be found in closer attention to overall disease environments.[31]

The existence of a specific microorganism in a given society can alert us to the probability of death and disease among some subgroups, but not among others. Some infections, especially dysentery and respiratory diseases, commonly lead to supramortality among young children. Chronic infections, such as amebiasis, tuberculosis, and malaria, would not be as likely to claim lives until an acute nutritional or infection crisis intervened. A tuberculous wet-nurse could infect many well-born babies, but usually children infected in the general community succumb later on when a nutritional, infectious, or possibly a psychosocial stress occurs. Chronic infections, and most acute diseases caused by intracellular parasites (viruses, malaria, and rickettsiae for the most part) take their heaviest tolls among older adults. The interplay of adult and childhood infections can have devastating effects on disadvantaged groups or classes, or can have paradoxical effects on elites. Much of the study on the pre-modern period has to rest on mortality studies rather than on an analysis of morbidity patterns. Inferences about illness from mortality crises has led to widespread assumptions about the autonomy of various infectious

31 Jean-Noel Biraben, *Les hommes et la peste* (Paris, 1976), 2 v.

diseases. Nevertheless, it is in illness, not in deaths, that the viciousness of hidden hunger emerges. There seems to be a synergism between disease and disease rather than between nutritional status and disease, in large part due to the social circumstances of infection.

The task for historical epidemiologists is not solely to describe and explain major killing infections of the past, but to analyze the rich ecological field of human and animal diseases contributing to the social and demographic make-up of past societies. The historical importance of the "synergistic package" will emerge, not from a hopeful link between famines and epidemics, nor from the demographic effects of differential mortality from specific diseases, but from the careful study of the social changes in human morbidity and mortality.

Roger Schofield

The Impact of Scarcity and Plenty on Population Change in England, 1541–1871

Scarcity is a relative concept, a state in which demand exceeds supply. But as Malthus observed almost two centuries ago, the critical characteristic of populations is their dynamic nature: they grow or decline. Consequently, scarcity for a population is a dynamic matter, determined by the relative *rates of change* of population and food supply. Living in an already densely settled country before chemical fertilizers had been discovered, Malthus, not surprisingly, regarded food production as subject to diminishing marginal returns (the "arithmetical ratio"). That is, the *rate* at which agricultural output could be expanded must inexorably diminish. Population growth, however, was subject to no such constraints; indeed it was compound by nature (the "geometrical ratio"). Thus in the long run, Malthus argued, population growth rates would inevitably outstrip the rate at which food could be produced; in such circumstances food prices would rise and, since money wages would be likely to decline, the standard of living must fall.[1]

At the limit this would lead to progressive overcrowding, malnourishment, starvation, and death: the positive check, which Malthus believed operated in populations of plants and animals. In human populations, however, and particularly in contemporary European societies, Malthus thought that this limit was short-circuited by the existence of another check, namely "a foresight of the difficulties attending the rearing of a family." This appreciation of a minimum viable standard of living, which obviously varied by social class, provided a "preventive check

Roger Schofield is Director of the Cambridge Group for the History of Population and Social Structure and is a fellow of Clare College, Cambridge.

1   Thomas Robert Malthus, *An Essay on the Principle of Population* (London, 1798; reprinted 1970), 70–77.

[which] appears to operate in some degree through all the ranks of society in England." Thus if population growth drove up food prices and the standard of living fell, more and more people would delay marriage, or never marry at all. This would reduce the level of fertility and so throttle back the rate of population growth to the point where it no longer exceeded the food supply. Indeed, it might overshoot the mark, reducing the population growth rate below the rate of increase in the food supply so that prices would fall and standards of living would begin to rise.[2]

The link between the standard of living and marriage could therefore provide the means by which a population might keep in balance with its food supply, avoiding runaway population growth and the terrible penalties of famine and catastrophic mortality that uncontrolled growth would ultimately entail. If Malthus were right, then the traditional societies of pre-industrial Europe had a significant advantage over those in the developing world today. For, in the latter, marriage takes place at an early and customary age (usually in the late teens) and almost everyone marries, often living initially in their parents' household. Consequently, fertility in these societies is high and unvarying. Since marriage is unresponsive to falls in living standards produced by too rapid population growth, the latter will continue unchecked until mass poverty and starvation result in very high death rates.[3]

Malthus' observations and theories, therefore, in addition to their contemporary relevance, raise interesting questions as to why the societies of Northern Europe may have been the first to break free of traditional constraints and attain self-sustained economic growth. Malthus himself thought that the operation of what he called the "preventive" check through marriage would come into play very slowly, so that there would be long periods of population growth and declining standards of living (or of population decline and rising standards) before population and resources were brought back into balance again. He believed that these "oscillations" would be too weak and long-term in nature

2 Ibid., 76, 89, 77.
3 John Hajnal, "European Marriage Patterns in Perspective," in David V. Glass and David E. C. Eversley (eds.), Population in History (London, 1965), 104–106. Hajnal, "Two Kinds of Pre-Industrial Household Formation Systems," in Richard Wall (ed.), Family Forms in Historic Europe (Cambridge, 1983), 65–104.

to be "remarked by superficial observers." Nor was he surprised not to find any mention of them in history, simply because "the histories of mankind that we possess are histories only of the higher classes."[4]

Malthus allowed some influence to mortality in determining the rate of population growth:

> The actual distress of some of the lower classes, by which they are disabled from giving the proper food and attention to their children, act as a positive check to the natural increase in population.

However, after a lifetime of study and investigation he concluded that:

> In almost all the more improved countries of modern Europe the principal check which at present keeps the population down to the level of the actual means of subsistence is the prudential restraint on marriage.[5]

Although some later scholars have agreed with Malthus, most recent writers have emphasized mortality rather than nuptiality and fertility as the dynamic demographic variable determining the relationship between population and the economy, at least until the demographic transition in the late nineteenth century. It has sometimes even been stated that changes in fertility could not have had any significant influence on the rate of population growth because fertility was already high and therefore unlikely to rise higher, and because the impact of these changes would be severely reduced by high levels of infant mortality. Although such an *a priori* dismissal of the role of fertility can be shown to be wrong, the lack of English historical data before the nineteenth century has precluded any clear appreciation of the nature and direction of long-term population trends and the role that scarcity may have played in determining these trends, whether through mortality or nuptiality.[6]

---

4   Malthus, *Essay*, 77–78.
5   *Ibid.*, 89; *idem, A Summary View of the Principle of Population* (London, 1830; reprinted 1970), 254.
6   For nuptiality see, for example, H. John Habakkuk, "English Population in the Eighteenth Century," *Economic History Review*, VI (1953), 121. For mortality see Thomas

Recently, however, it has proved possible to estimate, from a set of parish registers, national series of births, deaths, and marriages over a period extending back to the mid-sixteenth century. A method has been found of using these vital series to make quinquennial estimates of the size and age structure of the population, so deriving measures of population growth, fertility, nuptiality, and mortality over a period of three centuries. Taken in conjunction with data on wages and prices, these new estimates provide an opportunity to investigate the validity of Malthus' characterization of the long-run dynamic relationships between a population and its economic environment.[7]

Figure 1 shows the course traced out by the English population between 1541 and 1871, drawn on a semi-logarithmic scale so that rates of growth at different dates can be compared directly from the slope of the graph. There was a sustained rise in population during the sixteenth century with rates of growth of between 0.5 and 1.0 percent per annum. After 1600 the rate of growth slowed until it ceased altogether in mid-century. Between 1656 and 1686 the population declined in numbers, and then grew so slowly and hesitantly that by 1731 it was still smaller than it had been in 1656. When consistent population growth finally resumed in the mid-eighteenth century it did so at a level that

---

McKeown, *The Modern Rise of Population* (London, 1976); Michael W. Flinn, *The European Demographic System, 1500–1820* (Baltimore, 1981). Since 1955 McKeown has consistently denied that changes in fertility could have produced changes in population growth rates. McKeown and R. G. Brown, "Medical Evidence Related to English Population Changes in the Eighteenth Century," *Population Studies,* IX (1955), 119–141. For recent restatements see McKeown, *Rise of Population,* 40–41; *idem,* "Fertility, Mortality and Cause of Death," *Population Studies,* XXXVIII (1978), 537.

McKeown's arguments, however, fail to take account of the fact that at all times fertility was far from its maximum level and the effect of a rise in fertility on population growth rates would only have been reduced if it had entailed a countervailing rise in mortality as, for example, in the alleged higher mortality of high-parity children. However, when properly controlled to eliminate other factors, the effect of parity on infant mortality turns out to be negligible. These issues are discussed in Schofield, "Population Growth in the Century after 1750: The Role of Mortality Decline," in Rolf Ohlsson and Tommy Bengtsson (eds.), *Pre-Industrial Population Patterns,* forthcoming.

7 E. Anthony Wrigley and Schofield, *The Population History of England, 1541–1871: A Reconstruction* (Cambridge, Mass., 1981), 15–154, 192–199, appendix 15 (contributed by James E. Oeppen). The results appear robust in the face of alternative assumptions about the scale of error in the data or about age schedules of mortality and migration used in the estimated process; *idem.* 269–284.

Fig. 1 English Population Totals, 1541–1871

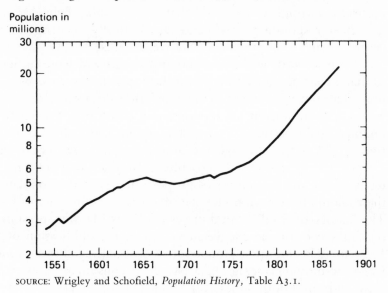

SOURCE: Wrigley and Schofield, *Population History*, Table A3.1.

was modest by sixteenth-century standards. Indeed, it was only after 1786 that Elizabethan rates of growth were exceeded. Population growth then accelerated to reach a maximum of 1.55 percent per annum in the early 1820s, falling back somewhat to maintain a level of 1.25 percent per annum until the late nineteenth century.[8]

There were, therefore, two periods of growth divided by a hundred or so years, from the mid-seventeenth to the mid-eighteenth century, when population numbers were stagnant. The lack of constancy in the growth rates argues against the relevance to England of the rather schematic view of pre-industrial populations sometimes encountered in the literature. Short-run crises apart, this view sees population growth as having been subject to virtually constant underlying schedules of fertility and mortality, the former determined by inflexible social rules concerning marriage

8   The figures in this article are reprinted from Wrigley and Schofield, *Population History*, by permission of the publishers, Harvard University Press, Copyright © 1981 by E. A. Wrigley and R. S. Schofield, and references in the notes to the figures refer to that work. For a fuller discussion, see *ibid.*, 207–215.

and reproduction. Rather, the long oscillation in growth rates that occurred in England suggests that demographic behavior may have been responding slowly and systematically to changes in the environment, as Malthus believed was the case.[9]

Both the scale and pace of population growth were sufficient to make considerable demands on the expansion of food production. Between 1541 and 1656 the population almost doubled (from 2.8 to 5.3 million) at an average annual rate of 0.6 percent. It doubled again between 1731 and 1816, and for a third time between 1816 and 1871 at average annual rates of growth of 0.8 and 1.3 percent respectively. If agricultural production had been perfectly elastic and had increased proportionately to the population, there should have been no long-term increase in the price of food. The history of English food prices confirms Malthus' pessimism on this score for the 250 years preceding the publication of his *Essay* in 1798. Figure 2 plots population totals against a twenty-five-year moving average of a basket of consumables. Between 1541 and 1656 both series rose, then fell for a period of about thirty years. For the next fifty years, when population growth was modest and halting, the price index tended to fall rather than rise. But when rapid and continuous population growth returned in the second half of the eighteenth century, the same positive relationship as' had existed before the mid-seventeenth century supervened between the two series. Prices rose rapidly under pressure of population growth, in both periods outstripping the pace of the increase in population.[10]

If there were a notable uniformity in the behavior of the two series relative to each other until the beginning of the nineteenth century, there was a remarkably clean break with the past thereafter. When the population doubled for a third time between 1816 and 1871, at an even higher annual rate of growth than in the preceding sixty-year period, the price of the consumables basket

9   See, for example, Ronato Freedman (ed.), *Population: The Vital Revolution* (New York, 1964), 3; Carlo Cipolla, *Economic History of World Population* ([London], 1962), 76–77.

10   Wrigley and Schofield, *Population History,* 528–529. In constructing the index, we gave food prices a weighting of 80 out of 100 (farinaceous 20, meat and fish 25, butter and cheese 12.5, drink 22.5). E. Henry Phelps Brown and Sheila V. Hopkins. "Seven Centuries of the Prices of Consumables Compared with Builders' Wage Rates," *Economica,* XXIII (1956), 296–314.

Fig. 2 English Population Totals Compared to a 25-Year Moving Average of a Basket of Consumables Index

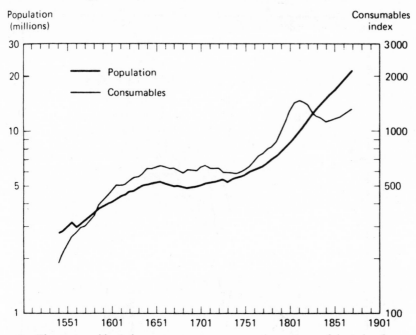

NOTE: The consumables index represents a 25-year moving average of the index figures centered on the dates shown.

SOURCES: Population totals, Wrigley and Schofield, *Population History,* Table A3.1; consumables index, Phelps Brown and Hopkins, "Seven Centuries of the Prices of Consumables," 194–196.

first fell and then leveled out. The historical link between population growth and price rise was broken: an economic revolution had taken place. By an ironic coincidence Malthus had given pungent expression to an issue that haunted most pre-industrial societies at almost the last moment when it could still plausibly be represented as relevant to the country in which he was born.

Throughout the pre-industrial period, however, there was also a striking uniformity in the elasticity of response of food prices to population change. Figure 3 plots the smoothed rates of growth of the two series at each date against each other. The grouping of the individual points is surprisingly close round a straight line running through the origin and rising or falling by

Fig. 3 Annual Rates of Growth of Population and of a Basket of Consumables Index

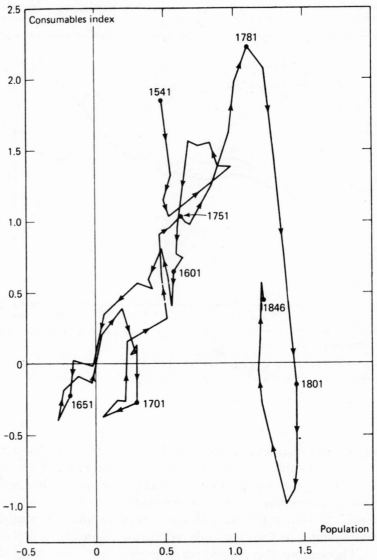

NOTE: The population growth rate was measured between any given date and a date 25 years later. The rate of growth of the price of consumbles was measured using the readings on a 25-year moving average of the index for the same dates as for population totals. Where a date is indicated it shows the beginning date of a 25-year period.

SOURCES: See Fig. 2.

three units on the vertical axis for every two on the horizontal. If population over a quarter-century period rose at 1 percent per annum, food prices rose by 1.5 percent per annum. Similarly, during a period of falling population, food prices tended to fall slightly faster.[11]

Yet if food production were far from being perfectly elastic in response to population growth, it was nonetheless capable of considerable expansion. In the early eighteenth century English agriculture not only fed twice as many people as in the mid-sixteenth century, but also provided a surplus of grain so that some 6 percent of output was exported. The next doubling of population was largely fed from home production, at least so far as basic foodstuffs were concerned, for it was only in the nineteenth century when the third doubling of the population occurred that imports of these commodities became significant. Moreover, the linearity of the relationship between the rates of change in population and food prices traced out in Figure 3 points to considerable powers of expansion in agricultural production, for neither great increases in the size of the population nor very fast rates of growth imposed an extra penalty through a disproportionate movement in prices.[12]

There were, therefore, long periods in English history when the cost of food rose or fell. And although there were considerable changes in the level of money wages, they were insufficient to counteract the impact of changes in food prices on the standard of living. In Figure 4 the rate of change in a real wage index is plotted against population growth rates. The same essential features emerge as in Figure 3 except that this time the relationship is negative; the faster population grew, the more the standard of living fell. Once again most of the points fall within a straight diagonal band, although the points curved sharply downward in the late sixteenth century as high rates of population growth brought abnormally large reductions in the real wage, because the

---

11 Exceptions are discussed in Wrigley and Schofield, *Population History,* 404.
12 Donald C. Coleman, *The Economy of England* (Oxford, 1977), 121. Imports rose from 1.4% of gross corn output around 1770 to 7.6% around 1820. Phyllis Deane and W. A. Cole, *British Economic Growth, 1688–1959* (Cambridge, 1962), 65. Imports of non-basic foodstuffs, such as tea, coffee, and sugar, were much more extensive. Ralph Davis, *The Industrial Revolution and British Overseas Trade* (Leicester, 1979), 116–123.

Fig. 4 Annual Rates of Growth of Population and of a Real-Wage Index

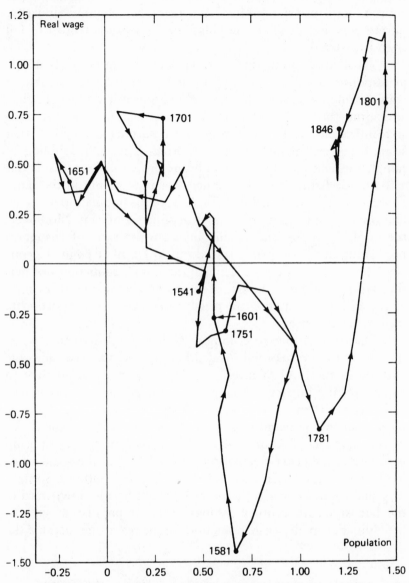

NOTE: The population growth rate was measured between each given census date and the census 25 years later. The rate of growth of real wages was measured using the readings on a 25-year moving average of the index for the same dates as for population totals. Where a date is indicated it shows the beginning date of a 25-year period.

SOURCE: Wrigley and Schofield, *Population History*, Tables A3.1, A9.2.

economy was unable to make effective use of the additional labor coming onto the market. And once more there was a radical break at the end of the eighteenth century: although population was growing significantly faster than at any earlier period, real wages, which had been falling sharply, recovered and began to rise more sharply than ever before. For the first time since the land had been fully settled, swiftly rising numbers proved consonant with rising real wages. An industrial revolution was under way.[13]

In the pre-industrial world, however, the graph of points showing the rates of change in the two series suggests that the early modern English economy was capable of sustaining a population growth rate of about 0.5 percent per annum without depressing real wages. Faster rates of growth entailed a fall in real wages, whereas more modest rates were associated with rising real wages. When the population was stationary, real wages rose by 0.5 percent per annum. If one may assume that the factor share of wages in total national income changed little in pre-industrial England, then it would appear that the economy was growing by about 0.5 percent annually and that the degree to which wage earners benefited was inversely related to the rate of population growth.

Although real wages were not the only element determining the standard of living, the market price of labor was likely to have borne a reasonably close relationship to general economic opportunity for the vast majority of the population in an economically differentiated society like early modern England. Thus, before 1800, the situation developed much as Malthus had insisted it must: the faster the population grew, the faster the price of food rose, the lower the standard of living fell, and the grimmer the struggle to exist became. As Malthus had postulated, there were indeed long, slow oscillations in the rate of population growth and in the standard of living.

How did the English population respond to these long periods of relative scarcity and plenty: did they react by varying the intensity of marriage, or did they wait passively for increased

13 For the construction of a real wage index from the Phelps Brown and Hopkins data, see Wrigley and Schofield, *Population History*, appendix 9. For a fuller discussion of the relationship between rates of population growth and rates of change in real wages, see *ibid.*, 409–412.

Fig. 5 Quinquennial Expectation of Life at Birth Data Compared with
an 11-year Moving Average of a Real-Wage Index

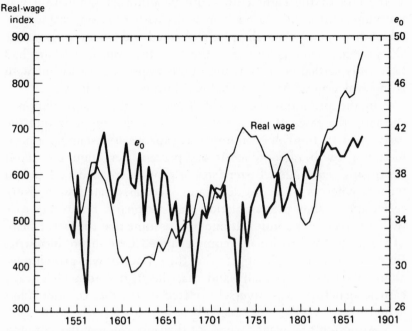

NOTE: The e_0 graph represents mortality in the 5-year period centering on the years shown.
The real-wage graph is an 11-year moving average centering on the years shown.

SOURCES: Wrigley and Schofield, *Population History*, real wages - Table A9.2; e_0s - Table
A3.1.

mortality to take its toll? Was England a country where the
preventive or the positive check prevailed?

Figure 5 compares changes over time in the real wage index
with the mortality history of England as measured by expectation
of life at birth. If the positive check were operating, there should
be a positive association between movements in the two series:
falling real wages should reduce expectation of life, and rising real
wages increase it. It is not easy to detect such a pattern in Figure
5, except perhaps in the sixteenth century. Yet, even when real
wages had fallen to their lowest point shortly after 1600, expectation of life was still at a relatively high level. For a full fifty
years after real wages began their long and sustained rise through
the seventeenth century, mortality continued to deteriorate. Between 1680 and 1740 mortality levels fluctuated rapidly while the

real wage index continued to rise to a high peak. And the final period of mortality improvement took place against a background of falling real wages up to the second decade of the nineteenth century, and of rising real wages thereafter. The relationships between the two series are disorderly and frequently contrary to expectation. Figure 5 provides little evidence that long-term trends in scarcity or plenty as captured by the real wage caused marked differences in mortality levels in early modern England.[14]

If the positive check is difficult to discern in the English historical record, is the preventive check any more in evidence? Figure 6 plots the long-run movements in real wages against nuptiality measured by an estimated crude marriage rate. The general parallelism in the directions of movement of the two lines on the graph, with turning points in nuptiality lagging behind turning points in real wages by thirty to forty years, suggests that secular changes in the standard of living were followed by secular changes in the intensity of marriage. Although the causal link cannot be proved, the graph looks very much like a picture of the "oscillations" of "retrograde and progressive movements" that Malthus outlined in his description of the operation of the preventive check.[15]

The changes in the intensity of nuptiality involved shifts both in the age of marriage and in the proportions ever marrying: when times were more difficult fewer married and they waited longer to do so. Since marital fertility rates varied little until the widespread adoption of family limitation toward the end of the nineteenth century, the movements in nuptiality were reflected, after a lag, by secular shifts in fertility. Moreover, in England, rates of illegitimacy and prenuptial pregnancy moved in sympathy with nuptiality, reinforcing rather than offsetting its effects. Thus it was the intensity not only of marriage, but also of sexual activity among the young in general, that responded to long-term trends in scarcity and plenty.[16]

---

14 A more extensive discussion can be found in *ibid.*, 413–416.

15 For the construction of the crude marriage rate and for modifications to the timing of the turning points, see *ibid.*, 425–428. Malthus, *Essay*, 77.

16 Wrigley and Schofield, *Population History*, 422–424, 258–264, 254–255, 266–267. See also Wrigley, "Marriage, Fertility and Population Growth in Eighteenth-Century England," in R. Brian Outhwaite (ed.), *Marriage and Society* (London, 1981), 155–163, 167–168; for the contrasting case of France, where movements in illegitimacy offset those in nuptiality, *ibid.*, 178–182.

Fig. 6 Crude Marriage Rates (marriages per 1,000 persons aged 15–34) Compared with a Real-Wage Index (both 25-year moving averages)

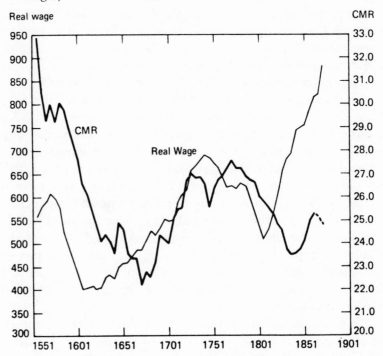

NOTES: Table A3.1 in Wrigley and Schofield, contains only broad age divisions of the population. The totals of those aged 15–34 at each date were taken from more detailed, unpublished output tables. The marriage rate per 1,000 aged 15–34 in the quinquennium 1869–1873 obtained from Mitchell and Deane was 25.26 compared with 25.53 from the back-projection data. The later rates based on Mitchell and Deane were adjusted upwards by the difference between the two figures (0.27) to ensure a good fit between the two series. The 25-year moving averages are centered on the dates shown. The CMR values which depend in part on data drawn from Mitchell and Deane are shown by a broken line.

SOURCES: Wrigley and Schofield, *Population History*, crude marriage rates—Table A3.1; real wages—Table A9.2. The marriage rates after the quinquennium 1869–1873 refer to England and Wales and were obtained from the census data and crude rates in Brian R. Mitchell and Phyllis Deane, *Abstract of British Historical Statistics* (Cambridge, 1962), 12, 45–46.

As a result there were marked shifts in the level of fertility in England between the sixteenth and nineteenth centuries, which combined with long-term trends in mortality to produce the long oscillation in population growth rates that occurred in pre-industrial England. The long squeeze of the high rates of growth in the sixteenth century down to actual population decline in the later seventeenth century was due in almost equal measure to a fall in fertility and to an increase in mortality. But responsibility for the subsequent sustained rise in population growth rates between the mid-eighteenth and mid-nineteenth century owed more to changes in fertility than in mortality, by a ratio of three to one. It was only fertility, through nuptiality, that appears to have responded to the changing conditions of scarcity and plenty wrought by previous rates of population growth. Secular changes in the level of mortality, although probably shaped to some degree by social and economic developments, appear to have been determined more by shifts in the patterns of disease than by changes in the standard of living.[17]

Thus pre-industrial England emerges as a society that was subject to the deleterious economic consequences of population growth that Malthus had postulated, but which responded through the preventive rather than the positive check. By modifying the intensity of nuptiality and early sexual activity according to the circumstances of scarcity or plenty, the English population corrected its rate of growth, bringing it back into rough equilibrium with the development of its economic environment. The adjustment lagged and was slow to take effect, so that England experienced long periods of falling standards of living, but in the end balance was restored and the country avoided the worst rigors of the positive check.

Yet, however successful a pre-industrial society might have been in securing a long-run balance between demographic and economic change, it still had to cope with the substantial annual fluctuations in fortune caused by variations in harvest yields. In a world where the land was the source of all food and of most of

17 In the early eighteenth century large swings in mortality had a dominant influence on changes in the population growth rate. Wrigley and Schofield, *Population History*, 236–245.

the raw materials needed by industry, a harvest failure meant distress and depression, an abundant harvest an interlude of comparative plenty. These annual fluctuations in scarcity and plenty caused an abrupt change in the balance between a population and its economic resources, which, if severe, could entail disaster rather than distress. Although England may have escaped the positive check in the long run, it may have been vulnerable in the short run, especially during those periods in the late sixteenth and eighteenth centuries when the standard of living was suffering a secular decline. If the preventive check operated in the long run, was nuptiality also sensitive to annual fluctuations in economic circumstances?

Because there are no direct observations of the size of the harvest each year, food prices and real wages have been taken as indications of annual fluctuations in scarcity or plenty. These fluctuations were substantial; annual deviations from a twenty-five-year moving average of real wages ranged from −36 to +28 percent, with a decadal mean absolute percentage deviation from trend lying between 5 and 15 percent before 1710, and between 5 and 10 percent thereafter.[18]

In considering the response of mortality and fertility to fluctuations in food prices or real wages, we first look for a general relationship between the movements in the series over the whole period, and for fluctuations of all amplitudes. We then look at the specific effects of highly deficient harvests, and consider how far the general pattern of relationships changed over time.

The disentangling of the relationships between short-run changes in series such as these is a complex matter, for not only may the effects be either simultaneous or lagged, but each series may also carry within it echoes from previous fluctuations. In order to study the effect of fluctuations in food prices on demographic behavior, therefore, it is important to remove the contaminations arising from the internal structure linking the fluctuations within each of the series. Otherwise one risks mistakenly claiming the existence of a systematic relationship between the

18 The money wage series was smoothed so that fluctuations in the real wage index reflect short-run movements in consumables prices. See *ibid.*, 639–641; also 317, 321. Note that the years are harvest years, running from July to June to maximize variation in prices: *ibid.*, 312.

fluctuations in two series when it may be a spurious artifact of similarities in their internal structures. Conversely, offsetting internal structures may mask a genuine relationship between short-run fluctuations.[19]

Moreover, what is at issue is not whether fluctuations in food prices *sometimes* affected mortality, fertility, or nuptiality, for in long and variable series some examples of any relationship are likely to arise by chance. It is rather a matter of the strength and consistency of the relationships. To address the question by piling up instances, as in so many studies, is clearly a futile exercise; what is required is a rigorous and systematic approach.

Unfortunately this type of approach is not easily achieved, partly because the main relationships of interest between fluctuations in food prices and demographic behavior are part of a complex network involving both inter-relationships between the demographic series themselves and fluctuations in the environment. Although the former are amenable to statistical control, there can be no guarantee that the latter can ever be captured adequately, for example by meteorological variables. Consequently, there is always a risk of drawing mistaken inferences from covariations that are properly attributable to common influences of unobserved variables.

Furthermore, the complexity of the subject requires sophisticated methods of analysis that make strong assumptions about the properties of the underlying economic and demographic processes. If these are misspecified, and it is often difficult to be sure that they are not, the apparently precise and detailed results may well be spurious. Under the circumstances it is advisable to adopt several approaches, varying in the complexity of their methods and the degree to which they make assumptions about reality. Fortunately there turns out to be a substantial area of common ground among the results obtained by different approaches to the English series. The following discussion is based mainly on a

19 Repercussions of earlier fluctuations might be positive or negative. For example, a rise or fall in vital rates, on the one hand, will alter the size of the stock of susceptible persons in subsequent years and could lead to compensatory fluctuations in the rates in subsequent years. On the other hand, the need to retain seed corn in deficient harvest years or the availability of storage in abundant years could lead to positive repercussions. See Wrigley and Schofield, *Population History*, 307, 344–348.

distributed-lag model analysis of transformed annual series of wheat prices, births, deaths, and marriages.[20]

First, taking fluctuations of all sizes, both upward and downward, and over the whole period, there was a statistically significant positive association between annual movements in wheat prices and in mortality. But the relationship was very weak; only 16 percent of the short-run variation in mortality was associated with price changes. Mortality fluctuations were overwhelmingly determined by other factors. Only when prices were exceptionally high did mortality rise in the same year; otherwise the upward or downward effect was delayed one or two years. The positive response to food prices was followed by a compensating negative echo. Except when prices were extremely high, the net, or cumulated, effect over five years was essentially zero. This suggests that most variations in scarcity or plenty merely advanced or delayed by a couple of years the normal pacing of deaths. These weak effects of price on mortality did not differ significantly by season, nor did runs of high prices have any significant additional effects on mortality.[21]

The effect of wheat price fluctuations on nuptiality was more pronounced: 41 percent of the short-run timing of marriages could be associated with variations in scarcity or plenty. Price variations had the strongest negative effect on marriages in the same year and to a lesser extent in the two subsequent years. The relationship was symmetrical, high prices inhibiting marriages and low prices encouraging them; and the degree of response was proportional to the magnitude of the price fluctuation. The cumulated effect over a five-year period was strongly negative; for example, a doubling of wheat prices in one year led to a permanent loss (and a halving of prices to a permanent gain) of 22 percent of the normal annual number of marriages.[22]

---

20 This analysis, carried out by Ronald D. Lee, and contributed by him as ch. 9 in Wrigley and Schofield, *Population History,* used wheat prices taken from several sources and aggregated into harvest years running from Oct. to Sept. *Ibid.,* 356. For a comparison with results from a nonparametric bivariate analysis, see *ibid.,* 348–355. Unreported analyses using autoregressive integrated moving average (ARIMA) methods found similar results.

21 *Ibid.,* 371, 377, 379–382.

22 *Ibid.,* 368–369, 375, 383–384.

In the short run, therefore, as in the long term, it was through the preventive rather than the positive check that variations in scarcity and plenty impinged upon the population history of England. However, annual fluctuations in wheat prices also had a marked and direct negative effect on fertility, independent of any indirect effect through nuptiality. Indeed, 64 percent of the annual fluctuations in fertility were associated with fluctuations in prices, a closer connection than obtained with either nuptiality or mortality. Once again the relationship was symmetrical, high prices inhibiting births and low prices encouraging them, and the size of the effect was proportional to the magnitude of the fluctuation in prices. As with marriages there was a compensatory positive echo at about two-years' lag, as biometric models of birth intervals would lead one to expect, and the cumulated net effect over five years was negative. The overall response of fertility to prices, however, was weaker, a doubling or halving of prices causing only a 14 percent loss or gain.[23]

The main impact of prices on fertility occurred in the same year and in the year immediately following. Although analysis on a monthly basis is necessarily imprecise because of a lag between birth and baptism, it suggests that the negative effect on births occurred between three and eighteen months after the fluctuation in prices. Thus it would seem that variations in wheat prices both affected fetal mortality, at least during the first two trimesters of pregnancy, and influenced the numbers of conceptions occurring during the following nine months. The latter effect may have been due to fluctuations in the level of nutrition on fecundity, or to variations in the level of sexual activity, whether physiologically or psychologically motivated. In the short run, therefore, fluctuations in scarcity and plenty may have had biological as well as behavioral consequences, but they affected life before, rather than after, birth.[24]

---

23 *Ibid.*, 369–370, 375, 383.
24 *Ibid.*, 370–371. Evidence for age at baptism in the sixteenth century is scanty, but points to baptism being performed very shortly after birth. By the late seventeenth century the median age at baptism was still only eight days, and the interquartile range was six days. By 1800 the median and interquartile range had risen to thirty and twenty-one days respectively. Bronwen M. Berry and Schofield, "Age at Baptism in Pre-Industrial England," *Population Studies*, XXV (1971), 458, 462. It is important to note that fertility also

The relative strengths of the connections between short-run changes in the food supply on the one hand, and fertility, nuptiality, and mortality on the other, are also visible in the years of most extreme relative scarcity. The lower panel of Table 1 displays the percentage deviations from trend in the demographic series in the twenty years when real wages fluctuated most violently below trend. Nuptiality and fertility were much more consistently affected than was mortality: both marriage and birth rates fell in eighteen of the twenty years, whereas death rates rose in only ten of them. This last result could well have arisen by chance even if there had been no relationship between scarcity and the direction of movement in the death rate.[25]

So far the discussion has been concerned with responses to fluctuations in scarcity and plenty over a period of three centuries from the mid-sixteenth to the mid-nineteenth centuries. During this time there were not only large changes in the level of the standard of living, but also profound transformations in the economy. How far were the relationships that have been discussed modified by these changes in the demographic and economic context? Dividing the period at 1640 and 1745 yields three subperiods (1548–1640, 1641–1745, and 1746–1834) that correspond roughly to the alternating secular phases of population growth and stagnation, with their attendant counter-movements in real wages. The response of the demographic series to fluctuations in wheat prices in each period can conveniently be summarized by the net elasticity cumulated over five years.[26]

In the case of fertility there was little change over time: the cumulative elasticities in the three periods were −0.134, −0.131, and −0.184. If anything, the biological, or behavioral, responses to variations in scarcity and plenty were slightly greater in the

---

responded negatively to fluctuations in mortality, net of the influence of prices. Mortality fluctuations affected fertility mainly in the same year and at one year's lag, and they did so more strongly than did prices. Monthly analyses suggest that deaths of pregnant women were not very important; most of the relationship should probably be associated with fetal loss. Wrigley and Schofield, *Population History*, 363–366, 375, 399. Consequently a scissors movement in birth and death rates can scarcely be taken as evidence of famine mortality, as is often claimed; it can occur in non-famine years and, in any case, is more likely to have been caused by an increase in morbidity.

25 Note that these results for years of extreme scarcity refer to bivariate relationships, the effects of other variables being uncontrolled. For a fuller discussion see *ibid.*, 320–332.
26 *Ibid.*, 373–377.

Table 1 Twenty greatest annual deviations above and below a 25-year moving average in each series, with contemporaneous deviations in other series

| REAL WAGES ABOVE | YEAR | ANNUAL PERCENTAGE DEVIATION ABOVE OR BELOW (−) MOVING AVERAGE | | | |
		REAL WAGE	DEATH RATE	MARRIAGE RATE	BIRTH RATE
	1821/2	27.55	1.68	5.64	5.93
	1654/5	22.88	11.60	36.05	9.28
	1690/1	22.04	8.40	10.95	1.08
	1557/8	20.75	60.54	5.00	−25.75
	1850/1	20.58	−3.85	6.17	1.60
	1706/7	20.38	−3.62	0.67	3.20
	1653/4	19.61	6.58	1.79	−2.38
	1603/4	19.47	21.04	3.73	5.88
	1627/8	19.16	18.56	6.52	4.56
	1851/2	19.04	1.71	5.60	1.74
	1849/50	18.75	8.04	2.60	−3.24
	1689/90	18.02	4.80	11.29	2.01
	1822/3	17.30	2.86	3.02	6.08
	1704/5	16.71	7.09	0.82	3.34
	1655/6	16.68	−16.91	67.52	10.33
	1592/3	15.92	29.80	3.65	1.10
	1643/4	14.80	29.27	−30.59	4.14
	1722/3	14.44	−3.32	12.19	3.08
	1833/4	14.23	−7.80	8.31	−2.53
	1570/1	13.91	7.28	−6.35	−1.15
BELOW	1596/7	−35.78	20.86	−15.33	−4.38
	1556/7	−33.66	7.30	−41.78	−12.79
	1710/1	−29.84	1.22	−12.21	−12.70
	1800/1	−29.43	4.94	−18.05	−11.16
	1555/6	−28.36	−28.18	−15.52	1.41
	1649/50	−24.55	−11.91	−15.29	−17.00
	1799/1800	−23.70	−4.56	−5.32	−2.93
	1648/9	−23.57	−6.07	−35.01	−5.84
	1597/8	−22.80	25.61	−9.10	−17.72
	1697/8	−22.06	−5.41	4.50	−1.57
	1545/6	−21.64	26.55	−14.53	−0.91
	1586/7	−21.56	1.46	−8.18	−6.69
	1698/9	−21.40	−3.26	8.17	−0.98
	1812/3	−21.10	−5.65	−4.34	−0.87
	1550/1	−20.51	−14.75	−11.18	10.97
	1709/10	−20.21	−10.07	−9.79	−9.97
	1647/8	−19.10	−11.04	−17.98	−4.32
	1740/1	−18.50	0.19	−15.30	−2.87
	1661/2	−18.47	6.52	−16.97	−4.07
	1630/1	−18.11	7.27	−14.66	−4.78

late eighteenth and early nineteenth centuries than in the period before the civil war. The response of nuptiality varied rather more, with a considerable reduction in the elasticities from a relatively high level to one roughly equivalent to that of fertility in the final period (−0.281, −0.206, and −0.155). The main reason for the low final figure is the emergence of a positive compensatory echo two years after the price fluctuation. One interpretation of this result is that from 1746 fluctuations in scarcity and plenty altered the timing of marriages over a much shorter time span than was the case earlier.[27]

But it was mortality that showed the greatest change over time in its response to fluctuations in wheat prices. The rather modest figure of 0.127 calculated for the whole period conceals the fact that, in the period of population pressure and falling living standards before 1640, the cumulative elasticity of response of mortality with respect to prices was much higher at 0.347. In the second period of stagnant population and rising real wages, the figure dropped to about a third of its earlier level (0.103). Even more remarkably, when population growth resumed in the third period to attain an unparalleled pace, the response of mortality to prices weakened to vanishing point. There was, therefore, a time when mortality in England fluctuated in sympathy with the harvest, but after 1640 this dependence was greatly attenuated, and by the mid-eighteenth century fluctuations in scarcity and plenty no longer found any echo in movements in the death rate.[28]

An examination of the local incidence of mortality crises throws some light on the nature of early vulnerability to harvest failure and on the probable reasons for its disappearance over time. The most severe upward fluctuation in food prices occurred in the period 1596/97 to 1597/98 when the national death rates were also considerably above trend. Yet not every community suffered to the same extent: only 28 percent of the parishes experienced a mortality crisis at this time. Moreover, the geographical distribution of these parishes suggests that difficulty of access to grain supplies may have played a significant role, every

27. *Ibid.*, 374, Fig. 9.7, second panel.
28 In fact the response of mortality to prices became negative (−0.133). This unexpected result weakened to −0.074 when fluctuations in temperature were taken into account. *Ibid.*, 376, 392.

parish examined in the north being affected, and almost none in eastern England and the central midlands.[29]

This pattern is very different from that which obtained in epidemics caused by airborne disease or plague. The contrast is brought out in Figure 7 which shows the geographical distribution of local crises during the period from November 1622 to December 1625. In 1622 the harvest was deficient, especially in the north, and local crises starting between November 1622 and December 1623 are distinguished on the map by the letter "x." As in the period from 1596 to 1598, the far north and the northwest were fairly heavily affected, with only a scattering of outbreaks elsewhere. Quite the reverse was true of the local crises beginning between January 1624 and December 1625, a period that was affected by fevers in the first year and contained a severe outbreak of plague in London from June to October 1625. Parishes experiencing a crisis beginning in this period are indicated on the map by the letter "y," and they were heavily concentrated in the southeast midlands, East Anglia, and the southeast, again with a scattering elsewhere. The areas in the far north and northwest that were affected in 1622–23 were almost entirely free from crises in this period. The relatively few parishes that experienced a crisis in both periods are indicated by the letter "z" on the map.[30]

Before the mid-seventeenth century there would therefore seem to be two Englands: one pastoral and remote, and the other engaged in arable farming but with a high degree of occupational specialization reflected in a relatively dense network of small towns. Although access to grain, together with ease of transport and the well-developed communications in the southeast, made the area much less vulnerable to harvest failures, its greater economic integration facilitated the spread of disease. The same contrast can be seen in microcosm in a county such as Devon, where crisis mortality in bad harvest years was largely confined to the

---

29 Real wages in these two harvest years (July to June) were 36 and 23% below trend respectively. *Ibid.*, 321. Of the 300 or so parishes examined, 18% experienced a crisis in 1596/97, and 19% in 1597/98. *Ibid.*, 653, 672. See Fig. 7.

30 The harvest was very deficient in Scotland, where mortality was very high in 1623. Flinn et al., *Scottish Population History from the Seventeenth Century to the 1930s* (Cambridge, 1977), 117–125. Creighton associates many of these fevers with typhus; Charles Creighton, *A History of Epidemics in Britain,* (London, 1965), I, 504–507. For the plague in London see J. Marshall, *Mortality in the Metropolis* (London, 1832), 66.

Fig. 7   Geographical Distribution of Local Crises Beginning November, 1622 to December, 1625

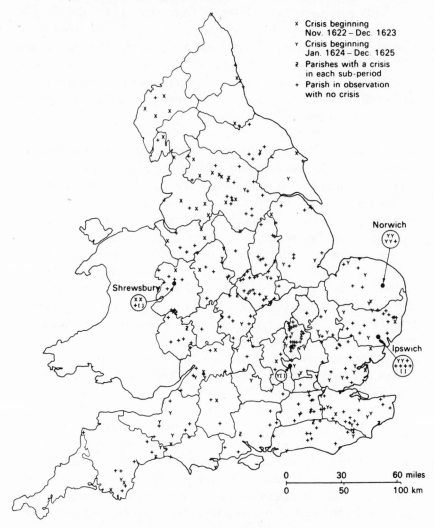

SOURCE: Wrigley and Schofield, *Population History,* Table A10.1.

remote upland parishes, whereas parishes in the mixed farming lowlands in the south of the county near the coast were infected in times of bubonic plague.[31]

The vulnerability of the upland northwest to harvest failure disappeared after 1623, but the greater susceptibility of the southeast to the spread of infectious disease continued throughout the seventeenth century. However, from the late 1720s the distribution of local crises no longer followed this division between a remote and pastoral northwest and an arable and more interconnected southeast.[32]

The demographic record, therefore, points to an increasing integration of market networks over the seventeenth and early eighteenth centuries. Recent research in the economic history of this period has uncovered considerable developments in information flows and marketing methods. Moreover, roads were improved and rivers made more navigable, greatly facilitating the transportation of bulky foodstuffs. Consequently regional specialization in agriculture could take place without regard for local self-subsistence needs, enabling upland and remote regions to exchange pastoral products for grain. In the case of wheat, regional prices were moving in a way that suggests the emergence of a national market by the 1690s. There were also changes in agricultural practices that increased output even in already highly productive areas such as Norfolk and Suffolk.[33]

An important consequence of crop specialization and market integration was an increased protection against the weather. Before the mid-seventeenth century prices of all grains increased

---

31 Paul Slack, "Mortality Crises and Epidemic Disease in England, 1485–1610," in Charles Webster (ed.), *Health, Medicine and Mortality in the Sixteenth Century* (Cambridge, 1979), 34–35, 45.

32 For the northwest see Andrew B. Appleby, *Famine in Tudor and Stuart England* (Stanford, 1978), 155. For the geographical pattern of local crises in the remainder of the seventeenth century, see Wrigley and Schofield, *Population History,* 677–681; see also 681–685.

33 John Chartres, "The Marketing of Agricultural Produce," in Joan Thirsk (ed.), *The Agrarian History of England and Wales,* V, forthcoming. Yields per acre increased between 1580 and 1660. Thereafter the introduction of four-course crop rotation increased the output of fodder crops and enabled pasture land to be ploughed up and used for grain cultivation. Mark Overton, "Agricultural Change in Norfolk and Suffolk, 1580–1740," unpub. Ph.D. diss. (Cambridge Univ., 1980).

steeply in years of dearth; but after this date the new balance between spring and winter cereals and the improved distribution network meant that, because not all grains failed at the same time, prices no longer all rose to famine levels and there were some grains available to the poor at prices that they could afford. Moreover, at least from the sixteenth century, both national and local authorities took steps to prevent famine occurring because of speculation, or because of a failure of purchasing power among the poor. Before 1650 these measures usually took the form of market regulation by local magistrates in favor of the individual consumers or, *in extremis,* through communally financed bulk purchases of grain. Social intervention to protect the poor from the consequences of high food prices became more sophisticated throughout the period: by the late eighteenth century many local authorities were linking their poor-relief benefits to the price of bread.[34]

Although England had developed a considerable degree of economic differentiation, with agricultural production for the market, long before the sixteenth century, the pressure of population growth in the second half of that century was sufficient to make remote areas vulnerable to variations in harvest yields, and mortality sensitive to variations in the price of food. With the social and economic developments and the stagnation of population growth in the seventeenth century, mortality crises were no longer common in the upland zone in years of high grain prices, and the general relationship between fluctuations in prices and mortality became much weaker. In the 1690s, when harvests were deficient and food prices high for eight successive years, mortality was remarkably unresponsive, in striking contrast to what had happened in similar circumstances in the 1590s, and to the soaring death rates in Scotland, Holland, Brabant, and France. By the

34 France continued to suffer from parallel increases in the prices of all grains in bad years, at least up to the mid-eighteenth century. Appleby, "Grain Prices and Subsistence Crises in England and France, 1590–1740," *Journal of Economic History,* XXXIX (1979), 865–887. Outhwaite, "Dearth and Government Intervention in English Grain Markets, 1590–1700," *Economic History Review,* XXXIII (1981), 389–406; Alan Everitt, "The Marketing of Agricultural Produce," in Thirsk (ed.), *The Agrarian History of England and Wales, 1500–1640* (Cambridge, 1967), IV, 577–586; Alan D. Dyer, *The City of Worcester in the Sixteenth Century* (Leicester, 1973), 167. Daniel A. Baugh, "The Cost of Poor Relief in Southeast England, 1790–1834," *Economic History Review,* XXVIII (1975), 50–68.

mid-eighteenth century the methods of production and distribution of food had so developed that, despite the intense pressure of renewed population growth, substantial annual variations in harvest yield had no effect on mortality.[35]

In England, therefore, the positive check was present at an early date as mortality responded to short-run fluctuations in scarcity and plenty. But it attenuated, and then disappeared, as methods of farming and marketing improved. Defined more widely to include fetal mortality, the positive check could be credited with some of the responsiveness of the live birth rate to fluctuations in food prices that persisted for three centuries, the remainder being attributable to the effects of nutrition on fecundity, or the intensity of sexual activity. In this way the positive check may have had a prolonged, but hidden and indirect, short-run effect on English population history. However, there is little sign of the positive check operating in the long run, since mortality failed to respond consistently to secular trends in the standard of living. The preventive check was far more in evidence: indeed the responsiveness of nuptiality to changes in scarcity and plenty, in both the long and the short run, was a dominant feature of the pre-industrial English demographic regime.

35 Wrigley and Schofield, *Population History*, 341. Death rates were actually below trend in the two worst harvest years (1696/7 and 1697/8). There was little evidence of government concern about the possible consequences of high prices, in marked contrast to the mid-1590s; Outhwaite, "Food Crises in Early Modern England: Patterns of Public Response," in Flinn (ed.), *Proceedings of the Seventh International Economic History Conference* (Edinburgh, 1978), 367–374.

Massimo Livi-Bacci

The Nutrition–Mortality Link in Past Times:

A Comment   Malnutrition increases the frequency, severity, and duration of infections and results in high mortality. This simple statement, which masks the complexity of the interrelated mechanisms linking nutrition to mortality, is variously used in interpreting past demographic trends.

Some affirm that, since mortality in past times was mainly determined by communicable infectious diseases, and since their frequency and severity were linked to the nutritional level, mortality would readily respond to changes in the patterns of nutrition. Others add that improvements in mortality in past times could only be achieved through improvements in the general level of nutrition. Others extend this concept further, affirming that until 100 years ago (or even less) other factors commonly cited as determinants of the modern decline in mortality, such as medicine and hygiene, have had little effect, the main factor having been the improvement of food availability and consumption. An interesting but extreme position is held by McKeown, who has stated that "the slow growth of the human population before the eighteenth century was due mainly to lack of food, and the rapid increase since that time resulted largely from improved nutrition." He thus plays down any possible impact of nuptiality and fertility in determining population trends.[1]

Many problems follow from the attempt to use the nutrition-mortality link to explain the past. Many of these problems have been analytically presented in the articles and commentaries contained in this issue. The following is a list of points and problems which need clarification:

Massimo Livi-Bacci is Professor of Demography at the University of Florence. He is the author of *A History of Italian Fertility* (Princeton, 1977).

Thomas McKeown, "Food, Infection, and Population," in this issue, 227.

1. There are considerable difficulties in constructing even an approximate measurement of the nutritional level (not to be confused with the availability of food) and of its changes in historical time.

2. The majority of the episodes of extraordinary and catastrophic mortality are independent of famine, hunger, and starvation.

3. Many infectious diseases (plague, typhoid, and malaria; and, to a lesser degree, typhus, smallpox, and syphilis) are independent of nutrition.

4. A population can gradually adapt to changes in the patterns of food availability either by changing the composition of diets, by modifying energy-allocating patterns (e.g., diminishing physical outlays when normal food intakes are unavailable), or by biological modifications.

5. There is a possible threshold level of malnutrition (a state of severe malnutrition) above which the degree of correlation between nutritional status and mortality is weak.

6. Cultural factors, such as child-raising practices and habits, could have a significant impact on mortality, particularly in infancy.

7. Climatic and environmental factors have an important and autonomous impact on many diseases (for example, malaria).

8. Changes in population density, or in the intensity and frequency of mobility, result in changes in exposure to infections.

9. The changing relationships among environment, parasites and viruses, and host resistance determine a changing pattern of survival of infections, which can be seen in the changing virulence of many diseases over the course of human history.

All of these facts make one think that the postulated relationship between mortality and nutrition may not be the only, or the most important one affecting human survival in past times. One is also led to question the assertion that an improvement in nutrition during the eighteenth and nineteenth century was the primary cause of the decline in mortality. Two additional points suggested by our current knowledge of historical population trends add further doubts about the real strength and primacy of the nutrition-mortality link. These two points can be formulated as follows:

First, if better nutrition improves resistance to infectious diseases and causes a substantial decline in mortality, then those favored and privileged groups which had no problems of access to nutrition should have exhibited a lower level of mortality than the general population, which was plagued by hunger and starvation during recurrent famines and had modest levels of nutrition during normal times.

Second, those populations with plentiful arable land, high agricultural productivity, and low demographic density, who enjoyed better nutrition in normal times and suffered from fewer famines, should have exhibited a level of mortality considerably lower than that typical of less fortunate populations.

The investigation of differential mortality is a complex enterprise today; it is easy to understand the difficulties that one may encounter when dealing with past times, the more so since the discriminatory variable is the nutritional level, the measurement of which is practically impossible. However, there are indirect ways to approach the problem. It is likely, for instance, that privileged groups like the aristocracies or other elites did not have problems of access to food. If we add that these elites probably enjoyed better-than-average environmental conditions, then a significantly lower-than-average mortality should be expected.

As far as we know, past experience does not lend support to this hypothesis. The British peerage studied by Hollingsworth exhibits a life expectancy at birth (e_0) for the cohorts born in each quarter of a century between 1550 and 1750 of between 30.0 and 38.8 for males and 33.7 and 38.3 for females. The estimates of e_0 made by Wrigley and Schofield for the same historical interval (and averaged for both sexes and each twenty-five-year period) oscillate between 33.1 and 38.7, levels that almost exactly match those of the aristocracy. It is only after the mid-eighteenth century that declines in the mortality of the nobility outdistance the general population.[2]

Unfortunately, the case of the British aristocracy is not matched by other elites, whose mortality levels cannot be com-

2 Thomas H. Hollingsworth, "Mortality in the British Peerage Families since 1600," *Population*, XXXII (1977), 323–352; E. Anthony Wrigley and Roger S. Schofield, *The Population History of England, 1541–1871* (Cambridge, Mass., 1981), 230. The average e_0 of the British nobility between 1750 and 1800 was 46.7 against 36.2 for the English population at large.

pared with those of the corresponding general populations whose mortality remains to be measured. However, the mortality of the favored groups is generally high, which makes it unlikely that they enjoyed appreciable advantages over the rest of the population. In the European ruling families studied by Peller, e_0 (both sexes) was 34.0 in the sixteenth century, 30.9 in the seventeenth century, and 37.1 in the eighteenth century. Among the *anciennes familles genevoises* studies by Henry, e_0 (both sexes) was 28.5 from 1550 to 1599, 32.1 from 1600 to 1649, and 35.0 from 1650 to 1699; it was only in the eighteenth century that a level of mortality that can be defined as low in the demography of the *ancien régime* was reached (42.6 from 1700 to 1749 and 47.6 from 1750 to 1799). For the *ducs et pairs* of France, e_{20} was estimated at 34.0, compatible with an e_0 around 30. The only exception in this survey appears to be the nobility of Milan, with an e_0 of 40.7 in the seventeenth century, which further improved to 43.7 in the eighteenth century.[3]

There is further example of a different nature in the mortality figures of the Jesuits in Italy. Those admitted to the order between 1540 and 1565 should have been in a favorable position for different reasons: first, they certainly enjoyed a better-than-average environmental and nutritional level; second, because the order rejected those with impaired health and constitution, theirs was a select group. These advantages, however, are not reflected in lower mortality levels since their expectation of life at age 20 was 31.5 years, a level compatible with an e_0 well below 30 years.[4]

The second approach to the investigation of the impact of nutrition on mortality requires a comparison of the mortality experience of populations with different nutritional patterns. Economic historians are in a position to indicate with some degree

3 Sigmund Peller, "Births and Deaths Among Europe's Ruling Families Since 1500," in David V. Glass and David E. C. Eversley (eds.), *Population in History* (London, 1965); Louis Henry, *Anciennes familles genevoises, étude démographique* (Paris, 1956). For Geneva, in the seventeenth century, a study by Perrenoud has shown large differentials according to social class, with an e_0 going from 18 to 36 years. However, Perrenoud rules out that these differences may be imputed to nutritional patterns, since problems of malnourishment and famines are unknown in Geneva after the sixteenth century. Alfred Perrenoud, "L'inégalité sociale devant la mort à Génève au XVII siècle," *Population*, XXX (1975), 239. Henry and Claude Levy, "Ducs et Pairs sous l'Ancien Régime: Caractéristiques démographiques d'une caste," *Population*, XV (1960), n.5; Dante Zanetti, "La demografia del patriziato milanese nei secoli XVII, XVIII e XIX," *Annales Cisalpines d'Histoire Sociale*, II (1972), 1–560.
4 Silvana Salvini, *La mortalità dei Gesuiti in Italia nei Secoli XVI e XVII* (Florence, 1979).

of accuracy those populations in the past who were fortunate enough to suffer only rarely from famines and to enjoy plentiful food supplies for all social strata. The few examples here are drawn primarily from the nineteenth century and deal with the American experience, under the assumption that American settlers, both in the North and in the South (Argentina) of the hemisphere, experienced very few of the structural nutritional problems that were still plaguing the European rural masses in the early nineteenth century.

Early French Canadian settlers (cohorts born between 1650 and 1720—"beneficiant d'un milieu naturel pratiquement vierge...n'ont guère connu de veritable famine") had an e_0 of 35.5, a level higher than that of contemporary France but not very different from that of contemporary England. The United States experience in the middle of the nineteenth century shows—according to various estimates—an e_0 in the high 30s or low 40s, a level almost exactly matched by the experience of Western European populations, in spite of the existence, on the old continent, of vast masses of impoverished peasants ready for migration to the New World. The case of Argentina shows that mortality was still high in the second half of the nineteenth century. In the city of Buenos Aires e_0 (both sexes) was 32.5 in 1855, 25.4 from 1868 to 1870 (cholera), and 31.7 in 1887; it was only at the end of the century that an expectation of life of 40 was reached. Estimates for the whole of Argentina made by Somoza confirm the picture; e_0 during the last third of the century (1869 to 1895) was 33.0.[5]

It would be interesting to pursue the analysis of the American experience and to extend our investigation to Australia, New Zealand, and other European settlements in the early part of the past century. But the impression based on the available data is that the areas of new European settlement, in spite of the large advantages that they enjoyed in terms of nutritional patterns, did not enjoy proportional advantages in terms of mortality.

5 Hubert Charbonneau, *Vie et mort de nos ancêtres* (Montreal, 1975), 125, 147; Michael R. Haines and Roger C. Avery, "The American Life Table of 1830–1860: An Evaluation," *Journal of Interdisciplinary History*, XI (1980), 85–86. The estimates of Haines and Avery for 1849–1850, for the white population, are 37.7 to 38.8 for males and 39.6 to 43.5 for females. Maria S. Müller, "Mortalidad en la Ciudad de Buenos Aires desde mediados del siglo XIX," in Conferencia Regional Latino Americana de Población, *Actas,* I (1972), 66–73. The Argentinian estimates made by Jorge Somoza appear in N. Sanchez Albornoz, *La Población de América Latina desde los tiempos precolombinos al año 2000* (Madrid, 1977), 191.

This superficial analysis of the mortality experience of elites and well-nourished populations can be summarized as follows:

(a) differential mortality in the past—with nutrition as the discriminatory variable—seems to have been modest, when visible at all;

(b) the mortality of the supposedly well-nourished elites was high before the mid-eighteenth century, with levels of expectation of life mostly in the low 30s; it was only in the latter part of the eighteenth century and in the nineteenth century that their rapidly declining mortality created and increased the gap between the elites and the general population;

(c) the experience of American populations was similar to that of contemporary European populations, in spite of the less satisfactory levels of nutrition of the latter populations.

Even a small difference in the mortality level, coupled with an unchanging fertility and nuptiality pattern, may determine, in the long run, a significant difference in population growth patterns. It is also conceivable that the small difference could be determined by a better nutritional pattern and could explain, for instance, the acceleration of demographic growth in many areas of Europe during the eighteenth and nineteenth centuries. In theory this is possible; in practice, when one interprets and compares historical trends of mortality, it is extremely difficult to distinguish the impact of the nutritional differential pattern from that of the other factors that caused variations in historical mortality rates.

There are two final conclusions. The first is that there are good reasons to believe that the achievement of good nutritional patterns did not cause (at least before the end of the eighteenth century) a significant fall in mortality. The second conclusion is methodological. The discussion in the preceding pages does not deny the role of nutrition in determining the level of mortality in the past. But the discussion questions the theory that the nutrition–mortality link is the sole key to the explanation of mortality trends and differentials in the past and the main determinant of population growth. Demographic analysis has done justice to many simplistic explanations of fertility; it is evident that mortality mechanisms are more complex.

Joan Thirsk

The Horticultural Revolution:
A Cautionary Note on Prices

Before too weighty a structure is placed upon a fragile foundation, we should remind ourselves of the crude measures used to establish the standard of living index, normally consulted by historians for the period 1264 to 1954. Some of the disorderly relationships which are noted in Schofield's article may well reflect the inadequacy of the sources on which that standard of living index was constructed.[1]

The index, constructed by Phelps Brown and Hopkins and published in 1956, set yearly wage rates against yearly food prices. The wage series was compiled from rates paid to building laborers in southern England, and Woodward has already put forward serious criticisms against using builders' wage rates as typical of laborers' wages generally in the sixteenth and early seventeenth centuries.[2]

For the index of food prices a "basket of consumables" was put together, and the items in the basket were separately priced year by year. In 1956 our knowledge of the regional diversity of agricultural production was deficient, and our knowledge of changing food habits was, and still is, totally inadequate. So the task of assembling a standard basket of foodstuffs was not easy. It was compiled from three pieces of documentary evidence: the first was William Savernak's account book, for 1453 to 1460, recording seven years of the weekly expenditure of two priests and a servant at Bridport in Dorset; the second document, compiled by two students of poverty, recorded the diet of sixty households in villages and small towns of southern England in

Joan Thirsk is Reader in Economic History at the University of Oxford and Professorial Fellow of St. Hilda's College, Oxford.

1   Roger Schofield, "The Impact of Scarcity and Plenty on Population Change in England, 1541–1871," in this issue.
2   E. Henry Phelps Brown and Sheila V. Hopkins, "Seven Centuries of the Prices of Consumables, Compared with Builders' Wage-Rates," *Economica*, XXIII (1956), 296–314.

the 1790s; the third record was the Board of Trade's estimate in World War I of the cost of living of working-class people in towns ten years before the start of the war, i.e. in 1904.[3]

The general framework of expenditures was established as follows: 80 percent of household expenditures throughout the seven centuries was attributed to food, and within that 80 percent, 20 percent was attributed to farinaceous foods, 25 percent to meat and fish, 12.5 percent to butter and cheese, and 22.5 percent to drink. The composition of these main categories was altered at two intermediate dates between 1275 and 1950, namely in 1500 and 1725. But the authors of the index do not give precise reasons for the changes which they introduced. They explained them thus: "sometimes we made these changes deliberately, to take account of shifting habits of consumption, or the entry of new products; more often our hand was forced by lack of materials. In general, we arranged the sub-weighting of such series as we selected or were all we had from time to time, according to the detail in the budgets already cited, and failing that, in the half light of general knowledge."[4]

As a pioneering effort, the cost of living index was a heroic achievement, but its weaknesses begin to obtrude in the light of deeper knowledge. For example, it ignores some considerable changes in diet in the course of the period 1500 to 1750, and introduces others which are scarcely credible. The index allowed for the consumption of 10 pounds of butter and 10 pounds of cheese in 1275, and the same amounts in 1725 and 1950, but none in 1500. Yet the dairy industry certainly did not disappear between 1500 and 1725. On the contrary, it underwent a remarkable expansion. The meat of 1½ sheep was allowed for in 1500, but in 1725 it was altered to the meat of half a sheep and 33 pounds of beef. Yet agrarian historians generally argue that declining wool prices in the seventeenth century promoted the keeping of sheep for meat, thus implying a rise rather than a fall in mutton consumption. Moreover, a notable increase occurred in pig-keeping, especially in towns, where production became cheaper than in the

3 Donald Woodward, "Wage Rates and Living Standards in Pre-industrial England," *Past & Present,* 91 (1981), 28–46, esp. 45.
4 Phelps Brown and Hopkins, "Seven Centuries," 180–181.

countryside as so many pigs were fed on tallow, brewers' grains, etc. Pork, however, does not feature in the index at all.[5]

Another major omission is vegetables and fruit. They are not included in the basket of consumables until 1950, when one hundredweight of potatoes appears for the first time. One historian has written of an agricultural revolution in the early modern period. If this is a valid term to apply to agricultural changes at that time, then space must also be given to a horticultural revolution. The expansion of vegetable and fruit growing was one of the farmers' responses to declining prices of cereals, wool, and other mainstream products in the seventeenth century. In 1688, Gregory King estimated the total value of fruit and vegetables at £1,200,000, compared with total agricultural output, valued at £22,000,000, i.e. 5.4 percent of the whole. Moreover, when fruit and vegetables entered the diet as supplements to bread, meat, and dairy produce, two fruit drinks, cider and perry, also began to occupy a larger place. Cider became an article of commerce, and was the subject of legislation in 1688, when it was allowed to be exported. Yet it is nowhere mentioned in the cost of living index. Drink is measured in terms of 4½ bushels of malt in 1500, and 3¼ bushels of malt, 3 pounds of hops, and 1½ pounds of sugar in 1725.[6]

Seventeenth-century writers gave much attention to the advantages of vegetable and fruit growing from the cultivators' point of view. They emphasized the monetary gain, as well as the much greater quantity of vegetables produced on one acre, compared with cereals. A more detailed study of changing diets in consequence of this development remains to be made. But Sir William Coventry summed up the essentials in the situation in 1670 when he described "the increase of the use of fruit, herbs, and roots, especially near all great towns, whereby an acre of garden will maintain more than many acres of pasture would have done".[7]

5   The evidence for these statements will appear in Thirsk (ed.) *The Agrarian History of England and Wales, V, 1640–1750*, forthcoming.
6   Eric Kerridge, *The Agricultural Revolution* (London, 1967); Thirsk, *Agrarian History, V*; idem, *Economic Policy and Projects* (Oxford, 1978), 177.
7   Thirsk and John P. Cooper (eds.), *Seventeenth-Century Economic Documents* (Oxford, 1972), 80.

Of course, dietary changes had a different impact in different regions of England. But in general, the production of fruit and vegetables spread out from London and the southeast in the late sixteenth century to leave its mark on the farming of most of southern England as far as the Trent by 1670. Thereafter interest in these foodstuffs crept more slowly north. The extent of dietary changes needs also to be differentiated by social classes, but that is a refinement yet to be undertaken. By 1700 it is fair to say that all classes were affected by dietary change, although not necessarily all classes everywhere.

The "horticultural revolution" slowed down after 1750 until 1880 and may even have retreated somewhat. This reduction implies another change in diet that needs to be more carefully investigated. Significantly, when Phelps Brown and Hopkins published their index, they remarked upon the similarity between Savernak's budget of 1453 to 1460, and that of 1904 to 1913. This similarity could well have existed, but similarities at two dates separated by 450 years could also mislead by masking substantial dietary changes in the intervening period.[8]

8 Phelps Brown and Hopkins, "Seven Centuries," 181.

Olwen Hufton

Social Conflict and the Grain Supply in
Eighteenth-Century France
In the history of hunger, of grain distribution, and of governmental policy toward the grain trade, the eighteenth century represents a universally acknowledged milestone in Western Europe. For France, it is the century which saw the disappearance of dramatic periods of starvation, sometimes accompanied by plague, which periodically caused sizable cutbacks in demographic performance. In Goubert's graphic phraseology, the *courbe tourmentée* of the seventeenth-century mortality graph was replaced by a *courbe sereine* in the eighteenth. The net result was a sustained population growth at the national (if not invariably at the local) level. The reasons for this trend have been variously attributed to a change in climatic performance from conditions which had previously jeopardized grain yields to better communications and centralized administration, which permitted more effective grain distribution to localities facing acute shortage.[1]

The focus of this article is not on the reasons for, but rather on the fact of, growth. There were by the most conservative estimates 5 to 6 million more mouths to feed in 1789 than there had been in 1720. Moreover, this growth occurred, as far as has yet been ascertained, without any increase in native grain production to match it. North of the Loire, in limited enclaves, some increase has been detected. Significant economic growth did occur in wine production and textile development which permitted an international trade in Baltic and Levantine wheat. Notwithstanding, taking France as a whole, evidence points heavily to the failure of French cereal production, at least in the short run, to meet demographic demands.

Olwen Hufton is Professor of Modern European History at the University of Reading. She is the author of *Europe: Privilege and Protest* (London, 1980).

1   Pierre Goubert, *Cent Mille Provinciaux, au XVIIe siècle. Beauvais et le Beauvaisis de 1600–1730* (Paris, 1968), 69. The socioeconomic background is summarized in Emmanuel Le Roy Ladurie, *Histoire de la France rurale* (Paris, 1975), II, 359–441; Hufton, *The Poor of Eighteenth-Century France, 1750–1789* (Oxford, 1974), 11–68.

Much of France was in the hands of small peasant proprietors who did not have the means to experiment. No technological breakthrough occurred to bring under cultivation previously unproductive land. Nor do we witness any radical departure from traditional cereal crops and patterns of eating. The mass of the people continued to eat the same kind of bread; or in some regions *galettes* (a kind of pancake made of coarse grains like rye); or starchy slops like oaten porridge; or barley, chestnut, or buckwheat gruel reinforced in spring and summer by vegetables such as cabbage, beans, onions; or in the Mediterranean regions an even wider variety. Much depended on where one lived, but cereals were ubiquitously considered the staple diet, and hunger was popularly identified with their insufficiency. Setting aside parts of the Midi which responded over time more favorably to dietary innovation than did anywhere else, most of France was singularly hostile to dietary change: "on mange mal le pain d'autrui" was as true of the eighteenth century as of any previous period, although by the mid-1790s radical readjustments were occurring.

Without lingering on how much slack existed in domestic production to cope with the new demand, or on the significance of grain imports, we can point to a substantial literature underscoring the fact that demographic growth without a concomitant increase in food production was behind a massive price rise—65 percent in the last two decades of the *ancien regime* as opposed to a speculative 22 percent rise in wages. The worst manifestations of the increase occurred between 1764 and 1775 (for wheat, the *setier de Paris* reached on average twenty-nine *livres,* whereas, in the previous five years, it had stood at fifteen). Between 1776 and 1786 the price of wheat fell to around twenty *livres,* but the *setier* again rose to over twenty-five *livres* after 1786. Attempts have been made to construct model family economies based on a bread ration of seven pounds of wheaten bread per day for a family of five, and such models have shown that bread could have accounted for between 60 and 80 percent of the budget of a wage earner's family by the end of the old regime.[2]

2 A broad interpretation of C. Ernest Labrousse, *Esquisse du mouvement des prix et des revenus en France au XVIIIe siècle* (Paris, 1933). For an excellent bibliography of grain prices, as well as of the bread riot, see Louise Tilly, "The Food Riot as a Form of Political Conflict in France," *Journal of Interdisciplinary History,* I (1971), 23–57.

It is artificial to use wheat prices alone as the measure of living standards. The poor did not eat wheat but cheaper, coarser grains and the prices of these commodities are less consistently recorded. Nevertheless, the movement of such prices generally conformed to movements in the price of wheat. In addition, in order to get a realistic notion about the quality of the diet, we need to know about the supply of vegetables or chestnuts which might have supplemented the poor family's consumption. Nonetheless, in the absence of this information we must content ourselves with the general trends profered by the wheat *mercuriales* which have preoccupied a long and distinguished series of French historians. Le Roy Ladurie has suggested that about one third of the adult male population subsisted on under 1,800 calories a day by the 1780s, without taking into account periodic reductions in yields such as those which occurred in the second half of the 1780s. An examination of stocks divided by the gross number of possible consumers reveals essentially the same point. In short, periodic starvation was replaced for a possible 30 to 40 percent of the total population (perhaps 60 to 70 percent in some regions) by long-term malnutrition, but the degree of deprivation must remain speculative.[3]

Furthermore, urban bread riots and peasant antiseigneurial demonstrations, highlighted by the events of 1789, bore witness to deepening social conflict over who controlled the produce of the land. The number of such disturbances varied considerably from one part of France to another, and the peasant antiseigneurial movement was also geographically circumscribed. This article explores the effects of price rises and of the growing contest for supplies upon towns and villages having different social structures and modes of tenure in an attempt to explain the intensity and diversity of conflict in a particular context.

We need to think in terms of a three-zoned France rather than a homogeneous national entity (Fig. 1). The first zone stretched from the Channel to the Loire (leaving out Brittany). This was the area of *la grande culture,* the granary of France, and

---

3 Le Roy Ladurie, *Histoire de la France rurale,* 438–440. See also, Michel Morineau, *Les faux-semblants d'un démarrage économique: agriculture et démographie en France au XVIIIe siècle* (Paris, 1971), 331–339; *idem,* "A la halle de Charleville: fourniture et prix des grains ou les mécanismes du marché (1647–1821)," *Actes du 95e Congrès des Sociétés Savantes* (Reims, 1970), 159–221.

Fig. 1 The Three Provisioning Zones of France

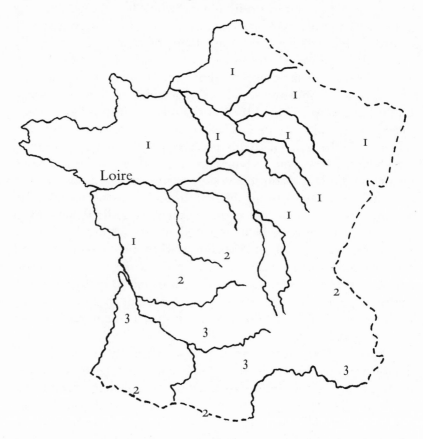

it had some very substantial farms, particularly in the Beauce, the Brie, the plain of Picardy, Champagne, and northern Burgundy. These farms were geared to the provisioning of the great northern cities, including the capital, which demanded supplies from an ever-widening radius. This zone also included the Seine valley, the Normandy Bessin, and the Cotentin, the last two being important dairy farming regions that catered to the moneyed markets of Paris, Rouen, and Caen. Burgundy, producing both grain and fine wines along the restricted area of the Côte, was subjected to the dual pull of the burgeoning Paris and Lyons markets. Burgundy had great religious foundations from Vézelay to Beaune, important noble houses, entrepreneurial bourgeoisie, and a number of substantial peasants, all commercially minded, interested in enclosure and engrossment, with an eye ever turned toward the city markets.

This zone also embraced Flanders, and Flemish agriculture was the most productive in Europe, for, although the farms were not large, they were abundantly fertilized. Flanders, like East Anglia, represented a balanced mixed agriculture that permitted vital soil replacement by the dung of cattle that were stall fed in winter. It produced grain yields of 18:1. The first zone was characterized by a diversified social structure which was conspicuous for the extremes of wealth and poverty it represented. At one end of the spectrum were the wealthy farms and tithe-owning religious houses, and at the other end were a proliferation of day laborers. Squeezed between them were a number of small-holders for whom debt or personal misfortune could mean falling into the ranks of the landless. The day laborer was one of the victims of rising bread prices and was condemned to watch the transit of needed grain to the city markets. Not surprisingly, this zone (and Burgundy in particular) was the heartland of the bread riot and of attempts to prevent grain from leaving the area.[4]

The second zone consisted in large part of the Massif Central, to which I have added, although they are not contiguous, Dauphiné, the Alpine regions, and the Pyrenees. This is mountainous, or at best hilly, France. It is also that of *la petite culture,* of small farms. Over 80 percent of the population in these regions were *micropropriétaires*: large exploiters in any village could be counted on the fingers, but so could the totally landless. It has been estimated that between 60 and 90 percent of holdings in this zone were too small to maintain a family throughout the year, and the farmsteads were therefore heavily dependent upon seasonal migration or upon patchy industrial outwork. Dietary standards in the second half of the century appear to have reached a nadir, with communities depending upon chestnuts as their staple for two or three months of the year. Nutritious as chestnuts might

4   The zoning pattern used in this paper is also used by Le Roy Ladurie, "Pour un modèle de l'économie rurale française au XVIIIe siècle," *Cahiers d'histoire,* XIX (1974), 1–25. Specific local studies relative to the *pays de grande culture* are Georges Lefebvre, *Etudes Orléanaises* (Paris, 1962); Michel Vovelle, *Ville et Campagne au 18e siècle* (Paris, 1980); Pierre de Saint Jacob, *Les Paysans de la Bourgogne du Nord au dernier siècle de l'ancien régime* (Paris, 1960).

be, they constituted a very risky food source because of the potential for devastation by wind or storm. Moreover, as the parochial enquiries of the 1770s revealed, those who ate them regarded chestnuts as a substandard diet. Statistics relating to the condition of the conscripts in the early nineteenth-century demonstrate that these hilly zones produced the puniest, and the highest percentage of rickety or deformed recruits.

The most conspicuous development in this zone over the eighteenth century was the multiplication of small-holdings by the fractionalization of already small units. An analysis of four villages in the Basse Auvergne, for example, shows that, whereas in 1700 there were 490 farms of under two and one half acres, by 1792 there were 870 of these tiny units. There was also, over the last fifty years, a massive rise in rentals (by 175 percent), a shortening of leases, and evidence of accumulating *rentes passives* (short-term extra rents to service and pay off debts). Markets existed: Clerment, Rodez, Le Puy, for example, were all large enough to demand provisioning, but they did not require vast stocks of grain. This zone was virtually free from market disturbances and attacks on grain convoys. However, it was the site of some of the most bitter, widespread, and prolonged outbreaks of violence directed by peasants against seigneurs, debt collectors, and *hommes d'affaires* that revolutionary France was to experience.[5]

The third zone encompasses the great regions of viticulture—Gascony and the Mediterranean regions of Languedoc and Provence. Gascony produced high-grade wines and good brandy that was appreciated by the finer palates of moneyed Europe and trans-Atlantic societies. Languedoc and Provence produced bulk, low-grade alcohol in the form of wine, *marc*, or *eau de vie*, which fueled the domestic market, the great cities of the north and south, and was important as an export commodity in a buoyant Mediterranean traffic that was closely integrated with Amsterdam, the Baltic market, and the Levant.

The seventeenth century had seen some extension of wine at the expense of cereal growth due to the availability of Baltic and Levantine wheat. The great ports of the Midi were largely provisioned from abroad. There remained important cereal-growing enclaves such as the Lauragais to the east of Toulouse, where

5 Le Roy Ladurie, "Pour un modèle," 1, synthesizes Abel Poitrineau, "Propriété et société en Haute Auvergne à la fin du régime de Louis XV: Le Case de Vic," *Cahiers d'Histoire*, VI (1961), 425; *idem. La vie rurale en Basse Auvergne au XVIIIe siècle* (Paris, 1965).

village society resembled that of the Beauce (in zone one) in having a large number of salaried day laborers, few small or medium farmers, and land and grain production that was controlled by a landed noble elite. Grain was also produced on smaller units in villages throughout Bas Languedoc (where terrain and climate allowed). The grain of Languedoc was highly prized. Sun-ripened and hard, it was vastly superior for sowing purposes to anything produced north of the Loire. Hence, a farmer might well produce grain to sell to the domestic northern market via the grain barges of the Garonne and the Canal du Midi, but purchase cheap imported grain himself. There was always grain in transit in Bas Languedoc, the Toulousain, and the Albigeois.[6]

Obviously, rural society in the Midi was highly varied. The olive, Europe's most valuable tree, flourished on mountain slopes where little else could grow and produced a crop of incalculable worth in terms of calories and vitamins to those who could obtain it. If we add to this the fish-producing capacity of the littoral, and the potential for purchasing Breton salt cod and Dutch salted herring as return cargo for wine and spirits or cloth, we are drawn to the conclusion that Mediterranean France enjoyed a richness and variety of diet unparalleled elsewhere in France (but which receded in both quality and quantity as the foothills of the Massif rose from the plain).

The well-being of the region was indissolubly linked to the traffic in wine (and hence to high wine prices) and, to a subsidiary extent, to the Levantine cloth trade. As long as it was possible to purchase from outside, and the means to purchase existed, the great cities of the Midi did not draw upon the produce of the hinterland to the same degree as did Paris, the northern cities, or Lyons. Yet, once wine prices slumped in the 1770s and 1780s, fierce urban bread riots developed over the price and the quality of this cheapest staple, and peasants moved to curtail the export of grain from the Lauragais, Albigeois, and other surplus-producing regions.[7]

This crude attempt at zoning blurs certain regional anomalies. Burgundy, for example, included both areas of capitalist agriculture and areas of small-holdings. It was the scene of bread riots, of demonstrations against the exit of grain toward the Paris mar-

6 Georges Frêche, *Toulouse et sa région, vers 1670–89* (Paris, 1974).
7 H. Bouderon, "La lutte contre la vie chère dans la généralité de Languedoc au XVIIIe siècle," *Annales du Midi*, LXVI (1954), 155–170.

kets, and of violent antiseigneurial movements among villages of *micropriétaires* exposed to exploitation through *rentes* and debts.

Any period of rising grain prices produces winners and losers. An obvious winner in these circumstances is the surplus producer or anyone who can exploit or cut into the increasingly profitable grain trade. Into the first category we can put the large farmers (whether owner-occupiers or tenants) who were known as *laboureurs* and who produced a large surplus for the market by direct exploitation. How many of these *laboureurs* were owners of their land is not important. Some farmers leased large territories from the clergy or from the nobility, and their presence is most significant in the first zone of *grande culture*.

Along with the surplus producer, the greatest beneficiaries of soaring grain prices were those who took rents in kind. Tithe owners were clearly paramount. The upper echelons of the ecclesiastical hierarchy (under 1 percent of the population) were in command of about 8 percent of France's total grain production without ever having to concern themselves with husbandry in any way whatever. A great amount of tithe gathering was leased to large farmers or bourgeoisie to spare the church the costs and inconvenience of collection. In this way, the profits of tithes were distributed over a broader social stratum which included at least some *laboureurs*. Nevertheless, some of the most impressive grain stocks of eighteenth-century France were found in the granaries of the great religious houses and cathedral chapters, in particular in the Seine Valley (Bec, Jumièges, Saint Wandrille, etc.); in parts of Burgundy (Vézelay, Cluny, etc.); in the Beauce, where the most affluent cathedral chapter in France existed at Chartres; in the Loire Valley; and to some extent in the Toulouse/Albi region—in short, in the great grain producing areas of the first zone. Each of these establishments was not only a tithe owner but also a massive land owner. As such, they controlled, directly or indirectly, the greatest grain stocks in France. Such stocks were intended above all for the provisioning of Paris and the great cities. They were large-scale enterprises that were fully commercial in orientation.[8]

8   Guy Le Marchand, "Les troubles de subsistances dans la généralité de Rouen (seconde moitié du XVIIIe siècle)," *Annales Historiques de la Révolution Française* (AHRF.), XXXV (1963), 401–427; *idem,* "Les monastères de Haute Normandie au XVIIIe siècle," AHRF, XXXVII (1965), 18–24. Vovelle, *Ville et Campagne,* 169–207.

The *seigneurs* were also in a position to cut into the produce of the land, but the degree to which they did so varied considerably. As a proportion of the gross product, seigneurial levies in kind took their greatest toll in the *pays de petite culture*. There are, for example, villages in the Auvergne where peasants parted with 25 percent of their crop.[9] Moreover, as a percentage of seigneurial income, the dues played a more significant part here than elsewhere. In 1760, Turgot, who knew the Limousin intimately, commented:

> Ces sortes de redevances en nature (les redevances seigneuriales) sont d'une tout autre importance dans la plupart des provinces meriodionales que dans les provinces riches, telles que la Normandie, la Picardie ou les environs. Dans ces dernières provinces, la principale richesse des gros propriétaires consiste dans le produit des terres qui sont réunies en grands corps de fermes, dont le propriétaire retire un gros loyer. Dans les terres les plus considerables, les rentes seigneuriales ne forment qu'une tres modique portion du revenu, et cet article n'est presque regardé que comme honorifique. Dans les provinces moins riches et cultivées d'après des principes differents, les seigneurs et les gentilshommes ne possèdent presque point de terres à eux; les héritages qui sont extrêmement divisés, sont chargés de très grosses rentes en grains, dont tous les cotenanciers sont tenus solidairement. Les rentes absorbent souvent le plus clair du produit des terres, et le revenu des seigneurs en est presque uniquement composé.[10]

In the second zone, the area of *la petite culture,* as much as 25 percent of the gross local product passed into the hands of a seigneur. (Since it was an area of multiple seigneuries this could be more than one individual.) This grain, although it constituted a surplus for the seigneur, did not provide the kind of wealth

9 J. L. Goldsmith, "Remarques sur le régime seigneurial en Haute Auvergne," in Albert Soboul (ed.), *Cóntributions à l'histoire paysanne de la Révolution Française* (Paris, 1977), 141–158; Michel Leymarie, "Les redevances foncières seigneuriales en Haute-Auvergne," AHRF, XL (1968), 229.

10 Michel Etienne Turgot (ed., G. Schelle), *Oeuvres* (Paris, 1923), III, 246–247. Note that, whereas in regions around Toulouse, Bordeaux, and Le Mans, seigneurial levies were only 5 to 8% of seigneurial income, in the Haute Auvergne they were 33%. Robert Forster, "The Survival of the Nobility during the French Revolution," *Past & Present, 36* (1967), 72; Leymarie, "Les redevances," 361.

which marked out an abbot of Vézelay or a Duc de Saulx-Tavanes, nor did it necessarily leave the locality. The bulk of it was probably destined to be returned to the community in the form of loans (with interest payments) when the *micropropriétaires* had exhausted the stocks that they retained. How soon that was depended upon the size of the holding, the state of the harvest, and the accumulation of debt repayments from previous years.

In most of the *pays de petite culture,* the *micropropriétaires* (60 to 85 percent of the population) lived on a sub-subsistence unit and were dependent upon seasonal migration or on semivagrancy for part of the year. Seasonal migrant farmers in Auvergnat would return at Easter for the spring sowing, having spent the winter heaving coal or wood in Paris or Lyons, with perhaps a few *livres* to their names. Their return would be the occasion for an interim reckoning: how much was left for sowing and to see their families through to the harvest or at least to chestnut time after the women, children, and the old had eaten out of the stock during the winter? Any money garnered in the town would be spent at this time buying grain back from the seigneur against the certainty of shortfall (actual or imminent). Some families would already have borrowed in the emigrants' absence. Many would not have enough money and would contract new debts against the next harvest. The sowing over, these farmers might leave again, tinkering, chimney-sweeping, etc.

In some communities, the emigrants' remittances were the only form of new wealth entering the villages; these were immediately absorbed into the small-holder's provisioning ecosystem and thereby shifted into the pockets of the seigneur or to those to whom he had subcontracted the collection of his dues. Evidence points toward the suggestion that no seigneur or *homme d'affaires* expected to realize all of his assets and was forced to let many of his debts ride, although not before making sure that they were recorded.[11]

Some of the *fermiers* (tax farmers) were also merchants in the

---

11 For some bibliographical background to the immense debt question, see Hufton, *The Poor,* 58; Saint Jacob, "L'endettement paysan au XVIIIe siècle: remarques de méthode," *Cahier Association Interuniversitaire,* I (1959), 15–20; Poitrineau, *Le vie rurale,* 486–496; Jean François Soulet, "A propos de l'endettement rural au XVIIIe siècle: Deux communautés du Piémont Pyrénéen," *Annales du Midi,* LXXXIV (1972), 29–50.

local markets. Towns in the Massif constituted the other outlet for the grain which has passed to the seigneur, although such places rarely exceeded 6,000 people, and most had only 3,000 to 4,000 inhabitants. In the *pays de petite culture,* grain did not usually travel farther than the nearest market.

Historians have indulged in considerable debate over the extent to which the grain trade was controlled by professional merchants, but there is no simple answer applicable to France as a whole. For the large cities—Paris, Rouen, Bordeaux, Marseilles, Lyons, Toulouse, etc.—the trade was obviously in the hands of a full-time, professional group of *négociants* whose existence was confirmed through registration by the relevant municipal authorities. These merchants were registered because the authorities feared the black market and speculative practices and wished to know where the trade was concentrated. For the same reason, it was necessary to keep track of grain exporters and importers. Since the Midi was partially dependent upon Baltic or Levantine wheat, the likelihood was that the grain traffic to modest towns like Castres, Carcassonne, Bedarieux, or Lodève would be controlled for the most part by a limited number of professional merchants, although that fact did not preclude the direct appearance of producers conducting their own business directly in the markets or with bakers, since many townspeople bought bread rather than grain or flour.

In the first zone, north of the Loire, the continuing pressure to feed Paris and the growing contest for supplies caused the number of middlemen to multiply as merchants scoured the grain-producing provinces for supplies. Some individuals sought to cut more directly into the system by negotiating the collection of seigneurial rights with the seigneur. This emerged very clearly in Burgundy:

> Il s'est élevé parmi nous une espèce de gens qui à l'aide de leurs courtiers se qualifient du titre de négociant pour envahir à quelque prix que ce soit toutes les fermes des seigneurs de 10 a 12 lieves à la ronde. Les seigneurs qui ont plus à coeur de servir leurs interêts que de faire végéter trois à quatre milliers d'individus livrent ceux-ci à l'ambitieuse cupidité de cette espèce de fermiers généraux.[12]

12 Archives Departmentales (AD), Côte d'Or B2. 242. Cahier de Châteauneuf.

Although the *pays de grande culture* produced the large-scale *négociant,* in the Massif, in addition to direct consumer/producer relationships, the *fermier* (tax farmer) turned *marchand* was more common, in particular in years of stress, when such a maverick figure would temporarily enter the market only to retreat into some other form of activity when the situation normalized. The Dihar family from Castillon provides an example. We can take Jean Dihar, a weaver who married a shoemaker's daughter in 1707, as founder of the line. His son, Pierre, combined the work of weaver with that of *marchand de laine,* making small grain purchases in Bordeaux between 1739 and 1745, probably in years of reduced local yields. He also built up a small *vignoble,* marketing the produce through Bordeaux. He was very much an amateur in the grain business and his main preoccupation was with weaving.[13]

His son, however, also a Pierre, abandoned weaving entirely and styled himself *marchand de laine* and *marchand de vin* in 1770. In 1785, however, after some very sluggish years in the wine trade and some indifferent cereal harvests, his main commercial interest for five years became the purchase in Bordeaux and distribution up the Dordogne (navigable as far as Siorac) of Spanish and Baltic wheat. The smaller the local harvests in the rural communities of the Perigord, the more extensive his investments in grain intended for the small towns became. Once local conditions improved, he shifted the emphasis of his business back to wool.

Other individuals chose to distribute grains that they had received as rents or debt repayments by personally selected means. An innkeeper's wife at Riberac who tried to send a small consignment to her son-in-law at Notron during the late summer of 1739 because he had informed her of a local scarcity and higher prices occasioned a minor riot in her town even though prices were steady at the local market. In the course of the ensuing police enquiry it emerged that she had discharged grain up the Dordogne in response to news from relatives dotted over the area. These included another tavern keeper, a locksmith, and a postman, who was especially helpful in telling her where hail or weevil had done their worst.[14]

13 AD Garonne, *Négociants,* Series U. Unclassified. Dihar.
14 Iain A. Cameron, *Crime and repression in the Auvergne and the Guyenne, 1720–1790* (Cambridge, 1981), 235.

In short, there is a great deal of evidence to suggest that an informal infrastructure of distributors and part-time merchants existed who worked within the formal provisioning structure and under the laws demanding registration of grain merchants. Their size increased with the penury of the times; shortage multiplied the numbers seeking to profit from rising prices by the distribution or redistribution of grain.

In picking out the winners in the price war we are locating those individuals who were popularly conceived to be the bogey men of the grain trade. In the *pays de grande culture* and in the Midi, these were the larger farmers and the tithe owners; in the *pays de petite culture,* the seigneurs, and their *fermiers* (tax farmers); and in all zones, the mercantile element, which played the market and the bakers who served the cities. To these "evil" people must, after 1764, be added the government and, increasingly, parts of the establishment which dealt with law and order. We are concerned here with the formal abandonment of paternalist theory.[15]

The paternalist model of grain distribution was founded on the belief that grain was a commodity too precious to the well-being of the community and the maintenance of public order to be left to the free play of market forces. Its sale and distribution, therefore, had to be through the channel of an official market and could not be sold by sample or by private treaty between merchants and producers. Also, precautions had to be taken to see that the market was always adequately provisioned and that holders of grain did not keep back their produce, thus denuding the market and creating a *disette factice* (artificial death) to push up prices. The flow had to be relatively constant, accepting that there was greater consumer demand in some months than in others.

In addition, grain could not seek out any market. Its distribution should have been tied to certain local markets, and all who dealt in grain, meaning merchants, had to be registered. The population had a right to protection from unfair business prac-

15 What follows draws heavily on Tilly, "The Food Riot"; Stephen Kaplan, *Bread, Politics and Political Economy in the Reign of Louis XV* (The Hague, 1976), which excels in the practicalities attached to the grain issue but is less strong on the psychological implications. The reverse is true of Richard Cobb, *The Police and the People, French Popular Protest, 1789–1820* (Oxford, 1970), 246–317. Kaplan never decides whether there really was enough grain to go around, and Cobb accepts the *sans-culotte's* own account that he really was a victim of peasant plots. Notwithstanding, Cobb's study justly remains a classic.

tices: the sale of dirty or diseased grain, short measure, or attempts to raise prices by false bidding.

These concepts of the regulated market were allied to that of the just price. This was a price acceptable to both consumer and producer. From the consumers' viewpoint, the price of bread had to bear a relationship to wages. The just price had to be a constant price not subject to sudden sharp rises which might put the vital commodity beyond the reach of significant sections of the population.

Students of the history of paternalist theory and practice insist that this model was never studiously applied. The provisioning of the capital and of the great inland cities like Lyon depended on an ever-widening radius which precluded the maintenance of a direct producer/consumer relationship and demanded that grain travel over considerable distances. Periodically, in years of dearth, government *arrêts* would remind the populace of the legitimacy of such action:

> Le commerce et le transport des grains de province à province du royaume a toujours été libre et permis à chacun sans que les officiers du lieu, gouverneurs et autres ayant pu sous quelque prétexte que ce soit empescher cette liberté et particulièrement pour les grains achetés et destines pour être amenés à la ville de Paris que sa Majesté et les rois ses prédécesseurs ont toujours voulu en être abondamment fournie.[16]

Implicit in such an *arrêt* was the assumption that the urban grain trade was in the hands of merchants rather than of farmers and that the central government and city authorities were not concerned over whether or not these merchants purchased in the marketplace or by agreement in the tavern. However, in support of a real expression of the paternalist model, there did exist in the first half of the eighteenth century something known as *la police des grains*. This term had always meant not policing as such but a state of vigilance among officials (understood to encompass town councillors, *jurats, consuls,* officials of the *bailliage* court who included a *lieutenant général de police*, the *maréchaussée, subdelegués,*

---

16 *Arrêt du Conseil d'Etat, le 16 Octobre 1708* cited by Michel Bricourt, Marcel Lachiver, and Julien Queruel, "La crise de subsistance des années 1740 dans le ressort du Parlement de Paris," *Annales de Démographie Historique,* n.v. (1974), 317.

intendants, and reaching up through them to the *Contrôle Général* in Paris). These officials had to look for *cherté* (rising prices) and determine whether such increases were the result of a real shortage of grain or of speculative practices creating *disette factice*. If the dearth were real, then the onus lay with the authorities (municipal, intendance, and central) to lay in more supplies from areas with a surplus. Alternatively, they might purchase grain in the ports before too much public inconvenience occurred or rumors inflated the shortage to such an extent that markets were stripped by speculators or left empty because farmers feared disturbances. If such a shortfall were deemed to be artificial, then the various officials had a number of options available. First, they could send the *maréchaussée* around to the larger farms to attempt to compel the resumption of a flow of supplies. Second, they could undertake token arrests of known speculators. Third, they could tolerate limited market disturbances which might force merchants and surplus holders to lower their prices.[17]

How effective were these approaches in dealing with periods of crisis? The question is difficult to answer, not least because the real crises came in the late 1760s, when the paternalist model was under official attack, and the 1780s, when the imbalance between supply and demand was chronic. However, the numbers involved in *la police des grains* were insufficiently numerous or powerful to confront the real giants of the grain business.

In January 1739, the *procurur fiscal* of Evron in the Maine noted:

> Il y a dans notre diocese du Mans quantité de seigneurs, gros fermiers, bourgeois et autres mêmes jusqu'à des abbayes, curés et autres maisons religieuses qui ont quantité de bleds dans leurs greniers, qui ne veulent point vendre dans l'attente et l'espérance qu'ils ont eu'en le gardant il viendra un grand prix et une grande cherté sur l'arrière saison. Ils [a religious house] ont fait refus de livrer au nomme Courtelle, boulanger de nostre bourg une demie chartée de bled froment, qu'ils lui avaient vendue ci-devant, à cause de l'augmentation des prix qu'il est arrivée depuis la vendition. Il n'a pas osé poursuivre les religieux pour avoir son froment à cause qu'ils sont seigneurs et qu'il n'aurait pas même trouvé un huissier pour leur en faire la contrainte.[19]

---

17 On this type of policing, see Cameron, *Crime and its Repression*, 233–235.

The tolerance of many officials for limited market disturbances resulting in *taxation populaire* stemmed partly from their inability to restrain an urban populace, partly from the need to intimidate speculators, and partly from the hope that reports of such disturbances might result in some help being brought to bear from the intendance or central authority. However, news of peasant attacks on grain convoys filled urban authorities with trepidation because such activity could jeopardize grain supplies to the towns and also because rumors of such attacks could only increase urban panic and the antipathy between town and country.

Protracted disturbances could have the effect of driving merchants from markets in the short term. However, setting aside the very particular instance of 1774 in the Paris provisioning zone, protracted market disturbances in any one center were almost unknown.[18]

The paternalist model was above all a public relations exercise. It cannot be said that it contributed in any degree whatever to increasing the grain flow or lowering prices. It never stopped prices from rising but it could contribute to holding them at a certain level. However, in so far as speculative practice was at the root of the trouble—and the important fact is that popular opinion held it to be so—the model contributed toward the maintenance of public order. The authorities were believed to be at one with the towns in the life and death struggle against unfair selling practices.

In 1764, and again in the period between 1774 and 1776, the government formally abandoned paternalism and declared itself explicitly to be a proponent of laissez faire. Why did it do so? In theory, through its use of reiterative *arrêts* relative to the provisioning of the cities, the government was already an exponent of freedom of mercantile action. Why did it need to go further? The 1750s had been a period of relatively stable prices and there had been little in the way of disturbances. Why change course at that point?

The answer probably lies in the condition of government coffers and the dilemma of a state drawing its revenues virtually exclusively from the agrarian sector. As France (and most other

18   George Rudé, "La Taxation populaire de mai 1775 à Paris et dans la région Parisienne," AHRF, XXVIII (1956), 139–179.

European countries) emerged from the most expensive intercontinental war in its history, the need to rebuild its army and navy, to hold onto the shreds of its empire, entailed a need for revenue reconstruction according to the physiocratic principles embodied in current economic philosophy. If wealth lay in land and its produce, the owners of land had an inalienable right to maximize their profits through the free play of market forces. Enhanced agrarian revenues would then in the long term produce healthy state coffers.[19]

In short, implicit in the advocacy of explicit laissez-faire principles was the recognition that prices would rise. However, it was not anticipated that they would do so on any considerable scale. The king's advisers believed that there was enough grain to go around and that supply and demand factors would even out prices at a realistic level. (They also believed in a stagnant population which would remain so until a new agrarian affluence created a new demographic environment.)

A formal commitment to laissez faire proved to be a grisly error for several reasons, some of which might have been foreseen, others being less predictable. Unforeseen was the state of the harvest—the late 1760s saw considerable short-term reductions in the grain supply. Predictable was the amount of ill-will generated among the consumers, especially in the sensitive regions north of the Loire, and in particular in the Paris provisioning zone. Consumers perceived themselves to be the sacrificial lambs of a producer-oriented philosophy with formal government backing, so that the government, rather than the immediate grain traders, was seen to be the architect of the shortage. From that point on, the politicization of the grain issue assumed a new bitterness.

Furthermore, as a direct result of the growth of Paris and of subsequent fluctuations in provisioning, attempts were made to build up a reserve granary for the city by insisting that the religious houses buy and warehouse stipulated amounts of grain for

---

19 For comparative material showing a similar tendency in other European nations, see Edward P. Thompson, "The Moral Economy of the English Crowd in the Eighteenth Century," *Past & Present*, 52 (1971), 76–136; Laura Rodriguez, "The Spanish Riots of 1766," *Past & Present*, 59 (1973), 117–146; *idem*, "The Riots of 1766 in Madrid," *European Studies Review*, III (1973), 223–242; Pierre Vilar, "El motin de Esquiâché y las crisas del antiguo régimen," *Revista de Occidente*, XXXVI (1972), 199–249.

sale either in an emergency or toward the end of the agricultural year. Merchants laying hold of this grain were interpreted as government agents, and Louis XV and Abbé Terray were perceived to be behind a *pacte de famine* to push up prices while lining their own pockets. A generation of consumers emerged in the sensitive zones north of the Loire in the closing decade of the old regime who believed that sound paternalist practice had once ensured fair provisioning. This concept, however, was variously interpreted: for consumers in the towns and cities it meant a free flow of grain at constant, reasonable prices; for those in the countryside and small towns within the city provisioning zones, it meant the retention of local grain to fill local consumption needs. The point of contact was the notion of *le bon vieux temps,* a clear conviction that political machinations had destroyed a harmonious past and that political change would be the vehicle for its restoration.[20]

It is logical to proceed from the collapse of the paternalist model and the problems of city provisioning in the first and third zones to a consideration of bread riots. First, however, we need to take into account another factor—the chronology involved in grain distribution, which will explain the timing of the riots and disturbances and reveal the socially derisive aspects of marketing and provisioning in the *pays de petite culture,* as well as in the areas of commercial agriculture.

The chronology of grain distribution throughout the agricultural year reveals vast social distinctions between types of buyers and types of sellers at any one time. Turgot and the physiocrats were aware of this chronology, and of the social aspects of marketing, but perceived them to be a part of a natural order ensuring even distribution over the year. Michaelmas (29 September) was the start of the distribution pattern. Small farmers marketed enough grain to pay taxes to the state, rent to their landlords, and any other debts contracted. (We shall call this phase A, and it stretched approximately from Michaelmas to December.) A second phase (B) extended to Easter. During this phase, the middling farmers marketed their grain, since their assets were not sufficient to enable them to hold back until phase C (Easter to the next Michaelmas). During the third phase, the giants of the

---

20 Kaplan, "Lean Years, Fat Years: The 'Community' Granary System and the Search for Abundance in Eighteenth-Century Paris," *French Historical Studies,* X (1977), 197–230; Gustave Bord, *Histoire du blé en France. Le Pacte de famine, histoire, légende* (Paris, 1887).

grain business—large farmers, seigneurs, tithe owners, merchants, and independent operators—would bring their grain into market, the more modest ones first, the most consequential last. Implicit in this order, the physiocrats recognized, was some movement in prices, slight or heavy depending upon the state of the harvest at the onset of phase A. During phase A, prices were at their lowest because the markets were abundantly provisioned. They began to climb during phase B, as the spring sowing approached. The most profits were to be garnered during phase C. In normal times (and physiocratic thought clung tenaciously to normality) the price rises in phase C should not be dramatic since no dealer would wish to be left with unwanted grain at the end of the agricultural year.

It is, however, worth examining this skeletal representation of the trade more closely to provide a more sophisticated account of what occurred. During phase A, when the small farmers marketed a part of their grain to pay their taxes and their debts, prices were at their lowest. Such individuals perceived their grain to be undervalued in the market, particularly if they had borrowed or purchased during the previous phase C. They were never in a position to profit from rising prices. Such individuals were not necessarily surplus producers. They knew that at some time in the not-too-distant future they would have to enter the market as consumers when others were making a profit out of the very grain that they had grown. This likelihood was increased by the knowledge that at Michaelmas tithe-owners and seigneurs stepped forward to take their percentage of the crop, and this 12 to 25 percent of the small-holders' total output disappeared into barns and granaries to await the end of the agricultural year. Added to this amount was whatever had been surrendered to pay off debts.[21]

Who were the purchasers of the grain sold in phase A? First,

---

21 There was a threshold below which participation in the market as a seller was unlikely. Morineau, using material from Champagne in the first zone, estimates that, with a yield of 6:1 on a 4 to 5 hectare farm, self-sufficiency was possible. Below a yield of 5:1, such a small farmer would keep out of the market (except to meet debts and small taxes at Michaelmas). The large farmers bore the brunt of royal taxation. Hence "La distribution du revenu céréalier obéissait à une modulation: en temps de crise, un groupe restraint de bénéficiaries se partageait un plus gros gâteau: en temps d'abondance, une masse de paysans recevaient chacun une somme beaucoup plus mince. Dans le premier cas, sélection sociale accentuée par le passage des démunis à la position d'acheteurs et concentration de la richesse; dans le second cas, nivellement relatif des chances et diffusion microfinée des profits." *Idem,* "A la Halle de Charleville, 186.

they were the wage earners of the towns and countryside who had no land and no monetary reserves to enable them to make bulk purchases. They attended market throughout the year, and the frequency of their appearances made each a walking tabulator of *mercuriales,* sensitive to the least shift in prices and sensitive also to the activities of three other kinds of purchasers who appeared in great numbers at certain town markets during phase A. The first of these buyers were institutions like the hospitals, running on very limited funds, and therefore concentrating their purchases in these autumnal months. The second group—and this depended very much on where one lived—was made up of merchants representing certain municipalities anxious to lay down stocks to stave off disturbances during phase C. The third group comprised any speculators, merchants, large farmers, etc., who were prepared to gamble on higher prices later in the year. Any rumor of harvests falling short of yields of, say, 5 or 6:1 was likely to bring out some such people. The sight of their buying, and even more of hospitals making bulk purchases, could give rise to October disturbances. These were generated by the regular small purchasers in the towns who expected low prices during these months and believed that bulk purchases caused a rise in price levels, which were never low enough. Also, convoys were halted as they went toward their destination by members of the communities through which they passed, who saw them as portents of future scarcity.

Phase B was, on the whole, a less tumultuous period. The subsistence farmer ate into his stocks and did not appear in the market, and there were no bulk purchasers to set nerves on edge. In any case, winter was not the time to shift goods.

Toward Easter, however, came the reckoning—a febrile, arithmetical exercise fraught with terrible fears for some and speculative profits for others. For the small-holders, the question at the end of winter eating was: would there be enough grain for sowing and what would that leave for families to eat for the rest of the year? A perceived shortfall of the quantity to be sown could mean recourse to the lenders of the old regime—large farmers, seigneurs, and grain merchants.

> Nos paysans pressés par ceux à qui ils doivent, iront trouver des marchands à qui ils vendent des denrées qu'ils ne sont point encore

sûrs de remasser, pour avoir de l'argent comptant; on leur en donne; ils en vendent souvent plus qu'on en peut recueillir dans les meilleures récoltes; les années manquent, les terms arrivent, ils n'ont plus de denrées; on les presse; ils courent, on exige jusqu'a trois louis pour les intérêts de cent écus, on ne leur donne encore que quelques mois pour finir; rien ne parait; l'huissier vient et dès lors, que de frais après les énormes intérêts qui ont déjà (été) donnés.[22]

Creditors wanted securities, which usually meant pledging a fraction of the harvest from the grain about to be sown or encumbering one's holding with a new *rente passive* (i.e., a long-term repayment for a contracted loan). Either way, such a debt meant an obvious deterioration in long-term living standards. Even if this situation reflected an abnormally poor previous yield, difficulties could be prolonged into the next normal year by the reduction in the amount of grain remaining to an individual when debts had been paid. Accumulated debt also carried with it the possibility of foreclosure.[23]

Whatever grisly calculations the small-holders made at the end of phase B, they could be sure that others were calculating as well. The level of stocks in this period was a fair indicator of how much grain was in the system, and those who were prepared to play the market had to make a number of decisions which all pivoted upon the questions of when and where to market. Even in a year drawing on good stocks there was something to be said for creating slimly provisioned markets at the onset of phase C which would create the impression that not much grain was about and could trigger an increase in prices. In normal years (for example in the 1750s) one could not afford to indulge for too long in such practices for fear of being left with stocks at the end of

22 AD Côte d'Or C 15. Le Curé de Villy-en-Auxois, 1785, cited by Saint Jacob, *Les Paysans de Bourgogne du Nord,* 508.
23 The issue of foreclosure appears in Saint Jacob, "Le mouvement de la propriété dans un village bourguignon à la fin de l'Ancien Régime, 1748–1789," *Revue d'histoire économique et sociale,* XXVIII (1948), 47; Georges Beaur, "Le Centième Denier et les mouvements de propriété. Deux exemples Beaucerons (1761–1790)," *Annales,* XXXI (1976), 1024–1032. Foreclosure, however, in areas where there were large tenant farmers, could cause the farming community to close ranks against attempts at eviction by refusing to recognize that the property was on the market. Hence, the *mauvais gré* of Flemish society and the virtual immovability of those who held land under *domaine congéable.* J. Timothy A. Le Goff, *Vannes and Its Region: A Study of Town and Country in Eighteenth-Century France* (Oxford, 1981), 197–201.

the agricultural year. In times of diminished returns, however, such a waiting period could be the precursor of substantial price rises and could generate considerable market apprehension. It is no accident that in difficult years the most extensive and serious market disturbances took place in April and May, when the suspicion of withholding in order to force up prices and create artificial famines was rife among the *menu peuple* at the market. It was possible, however, that such a dearth was real, and in this case the upward spiral would persist. Notwithstanding, the likelihood of market disturbances receded after the month of May.[24]

Amid fear, mistrust, rumor of shortage, and *de la crainte de manquer vient la disette,* the grain supply and its distribution was fraught with psychological as well as real problems. The lack of trust not only between rich and poor, landed and landless, but also between the consumers of the town and those of the country was crucial to creating such an atmosphere. Both groups believed themselves to be fundamentally at a disadvantage vis à vis the other. Those in the country believed that the people in the towns were cushioned by municipal bulk-buying and by the authorities' fears of municipal disturbances. Urban consumers believed that the proximity of the rural consumers to the soil and to the products of the earth ensured country dwellers of something which they did not in fact have—vegetables, chestnuts, roots, and mythical stores with which the cunning peasant could never be made to part. The peasant, as perceived by the town dweller, was mendacious, vicious, and vandalistic. In market demonstrations, it was sometimes possible to drive a wedge between rural and urban protestors by playing on their in-built hostility toward each other. A riot at Riberac, for example, in 1770 resulted in enforced distribution by the populace at *taxation populaire* levels. The *lieutenant de police* then bought off the urban rioters by persuading them to disassociate from the countryfolk who, if they lingered in town, might wallow in looting or threaten the existence of the next market.[25]

24 This version of playing the market was the one that the *maréchaussée* feared the most, and it was certainly the most dangerous from the point of view of causing riots. See, AD Dordogne B523. Procès-verbaux 10 April 1758. On the timing of riots, see Cameron, *Crime and its Repression,* 234; Bricourt, et al., "La crise de subsistance," 293–296
25 *Arrêt du Conseil d'Etat,* 19 May 1739: "The king being informed that the high price of Grain is principally the result of seditious alarms; etc." See Cobb, *The Police and the People,* 109–117, 216–218, 278–283. AD Dordogne, B608.

Rumors could wreak a different kind of havoc. The outriders of hunger often came several months in advance, and rural communities in particular were on the lookout for them. Usually by June there were indications of threats to the next harvest. Protracted rain or, conversely, drought, sudden dramatic hailstorms or the over-abundant appearance of insects which could rapidly reduce yields were portents of catastrophe which would occur months ahead. Yet responses were immediate and varied: subsistence farmers and those who fell below this level had recourse to pilgrimage and prayer; the parish bell pealed out to fend off hailstorms; the priest ceded to pressure to exorcise insects.[26]

Surplus producers and merchants responded differently. The one might review his current stocks with a view toward seeing what might last into the next agricultural year. This could cause prices to rise at the markets where provisioning was less abundant and could also provoke rumors about imminent dearth.

A merchant might indulge in risky if potentially profitable activities. Using Pierre Dihar (père, *marchand de laine*) as an example, a series of violent hailstorms in July through early August caused him on four separate occasions to go to Bordeaux to see what was left of last season's imports which could be snapped up at bargain prices before the news of locally reduced harvests passed into general circulation. The grain in question was of Baltic or Spanish provenance and, as such, having made a damp sea journey, was very prone to mildew. Dihar hoped to sell immediately in the bare late July/early August markets, when the news of a poor harvest to come would add value to whatever there was in circulation. Twice his activities doubled his outlay; once the grain turned so mildewed it was unmarketable; and once he misread the portents, the flattened local grain rose, and he had to sell his Spanish grain at cost.[27]

The country's anxieties were echoed in the towns. Hail and rain fell in the towns. Low-grade musty grain on sale in the town market heralded more difficulties to come in the popular mind.

---

26 Frank Tallett of the University of Reading is presently engaged in an analysis of requests for excommunication and exorcism in the diocese of Besançon in the seventeenth and eighteenth centuries. Insects form the most common target followed by rats and mice. The offending beasts were given official notice of their fate from the pulpit and, if they failed to depart, the service of exorcism followed one to three weeks later.

27 AD Garonne, series U, Négociants, Series U. Unclassified, Dihar.

It increased tension to the point that when phase A came, the sight of the bulk purchasers laying in their stocks became doubly menacing. When even small-town authorities took to laying in reserves, tension mounted further. How much was really around? Rumor invariably suggested either the worst or a producer's plot to create a *disette factice*. In the hope of preventing market disturbances, authorities had recourse to expedients such as leaving sacks of grain on wharves or in public places to create the impression of plenty and so forestall panic buying or riot.[28]

Any pronouncement, any suggestion, that change was afoot in traditional provisioning methods could give rise to wild rumors. The issue of the grain supply was so sensitive that open debate on policy became a very risky proposition. It did not matter what one said; the error was to speak at all. The mere notion of tampering could engender rumors of shortage and price rises, panic buying, withholding, and public fear.

We still do not know the extent to which rumors affected the outburst of market disturbances in the immediate aftermath of the announcement of official laissez faire in 1764 and 1774–1775. The immediate rise in prices was real enough, and the riots occurred during the months of April and May. Were grain holders deliberately retaining their grain to produce a *disette factice* and see what the new philosophy did for them when freed from police pressure? Turgot, like all economists confronted with the collapse of their model when put to the test, insisted that "his enemies" had gone out of their way to engineer panic buying or were withholding the grain to secure his downfall. He thus produced an alternative conspiracy theory to explain shortage and rising prices.[29]

Far more psychologically attuned to the problems arising from the enactment of measures to deal with the grain trade were Le Noir, chief of police in Paris, who persisted in believing that the police should ostensibly be for the people against the speculators, and Jacques Necker, who publicly decried laissez faire when confronted with a diminished harvest. Under such circumstances, the safest recourse for the government was to pay lip

28 AN F16i1. Calvados.
29 Rudé, "La taxation populaire," 176–179, examines the conspiracy notion and finds it groundless. Rodriguez gives more credence to a conspiracy theory priming the Madrid riots in "The Riots of 1766," 144–146.

service to a closed economy, punish a few hoarders and specula-tors, leave matters as they were, and discreetly lay in foreign stocks. To go beyond lip service and to attempt to give the paternalist model real form was beyond the capacity of any Eu-ropean government, as the period of the Terror was to demon-strate. The result was producer alienation; *disette factice* was ulti-mately real shortage.[30]

A decade ago, Tilly picked out the most striking features of eighteenth-century bread riots. She pointed to their specific lo-cation within the vast Paris/Lyons provisioning zone in the 1760s, early 1770s, and after 1785, and in certain parts of the Midi in the 1770s and after 1785—all of these clearly years of below-average yields. She emphasized that the simple equation dearth = hunger = riot had no validity. The fact of hunger, even chronic hunger, does not necessarily in itself produce revolt. We need to under-stand the growth, north of the Loire in particular, of a national market geared to the provisioning of major cities and above all to understand the gradual emergence in the markets of uniform pricing with the Paris market determining the levels.[31]

The consequence of these developments was the abandon-ment of a formal commitment to a paternalist model and, hence, the creation of a popular conviction that laissez faire was the progenitor of rising prices. We need to distinguish between the market riot directed against merchants and bakers and the insis-tence upon *taxation populaire* (distribution at a fair price) on the one hand, and *entraves* on the other—attempts by peasants or small-town dwellers to stop grain convoys from leaving an area in order to preserve local production for local consumption at reasonable (not Parisian) prices.

We must also acknowledge the emergence of certain problem areas even within the wider zone. The river valleys of the Seine, the Loire, the Garonne, and the Rhone were all areas of major disturbances in the communities which saw grain in transit des-tined for the city market, and *entraves* were intended to deflect

---

30 On Jean Charles Pierre Le Noir, see Robert Darnton, "Le Lieutenant de Police, J. P. Le Noir: La Guerre des Farines et l'approvisionnement de Paris à la veille de la Révolution," *Revue d'histoire moderne et contemporaine*, XVI (1969), 611–624.
31 One of the greatest services performed by Tilly's article was the insistence upon the gradual equalization of market prices in the Paris provisioning zone and the Midi markets. Variations continued to prevail in the third zone of underdeveloped markets.

that grain for local needs. The Seine, in particular, was crucial to Parisian provisioning. It brought not merely the grain of Normandy but any foreign stocks that the government might seek to lay hold of in times of dire shortage. Cobb and Rudé have demonstrated how riots could ripple along the valley, effectively reducing what appeared in the Parisian market.[32]

In a sense bread had always been a political issue, but it emerged as such in the second half of the eighteenth century with particular acuity. The switch to explicit laissez-faire policies served to alienate the masses north of the Loire from *ancien regime* government: during the Revolution, the hungry crowd became a vehicle for forcing constitutional change, and paternalist theory was perforce integrated into the policy of those politicians who looked to Paris for their support.

However, the bread riot was not the only expression of the increasingly bitter battle for supplies. Through local studies we are becoming increasingly aware of tithe warfare after 1760, as communities sought to contest ecclesiastical claims to a significant percentage of the crop. These contests were usually initiated by substantial farmers prepared to defray the costs when the church had recourse to the courts, but these individuals had no difficulty in persuading lesser farmers to join a tithe strike once they had agreed to bear the burden of litigation.[33]

More important is the certainty that the contest over the control of supplies lay behind the bitter antiseigneurial movement in the *pays de petite culture,* the second zone, between 1789 and 1792. The problem, visible above all in the Massif, was the accumulated indebtedness of farmers working units so small that the most fractional downward shift in yields could have disastrous consequences. In 1770, the Parlement of Bordeaux, in response to reports about the Aquitaine, or more specifically the Rouergue,

32 Cobb, *Terreur et Subsistances* (Paris, 1964); Rusé, "La taxation populaire"; Le Marchand, "Les troubles de subsistances dans la généralité de Rouen (seconde moitié du XVIIIe siècle)," AHRF, XXXV (1963), 401–427; François Lebrun, "Les soulèvements populaires à Angers aux XVII–XVIIIe siècles," *90° Congrès National des Sociétés Savantes,* I (1966), 136–139. The little towns of the valley, but not the city of Angers, were the scene of riots and *entraves.*
33 Jean Rives, *Dime et Société dans l'Archévêche d'Auch au XVIIIe siècle* (Paris, 1976), 145–162; idem, *La Grève Décimale* (Paris, 1976); Louis Ligeron, "La dime des Menus Grains," *Annales de Bourgogne,* LXV (1973), 117.

the Perigord, and the Quercy, called for a temporary suspension of seigneurial levies for that year, not only to permit the small-holder some prospect of surviving the coming winter, but also because there was an obvious fear among established authorities of peasant *jacqueries*.[34]

These areas (and to the same degree the Auvergne, the Velay, and the Gevaudan) witnessed plummeting standards for the small-holder throughout the closing two decades of the *ancien regime,* as holdings were fractionalized to meet debts, and foreclosure often forced not so much the eviction of a tenant as the renego-tiation of a shorter, harsher lease embodying new *rentes passives.* Whereas foreclosure in the *pays de grande culture* often led to en-grossment, in the *pays de petite culture* it multiplied the number of inviable units. At the same time, the difficulties of the small-holder and the need to raise money led to the sale of livestock, creating serious long-term consequences for soil replenishment.[35]

In Aquitaine (in contrast to the share-cropping contracts of Brittany and the Limousin) seigneurial levies were set at a fixed amount and were not a proportion of the yield. Frequently they were subcontracted to lawyers, *hommes d'affaires,* or *fermiers.* Why did the peasant protest not make itself felt until 1789? Several factors stood in the way of such a concerted protest. These were regions of non-nuclear villages with multiple seigneuries each drawing on a diffuse bureaucracy. Debts were personal affairs and sustained opposition or refusal to pay them might preclude further borrowing or lead to litigation in distant courts if it did not lead to foreclosure. These regions lacked the substantial farmers who were prepared to contest the tithes. Moreover, the strategy of the established individuals was designed to fob off revolt. First they were prepared to live with some debt if they could realize some-thing. Second, by subcontracting what dues they could, if a gen-eral refusal did occur, they were able to shift the blame onto the *fermiers* and retreat into paternalistic seigneurialism. Consider the remarks of de Hostange's steward at Saint-Alvere in the Perigord when he commented on the efforts of some *fermiers* to undertake litigation in September 1789 to recover debts:

34 Arrêt du Parlement de Bordeaux, 8 Mai 1770. *Bulletin de la société des lettres, sciences et arts de la Corrèze,* n.v. (1885), 680–685.
35 Goubert, "En Rouergue, structures agraires et cadastres au XVIIIe siècle," *Annales,* XXV (1953), 382–386.

Vos fermiers ont menacé d'établir des solidaires et de faire des saisies. J'ai vu le moment que ces démarches allaient occasioner de grands malheurs. J'ai calmé la fermentation en blamant les démarches des fermiers et j'ai eu l'air de prendre le parti des emphytéotes, ce qui m'a un peu rétabli dans leurs esprits.[36]

Even in normal years, the *intendants* would not permit the use of the *marechaussée* for debt collection, and it may well be that, if the Revolution had not precipitated events, the Parlements of Bordeaux and Toulouse would have temporarily suspended the payment of dues in 1789 as had been done at Bordeaux in 1770.[37]

The meeting of the Estates General initiated a rumor that the dues had been abolished. This led to the development of the movement known as the Great Fear in which a massive peasant attack was launched against the records of the seigneurie. This war was about papers, and it had peculiar force in Burgundy and in the *pays de petite culture,* but it had no meaning in the Beauce or in the areas of great capitalist agriculture.[38]

The attack, part of a battle of small producers to hold onto their produce, did not die in the Massif in 1789 when seigneurialism was declared dead. The peasants pillaged the property of the lawyers and subcontractors and, as late as 1792, fresh outbreaks were reported from the hills of the Quercy to the mountains of Provence. Why was this so? At least in part it was because debt was a part of the fabric of these small-holding societies and the elimination of seigneurial dues, although helping the sub-subsistence farmer, did not obliterate his constant need to borrow

---

36 Peter Jones, "Parish, Seigneurie and the Community of Inhabitants in South Central France," *Past & Present,* 91 (1981), 89–92, insists on the lack of coherence of these villages which followed upon their diffuse geographical distribution and differing seigneurial experience. The quotation is cited by Jean Boutier, "Jacqueries en pays croquant. Les Révoltes paysannes en Aquitaine, Décembre 1789– Mars 1790," *Annales,* XXXIV (1979), 766. This article is a remarkable exposé of the penury and indebtedness lying behind rural revolt in this area and includes a bibliography of relevance to the entire *pays de petite culture.*

37 On the attitude of the *intendant* at Riom toward peasants' debts and his refusal to let the *maréchaussée* help seigneurial agents to collect them, see Hufton, "The Peasant and the Law in Eighteenth-Century France," *Annales,* forthcoming.

38 Lefebvre, *La Grande Peur de 1789* (Paris, 1932); Philippe J. Hesse, "Géographie coutumière et révoltes paysannes en 1789," AHRF, LI (1979), 287–295.

throughout the year. Borrowing entailed securities (securities recorded by the rotary) and this took the form of a part of the crop or a *rente passive*. There is some evidence to suggest that the *bourgeoisie rurale* which had farmed the dues was still holding the threat of no more borrowing without the promise of backpayment over the heads of the *micropropriétaires* right into 1792. The nineteenth-century world of Eugène Le Roy is, after all, little removed from the one we are discussing even if the formal acknowledgment of seigneurial levies was no more.[39]

In the eighteenth century anyone who could not make that proudest of boasts, *il y a toujours du pain a la maison,* lived in fear and perceived himself to be victimized, a sacrificial lamb to someone else's interests. Sometimes he could give his enemy a face—the seigneur or his agents—sometimes he could point to the nearest town, sometimes he looked to the great gaping mouth of the capital. Conversely, the urban wage-earner saw peasant, merchant, miller, baker, and government as all locked together into a giant conspiracy to starve him. For everyone lacking in self-sufficiency, some kind of conflict was latent, although it could assume different forms and focal points. The Revolution of 1789–1796 merely converted the potential into actuality without resolving any of the fundamental problems involved in feeding 28 million French people.

39 Boutier, "Jacqueries en pays croquant," 780: "Si 50% de la récolte revenaient encore au métayer au début du XVIIIe siècle, il ne lui en reste plus que 25% vers 1800, 15% dans les années 1820–40," an indication that any breathing space gained from a repudiation of debt in 1789 was short-lived. On a similar situation in Provence, see Vovelle, "Les troubles sociaux en Provence, 1750–1793," *93° Congrès National des Sociétés Savantes* (Tours, 1968), II 325–372.

Louise A. Tilly

Food Entitlement, Famine, and Conflict

". . . last yeares famin was made by man and not by God."[1]

This pithy seventeenth-century analysis demonstrates the certainty of early modern English authorities that dearth and famine were caused by human acts, and could be prevented or corrected by public intervention. Their interpretation justified efforts to control merchants, markets, and the circulation of grain—a paternalistic role for local authorities in guaranteeing food at a fair price for ordinary people. Their belief that food shortages were a result of the actions of greedy speculators and middlemen, "evill disposed persons . . . without pity towards poore men, [who] by their engrossing of grayne and other abuses will make want amidst plentifulness . . ." provided them with a rationale for action.[2]

Historical traces of human acts offer important clues to understanding hunger in history. Since historians find it difficult to achieve the precision of contemporary medical and nutritional definitions of malnutrition, hunger, and starvation as individual human conditions, they must accept indirect evidence for hunger in the past. Analyses of systematic variations in proxies such as

Louise A. Tilly is Professor of History at the University of Michigan. She is the co-author with Joan W. Scott of *Women, Work, and Family* (New York, 1978).

The author thanks Charles Tilly, Fred Cooper, Bin Wong, and other members of the Collective Action/Social History group for their helpful comments.

1 Samuel R. Gardiner (ed.), *Reports of the Cases in the Courts of Star Chamber and High Commission* [for 1632] (London, 1886), 46, quoted in John Walter and Keith Wrightson, "Dearth and Social Order in Early Modern England," *Past & Present,* 71 (1976), 31.

2 *Acts of the Privy Council,* 1597, 30, quoted in Walter and Wrightson, "Dearth and Social Order," 31. The grain marketing control system of England is described in Edward P. Thompson, "The Moral Economy of the English Crowd in the Eighteenth Century," *Past & Present,* 50 (1971), 76–136.

mortality, food prices, and patterns of height and weight, all with reference to defined populations or groups, have been the historians' basic strategy.

Another approach, which examines the economic, social, and political *relationships* of those who suffer, and die, in famine, has been employed by Sen. In his study of contemporary poor countries, Sen concludes that

> market forces can be seen as operating *through* a system of legal relations (ownership rights, contractual obligations, legal exchanges, etc.). The law stands between food availability and food entitlement. Starvation deaths can reflect legality with a vengeance.[3]

Sen's interpretation, in common with seventeenth-century opinion, emphasizes the social and political context for famine. He makes a powerful case that starvation is not a simple matter of available food supply per capita, but rather a function of entitlement relationships, such as ownership exchange, employment, and social security rights. Even in famine, he shows, food is available; people starve because of inability to command food. They do not have the money to buy it or the socially and politically sanctioned right to receive it free.

There are several kinds of relationships which can give people command of food: inheritance or purchase of agricultural land to grow adequate food; employment which brings in wages to buy food; sociopolitical rights, whether they be religious or moral obligations of some groups to see that others are fed, or institutionalized government-sponsored welfare or social security rights. Starvation, Sen continues, is caused by the collapse of people's endowment entitlements (their earned or otherwise acquired set of entitlements to food) or of an unfavorable shift in the distribution of exchange entitlements.[4]

Understanding hunger and starvation as consequences of shifting social and political relationships does not deny their reality. Rather, it examines the context of these phenomena in search of an explanation in structural terms, of class, mode of production, political power, or change in these relationships. Such a relational approach can be a useful tool for comparing past and

3 Amartya Sen, *Poverty and Famines. An Essay on Entitlement and Deprivation* (Oxford, 1981), 160.
4 *Ibid.* This summary of Sen's argument is based primarily on 1–8, 47–50, 162–166.

present by tracing the effects of shifting food entitlements, as defined by law and enmeshed in political and social, as well as economic relations.

This article adopts Sen's entitlement approach to compare the historical relationships between food entitlement and conflict about food in England and France in the seventeenth through nineteenth centuries with the patterns of famine in contemporary poor countries. Both Sen and the seventeenth-century English analyst emphasize short-term, or what I will call "adventitious" effects, such as war, speculation, or business cycles outside food-producing agriculture, as causes of entitlement shifts, and hence, dearth or famine.

Large-scale secular structural change plays a vital role as well, however. The development of capitalism, with its large market systems, division of labor, and proletarianization of workers, and the rise of centralized nation states in Western Europe were accompanied by shifts in entitlement and, therefore, in some groups' increased vulnerability to high prices and shortage. This large-scale structural change, occurring over long periods of time, needs to be isolated and analyzed separately in contemporary poor countries as well. There is scope for public intervention in these matters that could be as important for relieving hunger as the short-term alleviation of shortage and assistance to those in need.

I focus on the historical political significance not of starvation, in the strict sense, or even of proxies which stand for hunger, but of the relationships between food entitlement and conflict about food. Both the patterns of food protest in Britain and France since about 1600, and the European protestors' own statements about the issues, show that they were concerned with precisely the same kind of entitlement shifts that Sen observes in case studies of contemporary famine. To be sure, conflict or collective action is another indirect indicator of distress, for, as Sen points out, it also reflects organization and militancy.[5]

---

5 Two interpretations of food conflict in political context are found in Louise A. Tilly, "The Food Riot as a Form of Political Conflict in France," *Journal of Interdisciplinary History*, II (1971), 23–57; Charles Tilly, "Food Supply and Public Order in Modern Europe," in *idem* (ed.), *The Formation of National States in Europe* (Princeton, 1975), 380–455. The present article looks at food entitlement, conflict, and structural change in a different comparative and theoretical perspective, with emphasis on late developing countries as well as Europe. Sen, *Poverty and Famines,* 98. The components of collective action are discussed in C. Tilly, *From Mobilization to Revolution* (Reading, 1978), 7.

SHORT-TERM, CYCLICAL OR ADVENTITIOUS ENTITLEMENT SHIFTS
Three striking examples of the way in which the collapse or shift
of entitlements led to dearth or conflict recur in historical and
contemporary accounts. These are climatic effects and their
echoes; the ripple effect of high food prices on manufacturing
employment; and wars and similar perturbations of international
trade and internal labor markets.

One of Sen's most illuminating discussions concerns the indirect consequences of climatic change in the Ethiopian famine of
1972 to 1974. The spatial pattern of deaths from deprivation
shows that upland areas of northeast Ethiopia suffered disproportionately. Drought had the direct effect of cutting food output in
much of Ethiopia but, in the northeast, drought had the indirect
effect of drastically reducing the ability of agricultural and pastoral
peoples to buy food. Agricultural tenants and small owners whose
crops failed had to buy food; since their crops were the source of
their income, they had no money to spend. Agricultural laborers
were dismissed by their employers who lacked money to pay or
food to feed them. They also had no money to spend on food.
Pastoralists, whose customary entry into food markets was via
their profit from the animals that they raised in hilly pastureland
and sold, lost out too. Their animals either died or were under-
weight; at the same time, the price for animals fell, as the price
of grain rose, and consumers could not afford meat. All of these
groups were unable to *buy* food; they were overrepresented both
among those who died in the camps where they sought aid, and
among those who marched to Addis Ababa to demand food.[6]

There are European historical cases which suggest similar
entitlement failures. Schofield shows that the excess mortality of
seventeenth-century English subsistence crises was concentrated
in upland, pastoral, remote areas. Although he credits transportation limitations as most important, entitlement constraints were
logically involved there also. Pastoralists had to exchange their
animal products for food. If the price of their products had fallen
in relation to the price of grain food, as happened in contemporary
Africa, the English pastoralists would also have had fewer resources with which to buy higher priced food. In the French

6 Sen, *Poverty and Famines,* 93–111.

Massif Central and Languedocian sheep-herding areas, Hufton notes that similar failures of command of food occurred. She also discusses a parallel case in the viniculture areas of the south of France, in which protest about food developed contemporaneously with a slump in *wine* prices. If wine could not be sold profitably, the wage earners of the whole region (including the cities involved in the wine trade) saw their ability to buy food greatly reduced.[7]

Workers in the manufacturing sector also indirectly experienced declining resources and reduced command of food in response to harvest shortfalls and uneven distributions of food. Sen notes that, as the rural economy of Bengal became more and more distressed in 1934, demand for urban goods declined sharply. Craft workers' income sank, and they lost some of their accustomed ability to buy food.[8]

The most well-known historical argument making a similar point for eighteenth- and nineteenth-century France was put forward by Labrousse. In 1788–1789, he writes:

> Bad harvests and rising prices caused the purchasing power of a large social group to collapse. The first to suffer were the peasantry . . . because they had precisely nothing to sell . . . On the other hand, the purchasing power of day labourers, who constituted the mass of agricultural consumers, collapsed because wages did not rise as fast as the cost of grain. . . . Imagine the effect of stopping up the outlets of the rural market on industrial markets entirely dependent on them.[9]

We have many historical examples of this kind of chain reaction. In Goubert's Beauvaisis, a community of rural industrial

---

7 Roger Schofield, "The Impact of Scarcity and Plenty on Population Change in England, 1541–1871," and Olwen Hufton, "Social Conflict and Grain Supply in Eighteenth-Century France," both in this issue.
8 Sen, *Poverty and Famines*, 78.
9 C. Ernest Labrousse, "1848–1830–1789: How Revolutions were Born" (orig. pub. 1948), in François Crouzet, William H. Chaloner, and Walter M. Stern (eds.), *Essays in European Economic History, 1789–1914* (London, 1969), 3–5. Labrousse' thesis is more fully developed in his *La crise de l'économie française à la fin de l'Ancien Régime et au début de la Révolution* (Paris, 1944). For a position questioning the validity of Labrousse' analysis, except in cases of extreme dearth, see David S. Landes, "The Statistical Study of French Crises," *Journal of Economic History*, X (1950), 195–211.

workers suffered much higher mortality in a subsistence crisis than did communities with a different economic base. An appeal for aid in seventeenth-century Lancashire ascribed the petitioners' distress to the cumulated effects of "dearth aggravated by . . . pestilence, and depression in the cloth trade." Ashton's classic account of the Industrial Revolution notes that contemporary observers, including Adam Smith, "assert quite plainly that dearness of food led to falling wages and lack of work." He argues, further, that although some cultivators must have profited from high food prices, they were slow to spend their gain. The consequence was that "poor harvests were usually followed by stagnation of trade, falling wages, and unemployment."[10]

War is another adventitious factor which seriously compromises food entitlements and contributes to hunger, or to collective action about food. The Bengal famine of 1943 is Sen's major example of the consequences of war, in multiple manifestations. Bengali fishermen's access to livelihood was severely compromised by wartime decrees removing boats from coastal areas to prevent possible Japanese capture; rice stocks were removed for similar reasons. Both of these actions reduced the coastal peoples' ability to buy food. Government policy also favored urban food supply and, in so doing, actually aggravated rural loss of entitlement. It hoped with this policy to guarantee that city workers, "on whose labour the Indian munitions and supply industries depend" would have privileged access to food markets.[11]

The short-term effects of war on entitlements played a role in European dearth and conflict as well. New outbreaks of fighting in the English Civil War in 1648 contributed to the dearth and depression of the Lancashire cloth trade of 1649; lost wages meant diminished food entitlement. In the French crisis of 1709–10, the provisioning needs of the army in Flanders cut deeply into the supply of grain of the eastern part of France. Military suppliers, large cities and small, sought grain in Burgundy and Champagne.

10   E. Anthony Wrigley, *Population and History* (New York, 1969), 66–69, citing Pierre Goubert, *Beauvais et le Beauvaisis de 1600 à 1730* (Paris, 1960), I, 56–57, and personal communication. Walter and Wrightson, "Dearth and Social Order," 39; Trevor S. Ashton, *The Industrial Revolution, 1760–1830* (London, 1960; orig. pub., 1948), 144–145.

11   Sen, *Poverty and Famines*, 67–68; Document 330 in Nicholas Mansergh (ed.), *The Transfer of Power, 1942–1947* (London, 1971), III, 464.

The countryside armed itself to prevent loss of vital supplies. A priest wrote, "There was an open war with the peasants to get their grain." During the French Revolution, the Maximum, which Rose calls the Jacobin version of "war communism," was a response to entitlement loss. Both in Paris, where the Sans-culottes mobilized to call for price controls, and in rural industrial areas, protest proliferated. Rose writes that "woodmen from the forest of Vibraye and glassworkers from Montmirail joined together and marched round the countryside gathering supporters and imposing a maximum."[12]

The end of the Napoleonic wars provoked more problems in both England and France. During the postwar demobilization, British industrial demand fell and unemployment was widespread. Food prices rose with the poor harvests of 1816 and 1817, and demand for manufactured goods fell further. Between unemployed workers and former soldiers crowding the labor market, the ability of British wage workers to buy food collapsed. There was a poor harvest in the same years in parts of France, followed by a wave of collective action. Chabert's study of the period shows that protest did not occur in the regions with the highest prices. Violence was more common in densely populated, rural industrial areas where there was a slowdown of manufacturing, and presumably reduced pay and unemployment.[13]

In the European cases of conflict over food, both the rhetoric and the ideology of the protestors and the spatial distribution of food protest events confirm that the issue was not one of absolute food shortfall but of entitlement. Thompson's analysis of the moral economy of the poor shows that, in eighteenth-century England, food rioters had a coherent ideology and a "legitimizing notion" for their action. They expressed a paternalistic theory of governmental responsibility to protect poor consumers in times of high prices. Thompson quotes contemporary reports of the

12 Walter and Wrightson, "Dearth and Social Order," 39; Pierre de St. Jacob, *Les paysans de la Bourgogne du Nord au dernier siècle de l'Ancien Régime* (Paris, 1960), 190; Robert B. Rose, "Eighteenth-Century Price Riots, the French Revolution, and the Jacobin Maximum," *International Review of Social History*, IV (1959), 439–443.

13 Ashton, *Industrial Revolution*, 152–153; Albert Chabert, *Essai sur les mouvements des prix en France de 1798 à 1820* (Paris, 1945), 410–414. See also Robert Marjolin, "Troubles provoqués en France par la disette de 1816–1817," *Revue d'histoire moderne*, VIII (1933), 426–427.

values and expressions of the protesting crowds. A magistrate wrote in 1631 that it was the sight of grain being exported from their community that "turned the impatience of the crowd into licentious fury and desperation." In 1709, a wheat dealer, assailed by a crowd, demanded why they rose "in such an inhuman manner to the prejudice of themselves and the country, but . . . they still cryed out that he was a Rogue and was going to carry the corn into France." Walter and Wrightson note that popular thinking frequently formulated the accusation that profiteers were shipping wheat away and creating dearth. They hold that popular collective action took place only when grain was being moved.[14]

In France, one of the major forms of food protest was the *entrave*, or blockage of the passage of grain. This form of collective action became common in the eighteenth century, after the crisis of 1709–10. Grain boats on canals and rivers, and wagons on the roads were fair game. The crowd in Burgundy in 1709 complained that "there is no justice if people die of hunger in Burgundy to feed the city of Lyon." The 1816–17 wave of protest, and that of 1839–40 consisted primarily of *entraves* as grain was moved from regions with surplus to urban markets. The form of the protest and its location at the frontiers of growing regions demonstrate that what was at issue was an entitlement question, not one of food availability in the absolute sense. Those with money to buy could attract grain from regions which grew it, even if it meant that those with weak or lost entitlement in that region would then be without adequate food.[15]

These European examples also suggest a range of problems in a much longer temporal perspective than that of Sen and the importance of large-scale structural change, as well as the cyclical or adventitious factors which Sen emphasizes.

LARGE-SCALE STRUCTURAL CHANGE   Food conflict, in the forms discussed here, is no longer common in Europe. The incidence

14 Thompson, "The Moral Economy," 95–97. Thompson's concept of moral economy may account for the ideology of food protestors, and for the form that their protest took, but as Dale Edward Williams has argued, it does not account for the spatial or temporal incidence of protest: see "Rural Proletarianization and Popular Disorder in Eighteenth-Century England," unpub. ms. paper (1982). Walter and Wrightson, "Dearth and Social Order," 30, 33.
15 The quotation is in Albert Payson Usher, *The History of the Grain Trade in France, 1400–1710* (Cambridge, Mass., 1913), 187. L. A. Tilly, "The Food Riot," 54–56.

of such conflict, in fact, is concentrated in a limited time period: in England, from the early seventeenth century through the first quarter of the nineteenth; in France, from the late seventeenth through the middle of the nineteenth century. Similar events can be identified in later periods, but most protests about food in the late nineteenth and early twentieth centuries take new forms: they are sponsored and carried out by formal organizations; they operate through planned meetings and demonstrations; and they are often indirect, channelled through struggles about wages and standard of living, rather than about food per se.

Food protest appears to have become more common in the first years of the period in which starvation—as measured by the impact of high prices on mortality—declined. Understanding the timing of the incidence of European food riots, their emergence in the early modern period, their clustering in the seventeenth to nineteenth centuries, and their disappearance or transformation, requires a dynamic structural framework. This framework can be found in the working out of two processes: the development of capitalism and the rise of centralized nation states.[16]

The development of capitalism is linked to long-term entitlement shifts in three ways: the expansion of market systems, the increasing division of labor, and proletarianization. Sen provides several examples of exchange entitlement loss linked to expanding markets. The pastoral populations of Ethiopia who suffered so severely in the famine of 1972 to 1974 were compromised by the growth of commercial agriculture. New areas were put into cultivation, displacing the pastoral peoples from their low-lying dry weather pastures. Worsening terms of trade in the exchange of meat for grain aggravated their loss. Sen concludes, "The pastoralist, hit by the drought, was decimated by the market mechanism." In the Sahel, also, commercialization of farming made agriculturalists vulnerable "both to output fluctuations and to shifts in marketability of commodities and in exchange rates."[17]

It is apparent, when we turn from famine to conflict, that Europeans who lived in times of shifting entitlements due to expanding market relations were very conscious of their new

16 Jean Meuvret, "Les Crises de subsistences et la démographie de la France d'Ancien Régime," *Population*, I (1946), 643–650; Schofield, "Impact of Scarcity and Plenty."
17 Sen, *Poverty and Famines*, 112, 126.

vulnerability. French conflict was linked less to dearth in the strict sense and more to reactions and objections to the expansion of markets and the movement of grain that went with it. Walter and Wrightson see a similar relationship in early modern England. They note, "years of dearth . . . were not marked by widespread rioting. . . . It was within the grain-producing regions which in normal years produced a surplus which went to feed other areas, notably the large towns, that grain riots were most likely to occur." In eighteenth-century France, grain prices in distant cities converged over time, suggesting the expansion of the area of the market for grain. At the same time, the old price and marketing controls were being dismantled. Responsibility for food supply moved from local to central authorities to the extent that governments were concerned at all. Older regulations against wholesale marketing practices were repealed in England in precisely the same period; Thompson writes that one such repeal "signalled a victory . . . for *laisser-faire* four years before Adam Smith's work was published."[18]

Eighteenth- and nineteenth-century French and English authorities were persuaded by the theory of political economists that free trade in grain would result in a national balancing of supply and demand, even in years of dearth. Sen notes that nineteenth-century civil servants in India were similarly confident that the market mechanism would solve food shortfalls. He adds, "Firm believers in the market mechanism were often disappointed by the failure of the market to deliver much." Sen shows that Adam Smith's proposition simply does not deal with "meeting a need that has not been translated into effective demand because of lack of market-based entitlement and shortage of purchasing power." The early converts to the theory of the market mechanism were expecting too much of it.[19]

The naïveté of this expectation is confirmed by the historical fact that grain moved in eighteenth- and nineteenth-century England and France, but not to those who had no or weak entitlements, unless the government intervened to supply them. Rather

18 Walter and Wrightson, "Dearth and Social Order," 26–27; L. A. Tilly, "The Food Riot," 35–45; Thompson, "The Moral Economy," 89.
19 Sen, *Poverty and Famines,* 160, 161. See Thompson, "The Moral Economy," 89, for similar beliefs and statements and 91, for his refutation of Adam Smith.

it moved to cities, favored (as, it will be recalled, were the cities of Bengal in 1943) by government policies, based on the belief that an adequate urban food supply was essential to public order, or to military units on campaign. The increasing division of labor and differentiation within the economy and society, a long-term effect of capitalism on entitlements, increased reallocation of food to nonrural populations.

The irony is that wage-earning populations were common in rural areas in eighteenth- and early nineteenth-century Europe, as well as in cities. The process of proletarianization, the essential link between the large-scale processes of capitalist development and the lives of ordinary people, had both a rural and an urban impact. Again, Sen describes wage earners as a group with precarious exchange entitlements: "The worker employed in wage-based farms or other occupations is, of course, particularly vulnerable . . ." In Bangladesh, a quarter of the rural population is dependent on wages: "For them a variation of the exchange relationships can spell ruin." Wage earning, the essence of being proletarian, is "[m]ore modern, perhaps; more vulnerable, certainly."[20]

In England both agricultural laborers and rural manufacturing workers were proletarians. The number of persons in these conditions rose markedly in the eighteenth and nineteenth centuries. In the southern and eastern grain producing areas, large farms were more often worked by day laborers from the late seventeenth century on. Agricultural payments in kind were replaced in the nineteenth century by money wages. The south and east were major regions of food protest from the seventeenth century onward. When food prices went up, or agricultural wages or employment went down (and, as argued above, these often happened in sequence), wage earners lost their command of food, in the very midst of a food growing region.[21]

English rural areas contained many industrial proletarians too. As Chambers and Mingay write, "With the growth in the

---

20 C. Tilly, "Food Supply and Public Order," 400–409; Sen, *Poverty and Famines,* 126, 150.

21 Jonathan D. Chambers and Gordon E. Mingay, *The Agricultural Revolution, 1750–1880* (London, 1966), 18–19; David Grigg, *Population Growth and Agrarian Change: An Historical Perspective* (Cambridge, 1980), 172–175.

countryside of such industries as textiles, mining, and iron manufacture, the level of employment was affected by booms and
slumps in trade." Cornish tin and copper miners, Black Country
colliers, nailers, and potters were frequently rioters. Confirmation
that coalminers and tinners were especially likely to act comes
from Thompson: ". . . the Cornish tinners had an irascible con-
sumer-consciousness and a readiness to turn out in force." Rose
concludes that "[f]or these groups popular price-fixing represented a well-tried form of industrial action, directed not against
the mine-owners, however, but against a more generalized target
of popular wrath, the food profiteer . . ."[22]

The situation in France was somewhat different. There the
more common pattern was for peasants to hang on to small plots
and supplement the inadequate subsistence that they were able to
grow by employment of themselves or their household members
in rural putting-out manufacture. Crude textiles and small metal
products like nails, files, or knives, were produced in peasant
cottages. Other non-food-producing rural workers, such as miners, forge workers, and wood cutters, lived close to and inter-
spersed with agriculturalists. These workers' command of food
was precarious, vulnerable to rising food prices and declining
industrial employment. They too appear to be overrepresented
among those who protested. In the "wheat basket" of the Beauce,
enough workers depended on their wages to buy food that they
were leaders in the rural demonstrations for the Maximum in
1792.[23]

In several of the entitlement shifts which occurred with the
development of capitalism, the state appears as initiator or me-
diator of change. Charles Tilly has argued that European state-
building most often accompanied expanded war-making, and
war-making forced states to find new revenue. Growth of taxation (or efforts to increase revenues) was one logical outcome.[24]

Eighteenth-century policies encouraged commercialization of
agriculture to tap the potential for tax revenue that it contained.

22 Chambers and Mingay, *Agricultural Revolution,* 102; Rose, "Eighteenth-Century Price
Riots and Public Policy in England," *International Review of Social History,* VI (1961), 285,
291; Thompson, "The Moral Economy," 99.
23 Rose, "French Price Riots," 442.
24 C. Tilly, "Food Supply and Public Order," 453–455.

The repeal of paternalistic grain-market controls which accompanied the nationalization of grain markets were, precisely, state acts which worked in this direction. So too were the English Corn Laws. Ashton argues that the passage of these laws after the Napoleonic Wars was "intended to preserve for the agriculturalists a structure of prices and rents that had been created by war." It had the effect of postponing "the fulfillment of the revolution in industry." He recognizes that the damage was done not only to capitalist entrepreneurs, whose revolution was delayed, but also to workers. Whether or not state action which continued to promote agriculture slowed industrial investment, it certainly affected the entitlements of many industrial workers by keeping food prices high and accentuating the boom and slump cycles in industry.[25]

The state also played an important role in favoring the food supply for urban areas at the expense of the rural areas. Urban food riots, especially those in capital cities, were quite another matter than the rural blockage of the movement of grain. Conflict over food became exquisitely political—and a dangerous threat to public order, or even to a regime—when it was urban. Such conflict was a political threat in the countryside only when it occurred in waves that joined it with demands for fundamental political challenge.

In the late eighteenth century, the food conflict around and in the French Revolution became even more political. Alleged speculators or officials responsible for food supply who were accused of incompetence could find themselves in physical danger.

Many of the revolutionary days saw elements of conflict about food, such as the well-known market women's march on Versailles in October, 1789. In July of that year one of the first acts in the rash of municipal revolutions in the provinces was the setting up of subsistence committees alongside the citizens' militia.[26]

Nevertheless, the Revolution was not simply about food. Food was just one of the issues activating some of the groups in what became a massive mobilization against the regime. Urban,

25 Ibid.; Ashton, Industrial Revolution, 153.
26 C. Tilly, "Food Supply and Public Order," 448–449.

professional, commercial, or intellectual members of the bourgeoisie and prosperous landowning peasants, for example, promoted the notion of free trade in grains as part of their political program. Urban proletarians and the rural landless poor or industrial workers supported the restoration of market controls. The temporal coincidence of these movements with the fiscal crisis of the old regime and the democratic ideology with which opponents were ready to challenge the very legitimacy of that regime made the revolution. The Third Estate took the first step to destroy that legitimacy when it declared itself the nation by the Tennis Court Oath, and claimed the right and duty to write a constitution for a new regime. There was a real potential for disorder in the loss of or long-term shifts in food entitlements, a disorder that had both political antecedents and consequences. Nevertheless, it was of a different order from revolution.

RESOLUTION AND/OR TRANSFORMATION OF CONFLICT ABOUT FOOD
Food protest had a place in European popular collective action for a limited period only. If such conflict is linked to shifting food entitlements caused by the twin processes of the coming of capitalism and of nation states, why and how did it disappear? Those two phenomena are still with us. Increased productivity and better transportation and communication probably made the redistribution of food supplies more efficient. Underemployed or unemployed rural laborers were able to migrate to cities, where they eventually were able to find more stable industrial or service work. There were increased possibilities of regular wage earning and higher wages: new entitlements were earned. All of these factors played a part. I would emphasize further the way in which groups renegotiated or rewon entitlements from the middle of the nineteenth century on.[27]

Several distinct groups—industrialists, workers, and reformers—seem most important. Industrial employers, whose workers were buffeted by high food prices in the nineteenth century, acted through national and local political channels for government policies to improve their situation. The long fight for the repeal of the Corn Laws in England, and the opposition to tariffs which

27 Ibid., 449–453.

exchanged agricultural exports for reduced entry duties for manufactured goods in France, were sponsored by industrialists.

In Milan's period of rapid industrial transformation, urban
politics was frequently embroiled over issues of food entitlement
for urban workers. Manufacturers opposed the conservative landowning urban oligarchy over schemes to increase municipal income through duties on food entering the city.[28]

The action of industrialists intersected that of workers, which
was directed more and more against employers, not against food
profiteers. Class-based organization and worker-collective action
came to focus on local power holders whose action could solve
their food entitlement problems—their employers. There was a
changeover of issues as well: from demands for food price or
marketing controls to better and more regular wages in which
the standard of living, including food, was subsumed. Class interest came to be represented by class-based organization which
in turn elaborated new forms of collective action, the strike and
the demonstration. When, in 1911, high food prices sparked protest in the northern industrial regions of France, it was quickly
"captured," organized, and translated into demonstrations and
strikes by labor unions. Nineteenth-century worker organization
and collective action was an effort to build new entitlements—
stable employment and adequate wages—within an organization
of production characterized by wage-earning.[29]

Both workers and employers—joined often by reformers—
urged state action which was aimed, not at guaranteeing food,
but at stable income, through social security schemes. Unemployment compensation, disability and sickness benefits, and old
age pensions eventually were accepted as state responsibilities in
Europe.

This rapid summary greatly oversimplifies the political process by which social security became law in each country, and
the group coalition which supported it. Some power holders
doubtless saw social security as a way to control working-class

28   The Milanese political struggles are analyzed in L. A. Tilly, *The Formation of an Urban
Working Class,* forthcoming.
29   *Idem,* "Women's Collective Action and Feminism in France, 1870–1914," in L. A.
Tilly and C. Tilly (eds.), *Class Conflict and Collective Action* (Beverly Hills, 1981),
222–223.

families and defuse potential worker protest; some workers opposed it as a sellout to the state. The point is not the precise detail of the politics of passage of such laws. Rather it is the way that the state's role altered with the changing organization of production, accompanied by a relatively unchanging motivation, the prevention of disorder. The outcome can be seen as both resolution and transformation.

There are still groups with uncertain entitlements in Britain and France, the most obvious among them being immigrants. These workers' legal entitlement to employment has become an issue in the economic downturns of the last ten years. They are vulnerable, less to direct hunger, than to loss of jobs and the legal right to earn. The consequence of this loss may be hunger.

This comparison of the role of entitlement loss or shift in famine in contemporary poor countries with its role in conflict about food in the history of England and France has shown remarkable parallels. The analysis of the role of secular large-scale structural change in Europe puts the entitlement approach in a long-term perspective. The European experience suggests ways in which governments can intervene to shape processes or protect their citizens from some of the consequences of change, to the extent that their political priorities and economic resources permit. Obviously, today's poor countries exist in a world capitalist system in which the operative political units are already established centralized nation states. These nation states are undergoing economic changes which are producing a set of problems not unlike those which European states faced earlier.

Although these states have access to modern transportation and world food resources, they have sometimes failed to deal effectively with food distribution problems and consequent famine. This outcome, and the state's role in it, is quite different from the West European experience in the centuries discussed here. Nevertheless, the parallels in entitlement shifts suggest that intervention should be shaped by questions such as: To what extent is the commercialization and growth in scale of agriculture depriving pastoral and agricultural peoples of formerly legitimate entitlements to farm or herd? To what extent is wage earning removing rural and urban workers from direct access or claims to food without assuring them stable incomes with which to buy food? To what extent is the political sensitivity of urban food supply causing government to favor food transfer from agricultural areas, to the detriment of less privileged groups in those areas?

The historical cases of England and France show that government policy often undermined the food command of rural people, even agriculturalists, and favored, for political reasons, reliable food supplies for the military and for urban populations. Capitalist markets moved food not necessarily to those who were hungry, but to those with money to buy.

The analysis of entitlements promises to complete the transformation of thinking about conflicts over food begun by Thompson, Rose, Walter, and Wrightson. Their work has discredited the simplistic interpretation of "riot" as a reflexive response to misery, and makes us recognize the crude rationality of blockages and other forms of struggle over food. Sen's treatment of entitlements allows us to specify who acquired an incentive to seize control over food when his or her title to that food became weak or contestable—and to discern how the titles shifted. The rise of a national market with strong claims as against local and regional ones neither deprived everyone of food nor dissolved everyone's entitlements equally. On the contrary, wage-earning proletarians and peasants and workers undergoing proletarianization felt the shift in entitlements most directly. They had the greatest incentive to coerce merchants and officials to hold grain in a locality or region.

If we enter entitlements into the equation, furthermore, it becomes less puzzling why, in a time of rising (or, at least, not falling) per capita production, the standard of living of proletarian and proletarianizing workers could actually decline. It was urban waged workers who first posed the issue of entitlement in the transformed form of wage demands, and who developed collective ways of organizing and acting on these demands. State-financed welfare entitlements were another response to fundamental changes in marketing arrangements, the organization of production, and the proportion of wage-earning proletarians. Entitlements are the mechanism which links ordinary people's experience to these large-scale processes.

Michelle B. McAlpin

Famines, Epidemics, and Population Growth: The Case of India

Since 1872, when a modern process of census taking began in India, there have been three periods with very different rates of population growth. In the first of these, from 1872 until 1921, the annual rate of growth was only 0.37 percent; from 1921 through 1951 it was about 1 percent; and since 1951 it has exceeded 2 percent a year.

The generally accepted view of this record suggests that the period from 1921 to 1951 represents a sharp break in the demographic patterns of the previous fifty years. It is the argument of this article, however, that the difference in growth rates between the first and second periods, rather than indicating any significant change in the factors which determined the ordinary levels of mortality, is due entirely to the absence in the second period of major famines and epidemics. Between 1872 and 1921 famines, plague, and influenza caused large increases in mortality, but in the decade 1881 to 1891, when all of them were absent, the rate of population growth was like that experienced between 1921 and 1951. It was only after 1951 that changes in the background levels of mortality became important in determining India's rate of population increase.[1]

CHANGES IN THE SIZE AND SHAPE OF INDIA'S POPULATION   India's first general census in 1872 was not taken on the same day or even in the same calendar year for all parts of India, but it was taken in almost all parts of the sub-continent. Because it did not follow the forms and categories which became standard for demo-

Michelle B. McAlpin is Associate Professor of Economics at Tufts University. She is the author of *Subject to Famine: Food Crises and Economic Change in Western India, 1860–1920* (Princeton, 1983).

1 Kingsley Davis, *The Population of India and Pakistan* (Princeton, 1950), 28.

graphic information from 1881, it is not directly comparable to succeeding censuses for most areas of enquiry.

Basic series (population, age, sex, civil conditions, etc.) from the census done each decade since 1881 are generally comparable *except* for frequent changes in the boundaries of administrative divisions. The paucity of information published in the 1941 census (taken under wartime conditions), the partition of British India and the Princely States into India and Pakistan in 1947, and the reorganization of Indian states largely along linguistic boundaries between the 1951 and 1961 censuses have made it difficult to construct consistent series for major units of the country. As a result, most people work either on the 1881 to 1931 or the 1961 to 1971 periods. Virtually the only work which presents data that apply to comparable geographic units for all of the censuses from 1881 through 1971 is Mukherjee's examination of age distribution.[2]

Table 1 gives the rates of population growth from 1881 to 1981 in the five zones now constituting the Republic of India. For India as a whole, population growth was sporadic until 1921. Wide variations occurred among the zones: growth in the Southern zone from 1891 to 1901 was over 1 percent per year while for the other four zones it ranged from a high of 0.24 percent per

Table 1 Rates of Population Growth: India and Zones, 1881–1981

YEAR	INDIA	EASTERN	CENTRAL	SOUTHERN	WESTERN	NORTHERN
1881–1891	0.95	—	0.86	—	1.44	—
1891–1901	0.18	0.24	−0.18	1.13	−0.13	−0.63
1901–1911	0.56	0.65	0.32	0.87	0.94	−0.16
1911–1921	−0.03	0.00	−0.26	0.19	−0.08	0.02
1921–1931	1.05	1.09	0.78	1.12	1.34	1.12
1931–1941	1.32	1.38	1.25	1.19	1.35	0.81
1941–1951	1.19	1.16	1.04	1.54	1.76	1.60
1951–1961	2.09	2.30	1.74	1.62	2.24	
1961–1971	2.25	2.31	2.05	2.05	2.51	2.57
1971–1981	2.24	2.24	2.29	1.92	2.28	1.86

SOURCE: Calculated from the Appendix.

2 Sudhansu Bhusan Mukherjee, *The Age Distribution of the Indian Population* (Honolulu, 1976), 9–43, for the problems of generating comparable series.

year to a low of minus 0.63 percent in the Northern zone. The decade 1901 to 1911 also showed wide variation, but for the decade 1911 to 1921 variation among the zones was considerably less. These differences were due to the nature of the demographic crises in each decade. No further decades of negative or near-zero population growth occurred after 1921 either for India as a whole or for any of the zones, although there continued to be variations in rates among zones.

Some of the differences in experience among zones were due to differential migration patterns, but the natural rate of increase also varied widely among them (see Table 2). The natural rates of increase varied at least as much as the overall rates of population growth among zones. Although data for all of the zones suggest a common pattern of low rates between 1891 and 1921, higher rates between 1921 and 1951 (although not in all cases higher than rates in 1881 to 1891), and another rise in rates after 1951, there was enormous variation among the zones in any given decade. For instance, rates of natural increase for males varied from 0.59 percent in the Southern zone in 1881 to 1891 to 1.77 percent in the Western zone. For females in the same decade the range was from 0.43 percent in the Eastern zone to 1.51 percent in the Northern zone. By 1951 to 1961, the range for males was from 1.67 in the Southern zone to 2.19 in the Northern. For females, the Southern zone also had the lowest rate of natural increase (1.56 percent) and the Northern the highest (2.17 percent.)[3]

Table 3 offers another view of demographic experience from 1891 to 1970 by presenting estimates of life expectancy at birth for males and females in the five zones. Estimates for 1891 to 1901 until 1951 to 1961 are from Mukherjee; those for 1951 to 1960 and 1961 to 1970 are from the Census of India, 1971. Census estimates for birth and death rates are generally lower and estimates of life expectancies are generally higher than Mukherjee's. The differences are due to the different methods of estimation; the Census of India demographers relied more heavily on the numbers before them and Mukherjee relied more heavily on model life tables.

---

3 Although I do not agree with all of Mukherjee's assumptions or methods of calculating his series, his are indubitably the best we have. They are also reasonable for the region I know best—the Western zone including the Bombay Presidency.

Table 2   Rates of Natural Increase of Males and Females: India and Zones, 1881–91 to 1951–61

DECADE	INDIA		EASTERN ZONE		CENTRAL ZONE		SOUTHERN ZONE		WESTERN ZONE		NORTHERN ZONE	
	MALE	FEMALE	MALE	FEMALE	MALE	FEMALE	MALE	FEMALE	MALE	FEMALE	MALE	FEMALE
1881–91	0.78	1.05	0.62	0.43	0.76	0.82	0.59	1.49	1.77	1.18	1.31	1.51
1891–1901	−0.07	0.02	0.47	0.43	−0.28	−0.15	0.75	0.74	−1.33	−1.10	−0.84	−0.84
1901–11	0.60	0.53	0.68	0.60	0.45	0.25	0.95	0.04	0.90	0.83	−0.08	−0.35
1911–21	0.01	−0.08	0.09	−0.10	−0.16	−0.14	0.26	0.02	−0.05	−0.16	0.02	−0.01
1921–31	1.06	1.01	1.16	0.97	0.83	0.77	1.12	1.08	1.30	1.27	1.09	1.19
1931–41	1.30	1.24	1.30	1.13	1.28	1.28	1.25	1.16	1.30	1.32	1.56	1.65
1941–51	1.30	1.31	1.20	1.16	1.03	1.03	1.51	1.55	1.36	1.54	1.49	1.63
1951–61	1.89	1.85	1.89	2.06	1.79	1.69	1.67	1.56	2.05	2.05	2.19	2.17

SOURCE: Mukherjee, *Age Distribution*, 159.

Table 3   Male and Female Life Expectancy at Birth: India and Zones, 1891–1901 to 1961–1970

DECADE	INDIA		EASTERN ZONE		CENTRAL ZONE		SOUTHERN ZONE		WESTERN ZONE		NORTHERN ZONE	
	MALE	FEMALE	MALE	FEMALE	MALE	FEMALE	MALE	FEMALE	MALE	FEMALE	MALE	FEMALE
1891–1901	20.1	21.8	21.7	22.6	19.9	23.9	26.5	27.8	—	21.1	17.5	23.1
1901–11	23.9	23.4	23.8	23.4	22.0	22.8	27.3	27.9	—	25.3	—	20.6
1911–21	20.1	20.9	20.1	21.8	19.7	19.2	25.0	25.9	20.2	23.3	—	20.8
1921–31	28.1	27.8	28.8	26.9	26.5	25.5	29.9	30.5	29.9	29.9	29.0	27.9
1931–41	33.1	31.1	30.6	29.4	34.6	30.6	31.0	31.2	33.0	31.7	33.6	27.6
1941–51	34.9	32.5	34.7	30.4	34.1	29.3	39.8	35.6	32.7	34.6	33.9	32.8
1951–61	37.9	37.7	36.8	38.0	36.8	34.7	36.5	36.6	40.6	39.9	42.4	38.1
1951–60	41.9	40.6	39.8	40.1	39.8	38.8	41.1	39.2	44.2	42.5	49.6	44.6
1961–70	46.4	44.7	46.0	42.8	42.2	40.7	47.5	46.4	48.6	49.0	50.6	48.3

SOURCES: 1891–1901 to 1951–1961, calculated from Mukherjee, *Age Distribution*, 198,202. 1951–1960 and 1961–1970 from *Census of India 1971, Series I, Paper 1 of 1977, Life Tables*, 6.

The estimates of life expectancies are consistent with the pattern that we have seen developing. Life expectancy at birth was low and fluctuating before 1921, for both males and females. Since 1921 the pattern has been one of sustained increases in life expectancy, again for both sexes. There are some minor exceptions to this pattern (Southern zone, 1941 to 1951, males; Central zone, 1941 to 1951, both sexes) for which I have no present explanation. I suspect that the Southern figure is an error. Generally, increases in life expectancy since 1921 have been greater for males than for females.

All of the demographic evidence examined shows the same broad patterns. Growth of population was slow until 1921; rates of natural increase and life expectancies were generally low and fluctuating through 1921. Since 1921 population growth has been sustained and it has accelerated since 1951. Rates of natural increase and increases in life expectancies also have been more rapid since 1951.

THE ROLE OF FAMINES AND EPIDEMICS IN SLOWING POPULATION GROWTH: EVIDENCE FROM THE BOMBAY PRESIDENCY   Although it is widely agreed that famines and epidemics were major forces retarding population growth in colonial India, little use has been made of the wealth of materials left by the colonial administration to ascertain the role of specific catastrophes in slowing growth. To do so for all of the regions that now form the Repulic of India would be a formidable task—especially since the quality of the vital registration data upon which estimates of mortality from famines and epidemics must be deduced varies substantially from one administrative jurisdiction to another.

The Bombay Presidency had an unusually elaborate land revenue establishment which was used in part to collect data on agriculture and vital rates. It also was the site of severe famines at the end of the nineteenth century, was the starting point for the plague epidemic that began in 1896, and was a region where the influenza epidemic of 1918 to 1919 was severe. The Bombay Presidency, therefore, seems a good place to estimate the importance of famines, plague, and influenza in population growth before 1921.

Table 4 presents estimates of deaths from famines, the influenza epidemic of 1918/19, and the plague epidemic that began in

Table 4   Effects on Population of Famines, Plague, and Influenza, 1891–
1921

	EXCESS MORTALITY				IMPACT OF LOWERED BIRTH RATE	COMBINED EFFECT
	FAMINES	PLAGUE	INFLUENZA	TOTAL		
1891–1901	687[a]	162	—	849	155	1,004
1901–1911	43	679	—	722	262	984
1911–1921	104	345	713	1,162	145	1,307

SOURCE: McAlpin, *Subject to Famine*, 80.

a   All figures in thousands.

1896. Deaths from famine and from influenza were estimated (by officers writing famine reports and by the Census) as the total excess of registered deaths over the normal registered deaths. "Normal" was defined as the average of the corresponding months in the last five or ten years (assuming that there had been no unusual experience in that period). The estimates of deaths due to plague were taken directly from the reports of the Sanitary Commissioner for the Presidency. Plague deaths were registered separately from shortly after the outbreak of plague in 1896; the Sanitary Commissioner added up the reports from all the sanitary circles to produce yearly totals. To the extent that there was underregistration of deaths in all years, and to the extent that this underregistration was more severe during a famine, a severe outbreak of plague, or the influenza epidemic, these figures underestimate deaths due to these causes.[4]

For the period 1891 to 1901, when the growth rate of the Bombay Presidency was minus 0.42 percent per year, these estimates indicate that deaths from famine and plague raised mortality by about 850,000. In the next decade, when growth in the Bombay Presidency was 0.52 percent per year, famine and plague are estimated to have again raised mortality by 722,000. In the decade 1911 to 1921, when the growth rate fell to minus 0.06, the estimated mortality from famine, plague, and influenza was 1,162,000. For the entire period, these estimates indicate that famine accounted for 834,000 deaths, plague for 1,186,000, and

4   For a fuller discussion of these data, see McAlpin, *Subject to Famine*, 50–51.

influenza for 713,000. Forty-three percent of total excess mortality (i.e., that estimated to be above normal levels) was attributable to plague, 31 percent to famine, and 26 percent to the influenza epidemic.

Catastrophes of this sort, however, do not just elevate the death rate—they also affect the birth rate. Because of the limitations of the vital registration data, it is not easy to discover either how large their effect on the birth rate may have been or, given the high levels of infant and childhood mortality, how important a decline in the birth rate was for the growth of population. However, using birth rate data and age-specific mortality data, the effect on population of declines in the birth rate after the period 1891 to 1895 have been estimated. The effect of these diminutions in the birth rate, suitably modified to reflect high levels of infant and child mortality, are also presented in Table 4. Over the entire period, reductions in the birth rate accounted for "lost" population of 562,000, with 29 percent of that loss occurring in the decade 1891 to 1901, 47 percent in the decade 1901 to 1911, and 26 percent in the decade 1911 to 1921.

The success of these estimates of increases in mortality and reductions in births due to plague, famine, and influenza in explaining the slow growth of population before 1921 is summed up in Table 5. Presumably, if we had captured all of the effects of these three crises, and if they were the only causes of slow growth of population, the reconstructions in Table 5 should yield rates of growth similar to those for the decades on either side that were free of these scourges.

The average compound annual rate of growth for the decades 1881 to 1891 and 1921 to 1931 was 1.23 percent. The reconstructed rate of growth for 1891 to 1901 was 0.26 percent, for 1901 to 1911 was 1.25 percent, and for 1911 to 1921, 0.87 percent. If we assume that the census of 1901, taken in the midst of a famine and a plague epidemic, was an undercount, then the rate for 1891 to 1901 should be higher and that for 1901 to 1911 should be lower. In addition, since we know that birth and death rates reflected considerable underregistration, we should adjust our figures up by some percentage for both births prevented and deaths. For instance, if we assume that the 1901 Census undercounted the population by 500,000 and that because of underregistration of births and deaths we should increase our estimates of the

Table 5 Actual and Reconstructed Rates of Growth

	COMPOUND ANNUAL RATES OF GROWTH	
	ACTUAL	RECONSTRUCTED
1891–1901	−0.57	0.26
1901–1911	0.45	1.25
1911–1921	−0.18	0.87

SOURCE: McAlpin, *Subject to Famine,* 81.

population impact of each by 25 percent, we can produce a new set of reconstructed growth rates that are about 1 percent for the decades 1891 to 1901 and 1901 to 1911 and about 1.1 percent for 1911 to 1921.

These reconstructed population growth rates are still below the rates of growth experienced in the Bombay Presidency from 1881 to 1891 and from 1921 to 1931, but they are approximately equal to or larger than the rates of growth for India as a whole and for the Eastern, Central, Southern, and Northern zones from 1921 to 1931. Indeed, these reconstructed rates are approaching the 1.19 percent rate at which total population increased from 1921 to 1951.

THE TRADITIONAL EXPLANATION OF SUSTAINED GROWTH, 1921 TO 1951   When we examine any estimates of vital rates after 1921, it becomes obvious that, although the temporary dips in the birth rate have vanished, most of the change in the rate of population growth has been due to declines in death rates. For the period 1891 to 1921, estimated death rates for all of India averaged 48 per 1,000 for males and 45 per 1,000 for females. From 1921 through 1951 these rates were 33 per 1,000 for males and 34 per 1,000 for females. For the decade 1951 to 1961 these rates are estimated to have been 25 and 27 per 1,000 respectively. For the following decade, the combined death rate is estimated by the Census to have fallen to 19 per 1,000; estimates place the death rate from 1971 to 1981 as low as 15 per 1,000.[5]

5 Mukherjee, *Age Distribution,* 197, 201; *Statistical Outline of India* (Bombay, 1982), 30.

Because the years from 1921 to 1951 have been, in many respects, the least studied period in India's social and economic (as opposed to political) history, hypotheses about the sources of mortality declines are rather sketchy. They are best summarized in Mitra's major work on India's population. He suggests several possible explanations for the decline in mortality although none of them are presented very fully, nor does he see very large gains *during* this perod (as opposed to the change between the two periods 1872 to 1921 and 1921 to 1951). He claims that there were wide-spread gains in productivity and "steady improvement in aspirations and economic activity," which he attributes to the stimulation to Indian industry provided by World War I, the boycott of British goods led by Mohandas K. Gandhi, and the "unprecedented efforts at improving all aspects of the economy from agriculture to finance, industry, and labour . . ."[6]

There is substantial evidence that industrial expansion in India was rapid between 1919 and 1939—possibly as high as 4 percent a year, which would indicate substantial increases in output per capita. Expansion of industrial production was accompanied by expansions in the industrial labor force and in non-agricultural employment. There was also some increase in urbanization, from about 10 percent in 1921 to about 17 percent in 1951.[7]

Among these changes urbanization may have had the greatest impact on mortality. Such rudimentary sanitation and public health services as India possessed at independence were heavily concentrated in urban areas. More recent evidence suggests that mortality among all age groups is much lower in cities than in surrounding rural areas. Employees of manufacturing concerns were frequently located in urban areas and may even have had unusually good access to medical care as part of their total compensation. The problem with attributing any significant overall decline in mortality to increases in non-agricultural employment and to increases in urbanization, however, is that they both affected small percentages of the population.[8]

6 Asok Mitra, *India's Population: Aspects of Quality Control* (New Delhi, 1978), I, 41–47, 36–37.
7 Alan Heston, "National Income," in Dharma Kumar (ed.), *The Cambridge Economic History of India*, II, forthcoming; Davis, *Population*, 127; *Statistical Outline of India*, 41.
8 Davis, *Population*, 50; Morris David Morris and McAlpin, *The Physical Quality of Life Index: Measuring the Condition of India's Poor* (New Delhi, 1982), 60–62.

Mitra dismisses the possibility (raised by others) that improvements in medical care and in public health and sanitation may have lowered mortality. There was, he argues, too little public health and medical care to have been of significance. In British India, the percentage of the population with protected water supplies was no more than about 10 percent in any major province; the population served by sewers was less than 5 percent; and the great majority of people who lived in rural areas had no protected water supplies nor any sanitary form of waste disposal.[9]

Efforts were made during this period to control smallpox with a vaccination and quarantine program. Registered deaths from smallpox had declined to less than .2 per 1,000 during the period 1937 to 1943. Since registered deaths from smallpox had never been more than .4 per 1,000 after 1900, its control could not have had large effects on mortality. Smallpox deaths, however, rebounded in 1944 and 1945 to almost .6 per 1,000, a level characteristic of the nineteenth century.[10]

Mitra is more sanguine about the possibility that improvements in nutrition may have contributed to lower levels of mortality. He bases his argument on harvests which were sufficient to glut markets in the early 1930s. But is there evidence that nutrition could have increased over the period?[11]

Table 6 compares trend rates of change in population and output and acreage of foodgrains from 1916 through 1946. These figures are drawn from Blyn's work on agricultural production

Table 6 Trend Rates of Change in Population and Output and Acreage of Foodgrains in British India, 1916–1946

YEARS	POPULATION (% CHANGE/YEAR)	OUTPUT (% CHANGE/YEAR)	ACREAGE (% CHANGE/YEAR)
1916–1926	0.45	−0.79	0.13
1921–1931	0.95	−0.17	0.06
1926–1936	1.07	0.06	0.21
1931–1941	1.19	−0.51	0.18
1936–1946	1.27	0.75	1.10

SOURCE: Blyn, *Agricultural Trends*, 327–328.

9 Mitra, *India's Population*, 36; Davis, *Population*, 50.
10 *Ibid.*, 47.
11 Mitra, *India's Population*, 36–37.

between 1891 and 1947, a work which remains our best source of reasonably clean agricultural data for all of British India. In Table 6 we see that population change was positive in each of Blyn's five reference decades, rising from 0.45 percent per year to 1.27 percent. Changes in output, however, were negative in three decades and barely positive in the fourth. This certainly suggests *declining* per capita availability of foodgrains. But all output figures are the product of yield and acreage statistics, and it has been argued that Blyn's yield figures may have spurious downward biases, which suggests that we should look at changes in acreage to see whether they kept pace with population growth. As seen in Table 6, changes in acreage planted with foodgrains were much lower than changes in population in all but the last of Blyn's overlapping decades.[12]

Because the quality of agricultural statistics for all of British India is not reassuring, it is possible that there are sufficient errors in Blyn's figures for parts of India to hide at least a constant per capita availability of foodgrains. Mitra argues that there were significant improvements in post-harvest technology, which could have increased the amount of consumable grain without changing output. However, we would need much more research on agriculture between 1921 and 1951 than we now have to confirm such a conclusion.[13]

Bhatia has argued that India became a net importer of grain after 1921 (having been a small net exporter in most years before 1921), which helped to eliminate famines and improve nutrition. Blyn, however, after a careful examination of the trade data, argues that imports had very marginal effects on availability because the international trade in foodgrains was small compared to India's own harvest. For instance, in the five-year period from 1936–37 to 1940–41, India's output averaged 47 million tons of foodgrains and her net imports averaged 1 million tons.[14]

It is possible that nutrition improved because of changes in crops and diets. To confirm this hypothesis we need to know the

12 George Blyn, *Agricultural Trends in India, 1891–1947: Output, Availability, and Productivity* (Philadelphia, 1966). Heston, "Official Yields per Acre in India, 1886–1947: Some Question of Interpretation," *Indian Economic and Social History Review*, X (1973), 303–332.
13 Mitra, *India's Population*, 37.
14 B.M. Bhatia, *Famines in India, 1860–1965: A Study in Some Aspects of the Economic History of India* (New York, 1967; 2nd ed.), 309; Blyn, *Agricultural Trends*, 103–104, 334.

degree to which cultivation of citrus fruits increased, the extent
to which potatoes and tapioca spread into everyday diets, and the
significance of shifts in the mix of cereals and legumes commonly
consumed. Answers to such questions still lie undisturbed in the
records of the Raj.

There is, thus, no very convincing evidence that the difference in the level of mortality between the period 1891 to 1921
and the period 1921 to 1951 was due to any of the commonly
cited factors—improvements in public health and sanitation, improvements in nutrition, or general growth of the economy.

A REVISED EXPLANATION OF SUSTAINED GROWTH, 1921 TO 1951
Plague, which had been raging in India since 1896, receded in
importance after 1921 for reasons that we do not know. At its
most severe, plague accounted for over 500 registered deaths per
100,000 population. But after 1921, registered deaths from plague
never exceeded about 150 per 100,000. After 1930, registered
deaths from plague were generally well below 10 per 100,000.
Registered deaths do underestimate actual deaths, but the system
of registration was, if anything, improving over this period so
that the sharp declines in mortality from plague appear to be
beyond question.[15]

Mortality from cholera was also lower in the period after
1921 than it had been in the earlier period. Although registered
deaths from cholera exceeded 200 per 100,000 in the seven years
between 1896 and 1920, they never returned to this level after
1920. The years in which cholera deaths peaked generally, but
not inevitably, correspond to years in which there were harvest
failures. The highest peak, of almost 400 registered deaths per
100,000 of population, for instance, occurred in 1900; that year
was also one of widespread harvest failure and declarations of
famine. However, the correlation of the scourges of famine and
cholera may well be due to the deterioration of water supplies
either in times of flood or drought, and to the increased movements of people seeking work and food, rather than to any direct
connection between hunger and cholera.[16]

Using evidence from the Bombay Presidency, it appears

15 Davis, *Population*, 46.
16 *Ibid.*

likely that mortality from severe harvest shortfalls had begun to decline by the end of the first decade of the twentieth century if not earlier. Rainfall had not improved, nor had changes in techniques of cultivation stabilized output. Rather, the society was developing in ways that sharply reduced the risk that an initial decline in food production would become a famine by generating major amounts of rural unemployment and sharp changes in the relative prices of food and all other goods (including labor). First, and a necessary but not sufficient means of containing mortality from food crises, came the creation of a dense and effective rail network that could quickly and cheaply move grain from regions of local surplus to regions of local scarcity. The famines at the end of the nineteenth century were terrible, but they were characterized by problems of organizing relief works and charitable aid and not by an absolute shortage of grain moving into the region. Barely twenty-five years earlier, in the famine of 1876–78, the southern part of the Presidency had suffered from an absolute shortage of grain which could not be ameliorated in the absence of any rail lines into the area.[17]

Diversification of the economy was the second important change that reduced the risk of famine. Once the capacity to move grain had been achieved, the next step was to put money to buy grain into the hands of those people who had lost their usual agricultural employment. The growth of construction work, the increased production of labor intensive crops in nearby areas, and the growth of the cotton textile industry in the cities of Ahmedabad and Bombay all changed the economic opportunities available to families in drought-prone regions. Income could be earned in agricultural slow seasons by migrating to other rural areas or urban areas for low-skilled jobs. If a family member could move to a factory job, his earnings became part of the cushion against a bad agricultural year. In addition, the regularity with which grain supplies moved among regions encouraged farmers to stop storing grain beyond their current year's requirements. They were able to sell grain that they might have stored or to switch land into higher value crops. In either case, they could accumulate monetary assets which could be used to survive bad periods.

17 This section draws heavily on McAlpin, *Subject to Famine*, 161–190.

Finally, the colonial government learned to recognize when intervention would be necessary to avert increases in mortality and to generate effective relief. They created employment by making loans to agriculturists for capital improvements and by starting relief works. For those unable to work, they generated systems of grants of food or occasionally of money.

All of these changes were intertwined—the transport network assured the availability of food; the diversification of the economy and government relief efforts provided money to buy food or, in a minority of cases, provided grants of food. By the end of the first decade of the twentieth century, harvest shortfalls in the Bombay Presidency no longer led to enormous rises in prices, large-scale aimless wandering by people unable to find work or food, and major elevations in mortality. What was true in the Bombay Presidency seems to have been generally true for the rest of India, but we lack the detailed research that would enable us to make a stronger statement. In general, mortality from famines was not an important force in slowing India's population growth after 1921.

However, the gains that had been made in the control of mortality from disruptions of food supplies were, and probably remain, fragile. Control of mortality depends upon the continued availability of a transport network, upon the vigilance of the government in providing both relief works and charitable relief, and upon the continued generation of employment opportunities for temporarily displaced agriculturists. When some or all of these pieces of the ring of containment of famines are missing, sharp rises in mortality can still occur. The Bengal famine of 1943 is the major example of a time after 1921 when there was widespread mortality due to disruptions of food supplies. Although there is not full agreement on the roles of various factors in precipitating this famine, it is generally agreed that the disruption of the transport network (both water and rail) by World War II, and the imperial government's ignorance of the conditions in the countryside (or their unwillingness to respond) contributed to the creation of crisis conditions.[18]

18   Paul Greenough, *Prosperity and Misery in Modern Bengal: The Famine of 1943–44* (New York, 1982).

The containment of famines may have been an important factor in reducing major outbreaks of cholera. By 1900 in the Bombay Presidency considerable care was taken in the administration of government relief works to prevent contamination of water supplies and to construct sanitary facilities. Outbreaks of cholera at relief works in earlier famines had become the center of epidemics when people fled the works and took cholera with them to their home villages and other locations. As the complexity of the economy increased and agriculturists became aware of a variety of alternative sources of employment in years of crop failures, there was also a diminution in the numbers of aimlessly wandering people who might become carriers and victims of the disease. The last pre-independence rise in the rate of cholera deaths corresponds closely with the Bengal famine of 1943. This famine was much like those before 1910 in that the paucity of government relief efforts does appear to have resulted in widespread movement as people searched ceaselessly for food or work.[19]

Although Davis and many others have been correct in noting that population growth in India ceased to fluctuate wildly after 1921, there is no evidence to suggest that there were any fundamental changes in demographic patterns between 1921 and 1951. The growth of population that occurred between 1921 and 1951 was the same kind that occurred between 1881 and 1891—only more sustained. What is significant about the period from 1921 to 1951 is that it was largely free from mortality crises caused by famines and epidemics. The administration and the economy had altered in ways that helped to prevent extraordinary mortality from most disruptions of food supplies. In addition, India, like the rest of the world, was fortunate that there was no recurrence of the influenza epidemic of 1918–19 and no introduction of other new epidemics like the plague. Declines in mortality (and the growth of population) since 1951 may well reflect some of the infrastructure created and maintained during the years before 1951. But the demographic experience of India since 1951 is different from that before 1951 in ways that have no earlier parallels.

19 *Ibid.*

APPENDIX
Population of India and Zones, 1881–1981 (in thousands)

CENSUS	INDIA	EASTERN	CENTRAL	SOUTHERN	WESTERN	NORTHERN
1881	212,327[a]	—	61,257	—	24,999	—
1891	233,322	57,419	66,702	51,646	28,847	28,692
1901	237,515	58,829	65,486	57,770	28,486	26,927
1911	251,167	62,753	67,593	63,023	31,278	26,493
1921	250,432	62,767	65,842	64,229	31,025	26,542
1931	278,051	69,969	71,132	71,816	35,449	29,656
1941	317,042	80,277	80,523	80,844	40,534	34,865
1951	356,787	90,083	89,287	94,185	48,265	—
1961	438,654	113,133	106,119	110,554	60,245	47,912
1971	547,950	142,192	129,995	135,852	77,184	61,754
1981	684,000	173,996	163,024	164,336	96,676	74,271

SOURCE: 1881–1971 Mukherjee, *Age Distribution of the Indian Population*, 65–70. 1981 *Statistical Outline of India, 1982* (Bombay, 1982), 33–34.

[a] Adjusted from Mukherjee's figure to include areas for which age data were not available.

Santhebachahalli G. Srikantia

Better Nutrition and India:

A Comment   The central point of the article by McAlpin is that the rate of change in India's population between the years 1921 and 1951 was due, not to a sharp, sudden reduction in the level of background mortality, but to a relative absence of famines. The fall in mortality rate came after 1951 and was followed by considerable population growth.[1]

The conclusion that frequent famines were responsible for the slow rate of population increase before 1921 is based upon data relating to one area in the country—the erstwhile Bombay Presidency. It is questionable whether what happened in Bombay Presidency represents what happened in the country as a whole. It is arguable that the magnitude of changes may vary from one region to another but that the direction of changes would be similar, given somewhat similar administrative and socioeconomic systems. This argument has to be viewed in the context of the growing evidence that geographically adjoining and apparently similar areas may have dissimilar demographic, economic, social, and morbidity profiles.

Changes in population growth in the five zones of the country as outlined in Table 1 of McAlpin's article, show an intriguing trend through time. Differences in the rates of population increase among zones are marked between the years 1981 and 1921, ranging from three- to fivefold; but thereafter they become more uniform and much smaller—not exceeding 1.5 times. Are these changes genuine or do they reflect methodological inaccuracies? If the changes are real, what do they mean? Answers to these

S. G. Srikantia is Professor of Food and Nutrition at the University of Mysore and is the former Director of the National Institute of Nutrition of the Indian Council of Medical Research.

1 Michelle B. McAlpin, "Famines, Epidemics, and Population Growth: The Case of India," in this issue.

questions would indicate whether conclusions drawn on the basis of data pertaining to one zone can be extrapolated to the country as a whole.

Famines can slow down population growth in two major ways—through an increase in the mortality rate and through a decrease in the fertility rate. These effects may, however, be expected to operate over a relatively short period. Under normal conditions, in situations wherein infant mortality rates are high—as in many developing countries—birth rates are also high. The reasons for this are twofold. The first is a desire on the part of the family to replace a lost child as soon as possible. The second is the shortened lactation period with its consequent relative loss of protection against conception.[2]

The duration of lactation does seem strongly to influence the duration of post-partum amenorrhea which, in turn, is a determinant of inter-pregnancy interval when contraception is not practiced. This relationship is particularly relevant to developing countries, where almost 95 percent of women in rural areas successfully breast-feed their infants for prolonged periods and breast-milk is the sole source of food for an infant often for up to twelve months, and not infrequently for up to fifteen months.

These considerations raise a question whether, as a result of the high infant mortality known to be associated with famines, once a famine ended there was not an increase in birth-rate. Did this not restore the population to the size that it was before the famine? How much of the effect of famine in a particular year would have been offset in the next year or two? It would have been interesting to look at birth rates in famine-stricken areas from this viewpoint.

A feature which India shares with several other Asian countries, in contrast to European countries, is a female/male ratio of less than 1. Since 1901, the sex ratio in India has shown a progressive fall. There were 910 females per 1,000 males in 1910 and only 845 in 1961 in urban areas. In rural areas it fell rather less conspicuously—from 980 to 963. High rates of maternal mortality and the culturally determined neglect of female children are

2 Roy E. Brown, "Breast Feeding and Family Planning: A Review of the Relationships between Breast Feeding and Family Planning," *American Journal of Clinical Nutrition*, XXXV (1982), 162–171.

among reasons given for the low female/male ratio. Both causes still apply, but neither is believed to be as strong as it was in earlier years. That the downward trend has continued, therefore, comes as somewhat of a surprise.

Mortality rates in India declined progressively from 1921 and McAlpin has sought out the possible reasons for this fall. Among the causes examined is the extent of urbanization and the contingent improved medical care, but McAlpin considers these factors of little consequence. She also agrees with Mitra's point that improved medical care and better public health practices could not be responsible for the drop in mortality rates, since no worthwhile public health programs were introduced during this period. This is largely true, but can one completely dismiss the possibility that, as a result of an increase in the numbers of medical personnel between 1921 and 1951, life-threatening situations were treated a little more effectively?[3]

McAlpin has carefully examined the suggestion that better nutrition played a role in lowering death rates between 1921 and 1951. Food production and availability data are often used to assess the nutrition status of countries and population groups, but there are genuine methodological problems in computing food production and the use of these data, even when reliable, to infer nutritional status should be seriously questioned. On the one hand, if the mean per capita availability of food, calculated from national food balance figures, is low, the chances are that the majority, if not an entire population, runs the risk of being malnourished. On the other hand, adequate or surplus mean per capita availability is no indicator of satisfactory food intake and good nutritional status, except when income and purchasing power show a normal distribution and do not become constraints.

In most developing countries, incomes and, therefore, purchasing capacity are highly skewed, with substantial numbers living below the poverty line. India is a good example of this phenomenon. Food grain production in the country increased from around 50 million tons in 1951 to over 130 million tons in 1981. In terms of per capita availability (*not* production), food grain production increased from around 350 grams per day to over 470 grams per day, and yet 40 percent of families, particu-

3 Asok Mitra, *India's Population: Aspects of Quality Control* (New Delhi, 1978), I, 41–47.

larly in rural areas today, consume diets which do not meet their energy needs.[4]

The inaccuracies of diet survey data are recognized and an estimate of the adequacy of energy intakes is difficult. These problems, however, do not alter the main point that the inequitable distribution of food (arising from any cause, including poverty) means that inferences about the nutritional status of people cannot be made from food production data.

A major problem that one faces in determining whether food intake and nutritional status between 1921 and 1951 improved and, in turn, lowered mortality, is the lack of quantitative or even qualitative data about food availability and food consumption at the family and individual levels. Data on expenditure patterns on food and information on nutritional status before 1940 are very limited. The earliest reported data on food and nutrient intake in India are from 1942. A comparison between data published then and data collected during the last decade shows that the rural poor had essentially similar intakes of energy and protein, despite the increase in per capita availability of food in later decades. What the situation was between 1921 and 1941 is anybody's guess. There is, however, little evidence to suggest that, during this period, food distribution was more equitable than in the years that followed. The growth of population in India between 1950 and 1980 has been considerable, and it is difficult to say whether any part of it can be ascribed to better nutrition. Neither the prevalence of frank deficiency signs nor the mean heights and weights of rural pre-school children, which are indicative of growth status, have changed over the three decades.

Evidence that the absence of famines contributed to the population rise between 1921 and 1951, as suggested by McAlpin, is reasonably strong. It is not that there were no famines between 1921 and 1951. Rather, the famines that befell the area were better handled and large-scale loss of life did not occur, except perhaps during the 1942 Bengal famine. It would be profitable to conduct microstudies of small, relatively isolated areas, which suffer from famine or near famine conditions, to determine the extent to which the rate of population growth is truly influenced by this calamity.

4 Indian Council of Medical Research, Annual Report of the National Nutrition Monitoring Bureau (Hyderabad, 1978).

Philip D. Curtin

Nutrition in African History
Nutrition has played a much more varied role in history than most historians consciously recognize. Some themes are taken as axiomatic. We can take it for granted that Europe came to be fed by the overseas world as part of the vast complex of change that goes by the name of the Industrial Revolution, just as we take it for granted that the Midwest's ability to feed New England somehow caused the abandonment of the homesteads the chimneys of which can still be found deep in the woods of the Berkshires and the White Mountains. Historians have also recognized the significance of the "Columbian Exchange"—to use Crosby's phrase for the exportation of Old World diseases, animals, and people to the Americas after 1492 in return for the New World crops like maize and potatoes that did so much to change the nutritional potential of the entire Afro-Eurasian landmass.[1]

Most historians, however, are not conscious of the ways in which hunger has molded the history of the non-Western world. Nor, for that matter, are historians aware of the great range of environmental possibilities that exist outside the familiar lands of North America and Western Europe. The African experience is relevant because of its difference from that of the West and because Africans adapted to nutritional deficits in significant and creative ways. Hunger in Africa has had something to do with phenomena as diverse as the origins of long-distance trade, the distribution of language groups, and the supply of individuals to the Atlantic slave trade. These developments may not be as grand as themes like the Industrial Revolution, but they illustrate the fact that

Philip D. Curtin is the Herbert Baxter Adams Professor of History at Johns Hopkins University. He is the author, with Steven Feierman, Leonard Thompson, and Jan Vansina, of *African History* (Boston, 1978).

1 Alfred W. Crosby, Jr., *The Columbian Exchange: Biological and Cultural Consequences of 1492* (Westport, Conn., 1972).

different environments have important effects on the human experience. If history claims to be the study of how human societies
change through time—not merely the story of how we came to
be as we are—historians will need to pay much more attention to
evidence from outside their own parishes.

DATE PALMS AND INCENTIVES TO TRADE   One of the oldest hypotheses about the origins of trade emphasized the importance of
ecological boundaries. People of the African forests had different
products from those of the savanna country. Exchange across the
savanna-forest boundary was therefore more common than was
exchange between households within the savanna or within the
forest. In much the same way, pastoral nomads and semi-nomads
along the desert edge had cattle to trade for the grain of sedentary
farmers in the sahel. Oasis dwellers were even more likely to
trade because they controlled a small island of ecological specialization in a much larger arid region. It is hardly surprising then
that they were active traders from an early date.

In Africa, those who pioneered the trans-Saharan trade, and
remained important in it to the end of the nineteenth century,
were almost all oasis dwellers by origin. More significant, they
came from a group of oases near the northern fringes of the
desert—oases where the date palm flourished. These were often
located where rivers coming down from the mountains to the
north flowed underground for some distance out into the Sahara,
providing a source of irrigation water.

In Morocco, to the west, the Wad Ziz and the Wad Draa
were both important. Another group of oases were located in
southern Algeria in the valley of the Wad Mzab, in the region of
Ouargla, and on into southern Tunisia. In Libya, the northern
oases like Ghat, Ghadames, and Kufra were also significant, as
were those in the Fezzan, farther out into the central Sahara. On
the upper Nile, Nubians from the desert reaches, where the valley
is so narrow as to be effectively an oasis, have also been prominent
as commercial pioneers far into the Nilotic Sudan. Farther south
and east around the Horn of Africa, similar cases can be found in
Somalia on the upper reaches of the Juba river as it flows down
out of the Ethiopian highlands. There, too, the oasis people have
been important traders between the highlands and the Somali
coastal ports.

The correlation between date-producing oases and commerce is negative as well as positive. Other Saharan oases, toward the southern fringe of the desert where the climate is too humid for good date production, are less significant commercially.

The date palm is part of the key to this pattern. *Phoenix dactrylifera* was one of the earliest trees to be domesticated for human use—in Mesopotamia by the third millennium BC. It is also one of the most productive of all food-producing trees: forty to eighty kilograms of fruit can be harvested each year from a single tree, with a yield of about 50 percent sugar by weight. The fruit is therefore valuable nutritionally, but not as a principal source of calories. The date palm requires a specialized environment: a hot, dry climate with temperatures around 30°C for several months of the year. In addition, it needs irrigation water, not rainfall, which at certain seasons can actually damage the fruit. The date palm grows best in the sandy alkaline soils characteristic of the desert edge.

All of the date-growing oases were surrounded by areas of sparse rainfall, mainly less than fifteen centimeters per year—too little for efficient use by cattle, even in the hands of nomadic pastoralists, but adequate for keeping camels. As the camel spread westward across Africa (reaching Somalia during the first millennium BC, but not arriving in southern Morocco until about AD 400), a new possibility arose. Camels are the most efficient of all beasts of burden. In conditions where they can live and work effectively, their cost per ton mile is less than that of oxen, donkeys, or carts. The oasis people probably grew and exported dates even before camels were introduced into northwest Africa around the fourth century AD, but the use of camels made it possible to grow dates almost exclusively in the appropriate oases and to sell most of the produce to people in non-oasis, arable farm areas in return for grain and other food supplies.[2]

The specialized characteristics of the date palm led in all of

---

2   See Richard W. Bulliet, *The Camel and the Wheel* (Cambridge, Mass., 1975), 7–27, 111–140. For calculations of transportation costs in the western Sahara, see Curtin, *Economic Change in Pre-Colonial Africa: Senegambia in the Era of the Slave Trade* (Madison, 1975), I, 278–285. For a general statement of the hypothesis about date-growing and the incentive to trade, see *idem*, chapter two of a thus-far-untitled book-length study of trade diasporas and cross-cultural trade in world history.

these instances to a very early commercialization of agricultural production. With the introduction of camels, short-range trade in food led to longer-distance trade. It would be foolish to claim that hunger for something other than dates caused this trade to develop, but it played its part.

IRREGULAR CLIMATES   Another important influence of hunger on history came about through the cultural responses of African peoples to the peculiar irregularity of many African climates. Europe and North America are comparatively fortunate. Their climates are variable; but harvest differentials from year to year were not notably great in comparison to those in other parts of the world. Even the supposed "little ice age" of 1550 to 1750 was not serious, as climatic calamities go in the tropical world. Chinese floods and periodic Indian famines have been notorious killers up to this century. Bryson and Murray recently reviewed the broader history of such "climates of hunger."[3]

Similar patterns of climatic fragility are a feature of many, but not of all parts of the tropical world just north of and south of the tropical forest. These areas experienced not just an occasional year of low rainfall but a pattern of great irregularity. Normally, a year's supply of rain fell within a two-to-four-month period, but great annual variations were also common. No rain at all might fall for three or four consecutive years. At another time, rain could be normal in quantity but so maldistributed that no crops could be harvested. At still other times, drought could turn into a season of floods.

These regions of erratic rainfall were also seriously threatened by desert locusts (*Shistocerca gregaria*), which depend on irregular rainfall, reappearing after years of dormancy. Swarms in recent years have been reported to cover as much as 500 square miles and have been known to eat as much as 50,000 metric tons of green vegetation each day. Their emergence from dormancy in the semi-arid desert edge is triggered by inordinately heavy rainfall. Satellite photographs are now used to spot unusual moisture

3   Reid A. Bryson and Thomas J. Murray, *Climates of Hunger: Mankind and the World's Changing Weather* (Madison, 1977). See also, Robert I. Rotberg and Theodore K. Rabb (eds.), *Climate and History* (Princeton, 1981).

as a way of predicting when and where locusts are likely to emerge. Thus, too much rain could cause hunger as easily as could too little.

Weather records for Africa are hard to come by before the colonial period, but Miller has gathered together impressive, if qualitative, accounts of climatic disasters for the southern savanna country centering on present-day Angola. More quantitative records from the arid zones of northeastern Brazil show the same pattern. There, three centers of especially severe climatic irregularity have been studied for anomalous rainfall over the century, 1835 to 1935. Rainfall variations serious enough to prevent normal economic activity occurred in more than half of those years.[4]

Fragile climates of this kind have affected African history seriously in a number of ways. One somewhat unexpected consequence has to do with the present-day patterns of language distribution. We can take two examples—Pulaar in west Africa and the Shari-Nile languages from Lake Chad eastward to the Nile and south into central and western Kenya.

THE FULBE   Pulaar or Fulfulbe speakers (also known variously as Peul, Fulani, and Fula, as well as Fulbe, the name they call themselves) are very widespread across the savanna belt stretching from Cape Verde in the far west to Lake Chad in the east. Dialectal differences are not very great, which indicates that the spread of Pulaar speakers was recent—probably within two millennia. In addition, most Pulaar speakers live scattered among people who speak other languages. They are often transhumant pastoralists, moving north into the sahel each wet season and then drifting south toward some secure year-round source of water in the dry period, which is about nine months of the year. Pulaar is a West Atlantic language, clearly related to others spoken in or near Senegal in the far west. The original home of Pulaar-speakers is taken to be the middle valley of the Senegal river, where the language is still spoken by transhumant pastoralists and sedentary farmers alike. Today, however, at least 90 percent of all West

4 Joseph C. Miller, "The Significance of Drought, Disease and Famine in the Agriculturally Marginal Zones of West-Central Africa," *Journal of African History*, XXIII (1982), 17–61: Friedrich W. Freise, "The Drought Region of Northeastern Brazil," *Geographical Review*, XXVIII (1938), 363–378.

Africans who speak it, or have a tradition of having spoken it in the recent past, no longer live near the Fulbe homeland.

The most plausible hypothesis to explain this distribution of Pulaar speakers begins with their practice of transhumant pastoralism, which is an adaptation to climatic irregularity. The Fulbe took their cattle for part of the year to places where they could not live all year round. Usually, this meant moving north to the desert edge, where the short annual rains would bring out enough grass for a few months' grazing. Sometimes, it meant going into places that had nearly enough rain for arable farming, but no groundwater or wells deep enough to carry through the dry season.

One environmental advantage of their original homeland on the banks of the middle Senegal was the fact that the river was fed mainly by rain that fell in the highlands of Fuuta Jallon, well to the south of the desert. The river's level did vary from year to year, but not in close synchronization with annual rainfall patterns. Because of this double chance for some kind of harvest, the Fulbe have a saying: "*Fuuta ko fetel jabaaji.*" "Fuuta [the middle Senegal] is a double-barreled gun." It thus escaped the worst of the annual variation in rainfall along the sahel.[5]

High rainfall in the southern savanna meant high water for irrigation farming. High rainfall along the middle Senegal meant successful rainfall agriculture that year and good grazing in the steppe country to the north and south. Low rainfall or no rainfall along the river, however, meant that only irrigation agriculture would produce a crop, and grazing would be bad. In a series of bad years, like the sahelian drought of 1968–1972, the pastoralists had to take their cattle and leave, moving their transhumant cycle farther south, to seek a new base with adequate year-round water and the possibility of some dry season grazing.

Having drifted off, many of these Fulbe pastoralists did not return. Instead, they continued a process of transhumant drift across West Africa, taking advantage of the fact that few if any of the other African peoples along the northern savannas occupied the same ecological niche. They were therefore able to enter into

5 Henri Gaden, *Proverbes et maximes peules et toucouleurs, traduits, expliquees, et annotes* (Paris, 1931), 310.

mutually profitable relationships as cattle-keepers for communities of sedentary farmers.

Once the drought was over on the middle Senegal, the local human and animal populations had a chance to recover for a few decades, or perhaps for a century, until the next period without rain again drove people and cattle away from the river. In this way, the Senegal valley became a kind of demographic pump that filled with people in good years and emptied out in periods of hunger.[6]

This pattern of eastward drift was not limited to the Fulbe herdsmen. Some of the sedentary Pulaar-speakers also left the middle Senegal, many of them Muslim clerics and religious teachers. They drifted eastward through the sudan, keeping in touch with their pastoral kinsmen, although they settled mainly in cities. In the nineteenth century, the Fulbe clerics led a series of religious revolutions. Their call was for religious reform, but they also appealed to Fulbe ethnic pride, and the Fulbe pastoralists gave significant military assistance. In the process, the Fulbe and their religious allies remade the political map of the savanna country from Cape Verde almost to Lake Chad, including among other new empires the Caliphate of Sokoto that unified what became northern Nigeria, the most populous part of the savanna. It would be going too far to say that the Fulbe adaptation to an irregular climate caused these revolutions, just as it would be inaccurate to say that the oasis dwellers' desire for variety in their diet caused them to initiate long-distance trade, but the course of history would have been far different if the Fulbe diaspora had not taken place.

CAUDATUM SORGHUM AND THE SHARI-NILE FAMILY OF LANGUAGES
The second example also involved a migration, but one that was more complex and even less well understood. Our knowledge of it is based on the research of a group of botanists at the University of Illinois. Their point of departure was a linguistic observation. Of the five principal varieties of sorghum bicolor now grown in Africa, one of the most restricted in its range and limited in its

6   Curtin, *Economic Change*, I, 13–23.

popularity is the race of caudatum sorghum. That particular race is grown almost exclusively by people who also speak one or the other of the Shari-Nile group of languages, and virtually all of those who speak those languages and grow any grain at all grow caudatum sorghum as their principal grain crop.[7]

Botanists assume that these different races of sorghum came about through a dual process of human and natural selection. Natural selection weeded out those varieties that could not survive in a particular environment. Of those that were known and could be grown, humans chose the race or races that they preferred, and that preference could depend on many things from the aesthetics of taste, to the quantity of the probable harvest, to the security of harvests in conditions of variable rainfall. Caudatum sorghum is the toughest of all common races of sorghum bicolor. It can survive under conditions of extreme flooding and extreme drought, where other races would produce no harvest at all. As though to balance these valuable characteristics, however, caudatum sorghum also yields a dark and bitter flour that people unaccustomed to it find unpleasant.

The best present hypothesis to explain the coincidence of caudatum sorghum and Shari-Nile languages is similar to the theory that explains the spread of Fulbe language and people across the western sudan. In both cases, the people who happened to speak a particular language also happened to invent or develop a technique for dealing with the uncertain rainfall of the sahel. For the Fulbe, it was transhumant pastoralism. For the original Shari-Nile speakers, it was combining the cultivation of caudatum sorghum with the keeping of particular breeds of sanga and zebu cattle, which produced a kind of agriculture that was both more secure against natural disasters and technologically more efficient than any other technique then known. As a result, speakers of these languages were able to expand westward from their presumed original home in the southern part of the present Sudan Repubic almost to the Lake Chad while others with the same original language and technology were able to expand southward into present-day Uganda and northestern Kenya, where their

7 Ann B. L. Stemler, Jack R. Harlan, and Jan M. J. Dewet, "Caudatum Sorghums and Speakers of Shari-Nile Languages in Africa," *Journal of African History,* XVI (1975), 161–183.

descendants still live as the Karamojong, Turkana, Luo, and Maasai, among others.

The Fulbe and the Shari-Nile migrations were similar in other ways. Fulbe migrations out of the middle valley of the Senegal began before AD 1000, continuing into the nineteenth century, and resuming in new circumstances with the great drought of the 1960s. Available evidence suggests that the Shari-Nile speakers began cultivating caudatum sorghum between AD 350 and AD 900, that the move westward along the sahel also came before AD 1000, and that the southward movement into Uganda and Kenya took place as late as 1500 to 1800.

These hypotheses suggest an important question without providing a very good answer. If these techniques were so effective as to allow one linguistic group to prosper and expand through their use, why were they not widely copied by their neighbors? Only a speculative answer is possible. Both techniques had serious drawbacks for people already conditioned to another culture, other tastes, and other habits. To take up the life of transhumant pastoralism meant giving up sedentary agriculture, since the cattle-keepers had to move away at precisely the time when planted fields needed most attention. Apparently, most sedentary farmers preferred not to do this, although there are many cases where the sedentary people entrusted their cattle to the Fulbe during the wet season.

The answer is more complex in the case of the cultivation of caudatum sorghum, since the developed technology involved a combination of cattle-keeping and the growing of certain pulses together with sorghum. The fact that those who did not speak Shari-Nile languages rejected caudatum sorghum (except occasionally for feeding cattle) suggests that they preferred their own food, as they preferred their own language—in short, that cultural retention for reasons of habit and culinary preference played a major role.

HUNGER AND THE SLAVE TRADE   Most people recruited in Africa for the Atlantic slave trade apparently were recent captives of war, political prisoners, or persons who were judicially condemned. Comparatively few were domestic slaves whose owners sold them for the sake of ready cash. Some evidence is beginning to emerge, however, to suggest that famines may also have been a major source of slaves. In times of famine in most parts of tropical Africa lineage heads could sell lineage members into slavery to save the lives of the rest. This included the sale of domestic slaves or other dependents—including one's children.

Evidence for this kind of sale into the trade comes almost entirely from the regions of extremely uncertain rainfall well to the north or to the south of the tropical forest. The bulk of it comes either from Senegambia or from the southern savannas of Angola. In neither case did the would-be seller simply search out the nearest slave dealer for direct negotiation. In both regions, the distribution of water was uneven, so that populations began starving in some places before others. In Senegambia, the reliability of water from the Senegal river, which was not dependent on local rainfall, caused starving people to go to the riverside and allow themselves to be sold, or sell their dependents so that the rest of a lineage could live. In the short run, this simply concentrated people where they could remain alive. When the drought became severe enough to threaten food supplies along the river, excess people were transferred into the slave trade—sold down the river to the European posts on the coast.

The situation was similar in Angola. Just as in the lands near the Senegal river, some parts of Angola also resembled a demographic pump, providing a place where populations could grow in years of good rainfall, only to find themselves driven out when the rains failed for several consecutive seasons. Without the cattle of the Fulbe, however, these refugees had to flee to places that were better watered even in bad years—places like the kingdoms of Kasanje and Matamba in the middle Kwango valley, parts of eastern Kongo, the Kunene floodplane, and portions of the upper Zambezi river. Those regions that still had food could add to the number of dependent retainers at little cost. Later, people who had first acquired the refugees might sell them into slavery down the trade routes that led to the coast.[8]

It would be foolish on the evidence now available to guess at the overall contribution of hunger to slave recruitment. At some periods and in some places, however, the correlation between high levels of slave shipments and prolonged drought is very

8   Miller, "Significance of Drought," 28–29; Curtin, *Economic Change*, I, 110–111.

clear, especially in Senegambia and Angola. Between 1746 and 1754, for example, Senegal experienced a series of chronically bad harvests. In 1754, the French exported more slaves from Saint Louis than they had ever done before, even though the average decennial level of slave exports from that port had been falling since the 1720s. Later, after the beginning of the Anglo-French war in 1757 brought an English naval blockade, the commander of the French garrison drove some 500 slaves out of the fort rather than have them die on his hands in captivity.[9]

The correlation is even more telling for Angola. In the 1780s, after a period of relatively constant levels of trade, the annual average number of slaves exported doubled, as French, Dutch, and English slave traders came south of the equator to join the Portuguese who had dominated that part of the African coast. Exports continued to rise on into the 1790s, coinciding with the worst drought of the eighteenth century in that region.[10]

For Angola, the connection between famine and political events can be traced into the nineteenth century, after the legal slave trade had ended. Rainfall disasters correlate with smallpox epidemics and with the pace of economic development, as might be expected. Hunger also had a strong effect on both the extent and the success of Portuguese military conquests in the late nineteenth and early twentieth centuries. Once the colonial regime was in place, hunger influenced both the frequency and severity of revolts, down to and including the attempted coup d'etat in Luanda of May 1977.[11]

These are only a few examples of the influence of nutrition on African history taken from a much greater number that have been recorded in recent research. Other examples are as diverse as the possibility of using known dates of famines to establish chronologies in oral histories and the impact of wildlife reserves on the possibilities of food production in the surrounding environment. In spite of the variety, these studies tend to have one element in common: in most, nutrition is not an independent

9   Curtin, *Economic Change,* I, 110, 166.
10   Miller, "Significance of Drought," 28–29, 31–32.
11   Jill R. Dias, "Famine and Diseases in the History of Angola *c* 1830–1930," *Journal of African History,* XXII (1981), 349–378.

variable, but rather a mediating element in man's relationship to his environment.

The oasis dwellers, for example, faced the problem of a specialized environment by growing a specialized food crop and realizing its potential through extensive trade. The Fulbe and the Shari-Nile speakers overcame the limitation of a difficult habitat through technical innovation that made it possible for them to expand far beyond their original homelands. Individuals who became a part of the slave trade through famine migrated for an opposite reason: they failed to solve the problem of a quixotic climate. The value of these examples, so different from the recent Western experience, is that they illustrate ways in which human creativity was able to manipulate the environment for man's use.

Ester Boserup

The Impact of Scarcity and Plenty
on Development
In all periods of human history wide differences have existed among societies which developed rapidly, stagnant societies, and societies which reverted from more developed to more primitive levels. Even today, we see sharp contrasts between communities of hunter-gatherers which have remained small in numbers, are illiterate, and apply stone-age technologies, and societies which, as a result of a long process of interrelated demographic and technological development, have large populations and have reached high levels of development with advanced industrial technology, general literacy, and a sizable, scientifically trained elite.

Were these differences in development related to differences in accessibility of food in these societies, and if so, was scarcity or plenty of food most likely to promote development?

Two centuries ago, the French Physiocratic School suggested that the development of human societies depended upon the size of the agricultural surplus which that society could produce and, since that time, this idea has been the focus of development theory. This agricultural surplus was the total food surplus produced in a given society, and the Physiocrats saw population increase as a means to increase this surplus. However, the classical economists, by developing their theory of diminishing returns to labor use in agriculture, focused upon the agricultural surplus per head of population. Malthus suggested that population increase would gradually reduce this surplus and end by eliminating the whole surplus, thus arresting development and causing starvation.[1]

Ester Boserup has held administrative and research posts with the Danish government and with the United Nations. She is the author of *Conditions of Agricultural Growth* (Chicago, 1965) and *Population and Technological Change* (Chicago, 1981).

---

1   Thomas R. Malthus, *An Essay on the Principle of Population* (London, 1798; reprinted 1970).

There was an escape from the Malthusian population trap. Technological improvement in agriculture could raise the productivity of land and labor, thus making it possible to feed a larger population. But, unless technological change in agriculture was rapid, as it is in industrialized societies, the escape was assumed to be only temporary, because the surplus created by technological progress would be "eaten up" by further population increase, due to improved nutrition.

This neo-Malthusian theory is unrealistic for more than one reason. First, technological progress in agriculture would not result in further population growth in cases where factors other than insufficient food supply were the effective restraints on population. Second, the malnourished were always the poor, and they would sometimes lose more than they gained by changes in agricultural technology, at least in the short run. Thus their mortality might not decline and might even increase. Third, and even more important, the Malthusian theory overlooks the effect of population increase on technological change. We have recent examples of this effect in the Green Revolution and modern birth control techniques. Both were developed as a result of research promoted by fear of rapid population growth in unindustrialized countries. Also, in earlier periods of history, the need to feed larger populations led to technology transfers from one society to another or to the invention of new methods and tools.[2]

Population increase has two different effects on systems of production: the one, on which the Malthusian theory focuses, is the negative effect of diminishing returns, when the existing agricultural system must feed more people. But this situation provides motivation for the introduction of more intensive systems of production and these changes may or may not raise the productivity of land and labor depending upon local circumstances. The other effect of population increase is to make it possible to build, and finance the building of, collective investments in physical and human infrastructure of various types, especially investment in water regulation, energy supply, and transportation. Because a larger population can afford more infrastructure, it can

---

2 Boserup, *Population and Technological Change. A Study of Long-Term Trends* (Chicago, 1981).

make use of technologies which would be inapplicable or uneconomical for a smaller one. The positive effects of this will often outweigh any negative effects of a higher man-land ratio on food supply and development.

In other words, because population increase motivated and often facilitated technological change, its effects on development were often positive. We have seen many increasing populations with sufficient food supply and rapid development, and many stagnant populations with sufficient food supply and no development. But we have also seen increasing populations with insufficient food supply and no development, and increasing populations with insufficient food supply, widespread malnutrition among the poor, and rapid development. We look below at some important examples of these different patterns of demographic, technological, and nutritional conditions.

A people could adapt to increasing numbers by means other than the intensification of agriculture and the introduction of technological changes. They could increase total food supply by changing the diet from food which uses land extensively, for instance meat of large animals kept on natural pastures, to pork, poultry, and cereals. Or they could replace such land-intensive crops as cereals with tubers or roots that have higher food-value yields per acre. Another possibility could be to use the increasing military strength of a growing population to conquer land from neighbors, or impose food imports from them as a tribute. Food could also be obtained in exchange for other products. Finally, growing populations could adapt population size to food supply instead of adapting food supply to population either by inducing a part of the population to emigrate to another area, or by birth prevention or infanticide. The effects on development would be very different according to which of these means of adaptation were used.

FOOD SUPPLY AND DEVELOPMENT IN THE ANCIENT WORLD   In a primitive society, food supply is plentiful when the man-land ratio is very low, but becomes scarce when the population becomes larger. Even in regions of poor soil and unfavorable climate, a very small population may be able to obtain sufficient food by applying primitive techniques. If climatic conditions preclude agriculture, a population which is sufficiently small and widely scattered can obtain enough food by hunting, pastoralism, or fishing, but in such a region food supplies will fall short as soon as the population density exceeds a very low level. In areas of better climate and soil, the limit between easy and difficult food supply will be at higher population densities, but there will be a limit where plenty gives way to scarcity, unless the methods of obtaining food are changed.

There can be little doubt that population trends in prehistory varied from one period to another, and from one people to another, as was the case in later periods for which we have better information. Some prehistoric peoples no doubt died out, either as a result of sudden catastrophies or because mortality exceeded fertility during long periods. Other peoples avoided an increase in the man-land ratio in their original habitat either by migration, by infanticide and exposure of children, or by high mortality from disease, war, or starvation. If their numbers did not increase, they were likely to continue as hunter gatherers or pastoralists, and as late as 1500 A.D. such peoples occupied most of the world, except for Europe and parts of Asia. However, some peoples increased their numbers slowly and adapted to increasing man-land ratios by eating new types of foods, and later by introducing systematic food production.[3]

Within the group of peoples who introduced food production, there were wide differences in population trends. Most of the early food producing peoples seem to have used long-fallow systems. Such systems are still widespread in Africa, Latin America, and parts of Asia, but they cannot support high population densities. If population increases, land which has been fallowed for the usual number of years becomes scarce, so that it becomes necessary to shorten the fallow period.[4]

However, fallowing serves many purposes; it preserves the land's fertility, reduces weeds and plant disease, and protects against erosion. Before industrially made chemicals and other

3 Richard B. Lee and Irven de Vore (eds.), *Man, the Hunter* (Chicago, 1968); Mark N. Cohen, *The Food Crisis in Prehistory* (New Haven, 1977).
4 Boserup, *The Conditions of Agricultural Growth. The Economics of Agrarian Change under Population Pressure* (Chicago, 1965).

industrial inputs existed, the shortening of the fallow period necessitated the use of additional labor to gather and spread fertilizing matter, weed, remove diseased plants, create mounds or terraces, and perhaps water the crops or drain the land.

The need for such additional labor and capital inputs was—and still is—a deterrent to the introduction of more intensive systems of agriculture, as long as the man-land ratio was low enough to allow the land to lie fallow for long periods. When fallow was shortened or abandoned, labor-intensive techniques had to be used. If such techniques were not known, or if they remained unused to avoid additional labor and capital inputs, crop yields declined and the land was often damaged. The result was starvation and malnutrition, unless the population was reduced by migration or infanticide, or unless food was imported or more territory could be conquered.

A number of peoples, widely scattered over the world, avoided these pitfalls when they shifted to more intensive agricultural systems. By gradually making land-use more and more intensive, they supported long-term rates of population growth, which may have amounted, with some large fluctuations, to an average of 0.1 percent annually.[5]

Some of these peoples, who in the millennia before our era increased from small numbers to more than a million, inhabited the Mesopotamian Plain and the surrounding mountains. A large number of excavations have shown that settlement began in the mountains with gathering and pastoralism, which were increasingly replaced by agriculture. As the population continued to grow, part of the increase was accommodated in the mountains through the intensification of agriculture and the development of small systems of flow irrigation. Another part of the population increase chose emigration to the plains, where it continued with irrigated agriculture and gradually, as the population continued to grow, built systems of flow irrigation.[6]

5 George L. Cowgill, "On Causes and Consequences of Ancient and Modern Population Changes," *American Anthropologist*, LXXVII (1975), 505–525.
6 Philip E.L. Smith and T. Cuyler Young, "The Evolution of Early Agriculture and Culture in Greater Mesopotamia," in Brian Spooner (ed.), *Population Growth: Anthropological Implications* (Cambridge, Mass., 1972), 1–59; Robert McC. Adams, *Land behind Bagdad* (Chicago, 1965); idem and Hans J. Nissen, *The Uruk Countryside* (Chicago, 1976).

The Mesopotamians and other peoples in Asia and the Mediterranean region, who had developments of this type, gradually invented, or imported from each other many techniques which intensified their agriculture. One of these techniques was flow irrigation, which solved both the problem of water supply and that of fertilization in regions like Mesopotamia, where the rivers carried silt, which was spread over the fields by annual overflows. Moreover, the Mesopotamians imported oxen, suitable for draft power, and iron, and they either invented or imported plowing techniques. Much later, they imported different methods to lift water, so that the irrigation networks could be further enlarged. It was long believed that these inventions enabled the Mesopotamian peasants not only to multiply many times, but also to produce food surpluses, which could feed at first a number of small towns, and later a number of large cities.

However, archaeological research in other parts of the world has revealed that large scale urbanization occurred also among peoples who did not benefit from any of these techniques. For instance, the Mayan people in Mesoamerica built their urban centers and huge temples although they only had tools of stone and hardened clay. They had no draft animals or plows, but relied exclusively on human muscle power and stone-age tools for all of their intensive agricultural operations and construction activities. Fertilization was not provided by the overflow of silt-laden rivers; instead the Mayans relied on labor inputs and performed the ardous task of handweeding. Recent research has shown that, in the period of high population density in the Mayan region, that is, in the first millennium A.D., the Mayas created walled and elevated fields and terraces, and dug canals in order to drain their fields and perhaps for transportation. In the Mayan area, transportation was effected exclusively by human muscle power, in contrast to Mesopotamia, where boats were drawn upstream by wind power and wheeled waggons were drawn by animals.[7]

No doubt, life was very difficult for the Mayan peasants, and some exhumed skeletons show signs of malnutrition; but the

7 William T. Sanders, "Population, Agricultural History, and Societal Evolution in Mesoamerica," in Spooner (ed.), *Population Growth*, 101–153; Peter D. Harrison and B.L. Turner (eds.), *Prehistoric Maya Agriculture* (Albuquerque, 1978).

example of the Mayas demonstrates that an urban civilization with monumental structures, a written language, and a large population, could be created by peoples with very primitive tools and difficult conditions of food production and transportation.[8]

If we compare the conditions of the Mayas in the period of urbanization with those of European peasants north of the Alps, it is clear that it was much more difficult for a Mayan peasant family to produce an agricultural surplus than it was for a European peasant family. The average population density in that part of Europe was still very low. According to the available estimates, there were only five to ten persons per square kilometer and long-fallow and pastoralism were the predominent food-supply systems. For many millennia, the Europeans had been importing food-supply techniques from Asia and North Africa. They used crops of Asian origin, scratch plows operated by oxen, and iron weapons and tools. Irrigation, and the heavy work and capital investment it required, was not needed because of the humid climate, and long-fallow techniques saved them from arduous labor with fertilization and weeding. Their animals fed on natural pastures and forests. If ever we could talk of ancient agricultural peoples who had plentiful food, the inhabitants of Europe would seem to be among them. They combined a low man-land ratio with advanced technologies—according to the standards of that time—while the Mayas combined a high man-land ratio with very primitive technology.

Nevertheless, it was the Mayas, with all their handicaps in food supply, and not the Europeans, who developed an urban civilization. In Europe north of the Alps indigenous urbanization appeared only in the beginning of this millennium. In the Roman period, agricultural surpluses north of the Alps fed only some Roman settlements, and even these seem, at least partially, to have relied on supplies of cereals that came from Rome by sea and by river transportation.[9]

The comparison between the Mayas and the inhabitants of Europe illustrates that the condition for development of an urban

---

8 Lawrence J. Angel, "Paleoecology, Paleodemography, and Health," in Steven Polger (ed.), *Population, Ecology, and Social Evolution* (The Hague, 1975), 167–190.
9 Moses I. Finley, *The Ancient Economy* (London, 1973).

civilization is not the ability of a population to produce a large agricultural surplus per family. The Europeans could no doubt have done that much better than the Mayas. In fact, the tribute paid by the Mayan peasants was not at a high level per family, but the number of families who contributed to the total agricultural surplus was very large, and this is what mattered for urbanization.

If man-land ratios were low in ancient times and the population was scattered, as it had to be in order to use labor-saving long-fallow techniques, food surpluses had to be moved over long distances in order to supply a town of more than a few thousand non-food-producing persons. But in ancient societies land transportation over more than some eight to ten kilometers was unfeasible or uneconomical, and only very densely populated regions could afford to build networks of canals linking producers to urban consumers. All economic historians stress the importance of transportation facilities for urbanization, but few have noted the close correlation between population density and the feasibility of creating transportation networks.[10]

A powerful empire could build strategic highways through sparsely populated areas, but long-distance bulk transportation of food on such highways was uneconomical with the primitive equipment of those times. Moreover, the highways and other roads deteriorated quickly if the empire lacked the power or the motive to use and repair them. Thus, because of the dependence of urban centers on food transportation, a certain population density was a necessary but not sufficient condition for urbanization. To judge from the few estimates of population density that are available, it seems that small towns were established in regions with some thirty to sixty inhabitants per square kilometer. Large cities of 100,000 appeared only in regions with much higher densities, or with exceptionally good possibilities for obtaining bulk supplies of food by long distance water transport, as was the situation with Rome and Athens.[11]

Peasants, like the Europeans, who were using long-fallow agriculture in sparsely populated regions, could not become sup-

10 Finley, *Ancient Economy*.
11 Sanders and Barbara J. Price, *Mesoamerica: The Evolution of a Civilization* (New York, 1968).

pliers of basic food to urban centers. For lack of transportation facilities, they remained isolated subsistence producers. Sometimes they produced surpluses for a scattered upper class who lived in small numbers in the villages, but these people did not benefit from the cross fertilization of ideas and the access to systematic training and education, from which elites living together in urban centers could benefit. So development occurred not where food was plentiful, but where population density was so high that many people lived together and created and maintained an infrastructure, which facilitated communication both within the centers and between different centers.[12]

THE BREAKDOWN AND DECAY OF ANCIENT CULTURES   The high man-land ratio in ancient urbanized societies made obtaining food difficult, but it was a necessary condition for building the infrastructure on which these societies depended. Given the labor-intensive technologies of those times, the cities with their walls, fortifications, huge temples, and palaces could not have been built had the dense populations not provided a large labor force. Also the necessary rural infrastructure, transportation facilities, and flow-irrigation systems required a large and densely settled population to perform the manual labor.

Most ruling classes in ancient societies created infrastructures by means of obligatory labor services performed by peasants when they were not needed in the fields. Part of such labor services was directly related to food production, such as the building, cleaning, and repair of dams and irrigation canals, or work on the agricultural holdings of the upper class. But other activities performed by peasant labor were the construction of temples, palaces, castles, city walls, and transportation facilities, and military service. As the peasants used more and more intensive agricultural systems in step with the increase in the man-land ratio, the seasons without work in the fields became shorter, and a conflict arose as to whether labor should be used in the fields, for irrigation and other agriculture-related activities, or for non-agricultural purposes.[13]

12 Gordon W. Childe, *New Light on the Most Ancient East* (London, 1952).
13 Karl A. Wittvogel, *Oriental Despotism* (New Haven, 1957).

The conflict became acute when flow-irrigation systems became extensive. As long as only the area with natural overflow was under cultivation, good yields could be obtained with a relatively small input of labor; but when a large system had to be cleaned and repaired each year after the annual floods, the process became labor-intensive for a lengthy period each year. This was true even for systems which used animal draft power. Draft animals are not an efficient source of energy, if population density becomes so high that the animals cannot be fed on natural pastures and human labor must be used to provide fodder for them. The mechanical energy supplied by animals is only a few percent of the energy contained in the fodder that they consume.

Moreover, the silt which fertilized the fields became a mixed blessing when the systems became large and the silt clogged the canals, ditches, and the river itself. Interference with the flow of the rivers meant that more and more of the silt was deposited before the rivers reached the sea, but the enormous silt deposits made cleaning the system more and more difficult.[14]

Comparison of an early stage of urban development in Mesopotamia with a late stage of development in China illustrates the magnitude of the labor problem. At an early stage of urbanization in Lower Mesopotamia, peasants had to perform labor services for temple building for four months each year; at that time the Mesopotamian irrigation system was not very demanding of labor. By contrast, when Buck in the 1920s surveyed the input of labor in Chinese agriculture, he found that the months free of field labor amounted only to one and a half on average for the whole of China, and most of this period was accounted for by winter unemployment in the dry-farming areas of northern China. The irrigated southern parts of China had hardly any periods during which peasant families were not fully occupied in fields and on farms.[15]

The causes of the breakdown of the Mesopotamian system in the twelfth century A.D. were war damage to the irrigation system and silting up the rivers. When wars disturbed a flow-irrigation system, or just prevented regular cleaning and mainte-

14 Adams, *Land behind Bagdad*.
15 John Lossing Buck, *Land Utilization in China* (Nanking, 1937).

nance, the whole system or parts of it broke down. The population had to emigrate or starve. Sometimes malaria appeared and made the region uninhabitable, as happened in the environs of Rome when the Empire broke down, and in Sri Lanka in the twelfth century A.D. after wars with India. In China, the silting up of the rivers which had been dammed with dikes resulted in huge floods in recent centuries. Damage to these dikes, due to war or poor maintenance, caused floods which killed millions by drowning or famine. In parts of India, salinization and ill-conceived British land reforms caused the decay of the flow-irrigation systems, because the landlords, who had financed maintenance and repairs by means of high crop shares, lacked both the means and the motives for maintenance, when rents were fixed and gradually diminished in value.[16]

Although the reasons for the breakdown or decay of many of the ancient civilizations are well documented, the reasons for the abandonment of the Mayan core area more than half a millennium before the arrival of Spanish conquerors remains unexplained. The high labor demand of agricultural work with primitive equipment could explain why the Mayas had to stop building temples, and why part or all of the excess population had to emigrate; but it could not explain why the whole population deserted the area, died out, or moved to neighboring mountain areas. It has been suggested that low-lying areas had once been shallow lakes, which silted up. If so, waterborne diseases or devastating epidemics due to new contacts may have induced the population to leave the area, but there is no evidence to support these hypotheses.[17]

FROM PLENTY TO SCARCITY IN WESTERN EUROPE   Heavy investments in infrastructure for agriculture made urban civilizations with flow irrigation vulnerable to demographic change. Decline in population was likely to cause a catastrophe, because the labor force became too small to maintain the network. Its humid climate saved Western Europe from such catastrophes when population

16   E.L. Jones, *The Economic Miracle. Environment, Ecology, and Geopolitics in the History of Europe and Asia* (Cambridge, 1981); Boserup, *Agricultural Growth.*
17   Harrison and Turner, *Maya Agriculture.*

declined. Both in the first millennium A.D. and in most of the second, population size in Western Europe fluctuated as a result of wars and epidemics, but such events caused no permanent damage to the food supply system. When population increased, fallow was shortened and pastures and forests were transformed into fields. When population declined, fallow periods again became longer, and some of the fields reverted to permanent pasture and forest, until the next period of population increase once more reversed the trend.[18]

The population of Western Europe seems to have adapted to these changes by consuming less animal and more vegetable food per head when population increased, and the reverse when it declined. These shifts in consumption seem to have been induced by changes in the relationship between wages and prices of cereals. In times of population increase, prices of cereals increased more than wages, thus forcing wage earners to reduce their intake of animal products, whereas high wages in relation to prices of cereals, for instance in the period of low population density after the Black Death, made more money available for the purchase of animal products.[19]

The major shifts to more intensive food supply systems in Western Europe occurred during two long periods of population growth. In the first, between the ninth and the fourteenth centuries A.D., during which population seems to have doubled twice, pastoralism and long-fallow agriculture were gradually replaced by short-fallow systems, except for the Low Countries, which had higher densities than elsewhere and introduced annual cropping. The second large wave of population increase occurred in the eighteenth and nineteenth centuries, in which numbers again doubled twice or more in most countries. This multiplication of population was accompanied by a gradual change from short-fallow systems to annual cropping with fodder production. In both periods there was population pressure in some areas, before the existing systems were replaced by more intensive ones

18 B.H. Slicher van Bath, *The Agrarian History of Western Europe, A.D. 500–1500* (New York, 1963).

19 Jean Fourastie, *L'Evolution des Prix a Long Terme* (Paris, 1969); E. Henry Phelps Brown and Sheila V. Hopkins, *A Perspective of Wages and Prices* (New York, 1981).

but, by and large, Western European agriculture adapted flexibly to the demographic changes.[20]

This adaptability of the populations to changes in density does not mean that there was neither malnutrition nor famine in Europe in the period of preindustrial urbanization. We must distinguish between long-term scarcities of food caused by increasing population pressure, and short-term scarcities due to climatic fluctuations, interruptions in agricultural operations, and other disturbances in years of wars or epidemics. Such events would cause famines in regions with abundant reserves of cultivable land, and the food scarcities in Western Europe in the period of preindustrial urbanization seem to have been mainly of this type.

In the last centuries before the Industrial Revolution, these short-term food scarcities were serious, but they were due not to shortages of cultivable land, but to shortages of agricultural labor. Food became scarce either because the non-agricultural population grew more rapidly than the agricultural labor force, or because the agricultural labor force declined in periods when the overall population size remained constant. Urbanization had been late north of the Alps due to low population densities, but when it finally appeared in a period of increasing population density in the twelfth and thirteenth centuries A.D., there was a burst of activity during which imports of techniques and knowledge from more advanced parts of the world supplemented indigenous inventions.

The building of the towns with their cathedrals, palaces, universities, and fortifications, and the manning of arms factories, workshops, trading firms, and other urban activities were made possible by pulling labor out of agriculture. Armies also drew labor from agriculture in times of both peace and war. Although European agriculture could adapt flexibly to parallel changes in the demand for food and the supply of labor, that is, to overall population growth, it was much less flexible when it had to raise output per worker than when it had to raise total output by using additional labor.

The mulboard plow, equipped with a piece of iron which turned the soil, had been introduced and there had been other

---

20 Boserup, *Population and Technological Change.*

technical improvements during the first wave of population growth. But in the centuries before the Industrial Revolution there were few, if any, agricultural changes which improved labor productivity. Therefore, the effective restraint on food production was the lack of labor to utilize the existing potential for increase in output. For lack of labor, the area sown with crops was sufficient only to feed the population in years of normal harvest, but when the harvest was small, for climatic or other reasons, food became scarce, prices soared, and the poor went hungry. Also, peasants starved when they were unable to retain sufficient stocks for themselves, because these were confiscated for use by the army and the urban population, as happened in France in 1709–10.[21]

The development of London between 1500 and 1700 provides an example of the problem. Its population increased from some 50,000 to more than 500,000, and the whole urban population of England seems to have increased eightfold. But the rural population only doubled, and the agricultural labor force grew even less. Although more and more distant areas were drawn in as suppliers of London, the food situation was precarious, and in years of bad harvest the needs of London were met by reducing the food supply of the rural population.[22]

It was suggested earlier that the plentiful food supply in Europe in the pre-urban period had not facilitated development. In the urban period, with its frequent short-term scarcities, these food scarcities did not prevent the rapid urban development that took place. Food scarcities were the result of the rapid urban development and the armaments race in Western Europe, which accompanied increasing urbanization.

FOOD SUPPLY AND THE INDUSTRIAL REVOLUTION   Much of the discussion of the impact of food scarcity or plenty on Western European development is focused on the role of agriculture in the Industrial Revolution. Some historians have suggested that agri-

21 David B. Griegg, *Population Growth and Agrarian Change. A Historical Perspective* (Cambridge, 1980); Louise A. Tilly, "La Revolte Frumentaire, Forme de Conflit Politique en France," *Annales,* XXVII (1972), 731–757.
22 James D. Chambers and G. E. Mingay, *The Agrarian Revolution, 1750–1880* (London, 1966).

culture played a leading role. An agricultural revolution starting in the eighteenth century, or even earlier, should have stimulated the beginning of the Industrial Revolution by raising agricultural productivity, thus ending the period of Malthusian food shortages and permitting large transfers of labor from agriculture to industry.[23]

To evaluate this theory, we must try to answer two questions. Did the changes which have been labeled the "Agricultural Revolution" increase productivity, not only of land, but also of labor? And, did the changes which culminated in the Industrial Revolution originate in the agricultural sector? We begin with the latter question.

The Industrial Revolution was brought about by an acceleration of the rapid technological changes in Western Europe in the period of pre-industrial urbanization. Recurrent food shortages in this period had not prevented the growth of non-agricultural activities, but had been the result of it. That period had not, as is often believed, been one of labor surplus, but one in which urban activities and a demand for soldiers had competed with agriculture for labor. Therefore, the urban sector had not always found it easy to recruit the necessary labor, which had provided the motive for experiments with labor-saving techniques. Such techniques became more and more widespread even before the Industrial Revolution, but their use increased during the Industrial Revolution and after.

Moreover, as cultivation expanded in response to population increases, forest areas, and thus timber, fuel, and charcoal for iron production, became more and more scarce, just as the technological changes raised the demand for these products. Experiments with the use of coal for iron production had been going on over a period of 200 years, and when they finally succeeded toward the end of the eighteenth century, the shortages of energy and raw materials were overcome and the Industrial Revolution became possible. Industrial changes, therefore, had their origin in the industrial sector and not in the agricultural one, which only adapted to the industrial changes, but did not release them.[24]

23   Paul Bairoch, *Revolution Industrielle et Sous-Developement* (Paris, 1969).
24   E. Anthony Wrigley, "The Supply of Raw Materials in the Industrial Revolution," *Economic History Review*, XV (1962), 1–16.

As to labor productivity in agriculture, it is generally agreed that the agricultural changes which had major labor-saving effects, that is, the use of non-agricultural inputs like chemical fertilizer and oilcake, and horsedriven mechanization, only became important in the middle of the nineteenth century, or later. The changes in the eighteenth century and the beginning of the nineteenth century, among which the elimination of fallow and the introduction of fodder production were the most important, were of the type which raised total output by means of additional labor inputs, so the agricultural labor force continued to increase. Because the rate of population growth accelerated, the non-agricultural population could also increase.

The change to fodder production was prompted by an increasing demand for meat and dairy products from members of the new urban middle class. This demand raised prices of animal products so much that fodder production became profitable; as a result livestock numbers, the output of livestock products, and the availability of manure increased. But much additional labor was needed to produce grains, turnips, potatoes, and other fodder in areas which had been devoted to fallow and natural pasture. Some of this labor was supplied by population increase, and some was provided in seasons which had hitherto been idle. Women, children, and other family members who had previously done little agricultural work had more to do. Some of these family members had produced textiles and other non-agricultural products for home consumption, but when the prices of such products declined steeply, home production was replaced by the purchase of industrial products. Home workers either gave more help in agriculture, or they began to work in or for the new factories.[25]

In this period, peasant families obtained higher real incomes mainly by working many more hours in agriculture, while real output per work hour probably declined, due to the intensification of agriculture, especially fodder production. Some figures are

---

25 Phelps Brown and Hopkins, *Perspective*; D.M. Snell, "Agricultural Seasonal Unemployment, the Standard of Living, and Women's Work in the South and East, 1690–1860," *Economic History Review*, XXXIII (1981), 407–437; Eighth International Economic History Congress, *Female Labour Before, During, and After the Industrial Revolution* (Budapest 1982).

available for Denmark: during the period 1818 to 1836, agricultural output per male worker in Denmark declined 0.1 percent annually; during the whole period 1818 to 1876, it increased only 0.2 percent annually. If account is taken of the increase in labor input per male worker and per family due to the change in the seasonal patterns of work and the increasing use of female labor, there must have been a substantial decline of output per work hour, especially in the period first mentioned. But living standards increased for the agricultural population as a whole, due to an annual improvement of more than 1 percent in sectoral terms of trade and terms of trade with other countries. (Denmark exported agricultural products and imported industrial manufactures.)[26]

Many historians have described the agricultural changes in the eighteenth century as a revolutionary change from a Malthusian to a post-Malthusian era. This is no doubt because acute short-term food scarcities ceased, except for the Irish tragedy. Famines disappeared in Western Europe, partly because the potato now provided a hunger crop for the poor, and partly because the feeding of domestic animals, especially pigs and poultry, on grains provided a buffer stock in years of poor cereal harvests. Previously, soaring grain prices in years of poor harvest had forced the poor to starve. Now, fluctuations in grain prices between good and poor harvest years became smaller, because pigs, poultry, and grain-fed cattle were slaughtered in years of poor harvest, and the stock was replenished in years of good harvest. Moreover, improved transportation and increasing intro-European trade in agricultural products averted regional and national short-term scarcities.[27]

Apart from the disappearance of the famines, it is doubtful whether the nutritional conditions of the lower classes improved. Income inequality increased during the Industrial Revolution, and the increase in production of animal food went mainly to the growing middle class.

ABUNDANCE AND DEVELOPMENT IN NORTH AMERICA   For the European settlers, North America was an area of plentiful food

---

26   Svend Aage Hansen, *Økonomisk Vækst i Danmark* (Copenhagen, 1972).
27   Griegg, *Population Growth*; Phelps Brown and Hopkins, *Perspective*.

supply, but in contrast to ancient Europe and other sparsely populated regions, for instance Africa, the plentiful food supply did
not delay, but promoted development. The difference between
ancient Europe and Africa, on the one hand, and North America
on the other, is explained to a large extent by the differences in
the pattern of settlement. The population in ancient Europe—like
most of the African population—was widely scattered, which
prevented the development of transportation networks and urbanization. In North America a minority of the early immigrants
scattered as hunter-gatherers in the large forests, but most of the
immigrants concentrated in areas close to the harbors of arrival
or in places linked to these by water transportation. They were
accustomed to a certain standard of infrastructure in their European villages and towns, and they made a compromise between
the desire for larger land holdings than those of European peasants, and a not too widely scattered settlement, which made some
infrastructure investment feasible. In this way, they were able to
choose the man-land ratio which was optimal for the technology
at their disposal. As a result their agricultural system was less
intensive than that of Europe, their output per worker was higher,
and the output of land was much lower—which did not matter,
since land was plentiful.

I am not aware of any quantitative comparisons between
American and European agriculture in the period of early settlement, but a comparison for 1880, when mass exports of cereals
from America to Europe began, is reproduced in Table 1.

In 1880, the agricultural area per male worker in the United
States was three to four times that of continental Western Europe.
Output per hectare was half as large and output per male worker
was larger. Land had remained plentiful in North America in spite
of the extremely rapid increase of population because gradually,
as immigration continued, the settlers had moved further west in
step with the creation of the necessary infrastructure. A plentiful
supply of land had provided the motivation for the improvement
of farm equipment, which was lacking in most of Western Europe
because of the small size of agricultural holdings. Mechanization
of agriculture took place much earlier in America than in Europe,
and the westward movement was accompanied by a gradual increase in the size of farms in the newly settled areas compared to
the areas of early settlement on the East Coast. Large farms in

Table 1   Agricultural Output in Seven Countries

	HECTARES PER MALE WORKER		OUTPUT PER HECTARE		OUTPUT PER MALE WORKER		FERTILIZER KILOS PER HECTARE	TRACTORS NUMBER WORKERS PER TRACTOR
	1880	1970	1880	1970	1880	1970	1970	1970
United States	25	165	0.5	1	13	157	89	1
England	17	34	1	3	16	88	258	—
Denmark	9	18	1	5	11	94	223	2
France	7	16	1	4	7	60	241	3
Germany	6	12	1	5	8	65	400	—
Japan	1	2	3	10	2	16	386	45
India	—	2	—	1	—	2	13	2.600[a]

NOTE: Hectares refer to agricultural area, i.e. to all land in farms. Agricultural output refers to output of both crops and animal products (excluding fodder consumed by the farm animals). This output has been recalculated in wheat units, equivalent to one ton of wheat, by Hayami and Ruttan (see source note below). Workers include adult male workers, but not women and children. The kilos of chemical fertilizer are measured in fertilizer content per hectare of arable land, i.e. agricultural area minus pasture and fallow.

SOURCES: Hans P. Binswanger and Vernon W. Ruttan, *Induced Innovation, Technology, Institutions, and Development* (Baltimore, 1978); Yujiro Hayami and Ruttan, *Agricultural Development: an International Perspective* (Baltimore, 1971); UNRISD, *Data Bank of Development Indicators* (Geneva, 1976); United Nations, *Implementation of the International Development Strategy* (New York, 1973).

a   1961–1965 average.

the Midwest and on the West Coast of America had a much higher output of labor in cereal production than European farms, and when technological improvements in transportation equipment reduced the price of bulk transportation over the oceans, North America became so competitive that a serious crisis in European agriculture resulted from the mass imports of cheap American cereals. This crisis led to a further delay in the modernization of European agriculture, except in a few areas which specialized in animal production based upon American fodder grains and oilcake.

Because the immigrants concentrated in the East, before they moved further west, it did not take long for the East to reach sufficient densities for both urbanization and industrialization. Due to high rates of population growth, the development of both industrial and agricultural production was much more rapid than in Europe. The technological gap between American and European agriculture widened between 1880 and 1970, as can be seen from Table 1. In 1970, the agricultural area per male worker in the United States was five to ten times larger than that in Western Europe, output per hectare was one third to one fifth, and output per male worker two to three times larger. Much less fertilizer and more mechanized equipment were used in America. Demand for rural transportation over longer distances than in Europe and for mechanized agricultural equipment helped to develop motor vehicles, which became a leading sector in American industrialization that soon overtook that of Europe.[28]

FOOD IMPORTS AND DEVELOPMENT IN THE THIRD WORLD   We have seen that the link between agricultural surplus and development is much more complicated than is usually assumed. In some cases, plenty of food has been an obstacle to development; in other cases, development has been rapid under extremely difficult conditions of food supply. We began by distinguishing between attempts to adapt food supply to increasing demand due to population growth and attempts to adjust demand to supply. The first alternative often promoted development, whereas effects on development of the second alternative, that is, emigration and birth control, were less positive and sometimes negative. But the effects of such measures vary widely according to the rate of growth of population, the technological level, and natural resources.

When we note that adaptation of food supply to demand often had positive effects on development, it should also be noted that there seems to be one important exception: in several cases, attempts to adapt food supply to increasing demand by means of large scale food imports discouraged local food production and had negative effects on development. When Rome was supplied with food from the colonies, the Roman peasants were ruined and went to live in Rome on food aid. European food imports from America retarded the modernization of European agriculture, as mentioned above, and a similar phenomenon has occurred on a very large scale in many developing countries in recent decades when rates of population growth accelerated and increasing demand was met by large scale imports of basic food on commercial or concessional terms.

28 Douglass C. North, "Industrialization in the United States," *Cambridge Economic History of Europe* (Cambridge, 1966), VI, 673–705.

When the demographic transition in the developing countries accelerated after World War II, it was generally believed that widespread famines would be unavoidable—some said before 1980—or that birth control was the only means to avoid them. Most economists assumed that agricultural output was unresponsive to population growth, because there was assumed to be a large labor surplus in agriculture in unindustrialized countries. Many Asian countries were densely populated and there was little appreciation of how far agriculture could be intensified with traditional means. Many other countries were sparsely populated, but because of the general belief in the Malthusian population theory, these countries were assumed to have sub-marginal land which could not feed large additional populations.[29]

These opinions had important effects upon agricultural policy. Since the scope for additional food production was grossly underestimated, little was done in most of the developing countries to promote investments in agriculture and in rural infrastructure. Government policies were aimed at encouraging urban development in order to move as much as possible of the rural surplus labor into urban employment. The resulting rapid increase in urban demand for food was filled by imports and aid. In the industrialized countries, income support to agriculture had encouraged the production of increasing surpluses. It was believed that the transfer of these surpluses by aid or trade provided the best means of preventing famines and malnutrition in the developing countries.

As a result of the urban bias in government policies in most developing countries and the increasing food imports, income differentials between urban and rural areas widened in the food importing countries. Rural-urban migration was large and the growth of food production sluggish and often less rapid than population growth. The gap between urban demand for food and its supply was filled by further increases in food imports. The cereal imports of developing countries increased from 40 million tons in the early 1970s to 96 million tons in 1980/81, and it has

29 René Dumont and Bernard Rosier, *The Hungry Future* (London, 1969); Boserup, *Agricultural Growth*; idem, "Food Supply and Population in Developing Countries," in Nurul Islam (ed.), *Agricultural Policy in Developing Countries* (London, 1974), 164–176.

been suggested that they may increase to 333 million tons in 2030.[30]

The neglect by governments in developing countries of rural infrastructure had the worst effects in sparsely populated countries, in which the existing rural infrastructure was much poorer than in most of the densely populated countries. The densely populated countries have at least some regions with good transportation and other infrastructural facilities which are necessary for commercial production and even more for the modernization of agriculture. Moreover, because of the belief that land reserves were small everywhere, research in agriculture focused on raising crop yields by means of large purchased inputs, especially fertilizer. The result has been a very rapid increase in food output in some densely populated regions with a better infrastructure than is usual for rural districts in developing countries, but not in both sparsely populated areas and densely populated ones with a poor infrastructure where the new techniques have not been applicable. Therefore, densely populated regions of East Asia and some districts of India with a good infrastructure have had extremely rapid increases in food production and both rural and urban industrialization, whereas most of Africa and Latin America, with their much larger unutilized potentials for food production, have had much less expansion, and sometimes declines of output of cereals, due to competition from imports.[31]

It was indicated above that, in India, progress in food production varied between districts with good and poor infrastructures. Around 1970, 15 percent of the districts in India employed 80 percent of the chemical fertilizer used in the country. The level of fertilizer application per hectare in these favored districts was around one third that of Western Europe, whereas the rest of India used some three kilos per hectare, which is the same as saying that they did not use chemical fertilizers on food crops. The low level of fertilizer consumption largely explains the rural misery and malnutrition of large parts of India. The area of arable land per inhabitant in India is in the same ratio as in Western

---

30 Boserup, "Population and Agricultural Productivity," United Nations (ed.), *The Population Debate* (New York, 1975), I, 498–501. F.A.O. figures quoted from OECD, *Development Cooperation, 1981 Review* (Paris, 1981). Nurul Islam, "Food," in Just Fåland (ed.), *Population and the World Economy in the Twenty-First Century* (Oxford, 1982).

31 Boserup, *Population and Technological Change.*

Europe but, primarily because of the lack of fertilizer and high yielding seeds, output per hectare is as low as that of Western Europe in 1880, that is, before massive fertilizer inputs were applied there (see Table 1). In 1970, output per hectare in Western Europe was three to five times that of India, and Japanese output per hectare was ten times that of India. Because of the low per hectare output and poor equipment, production per male worker in India was one eighth that of Japan, and only 2 to 3 percent that of parts of Western Europe with similar population densities to India.[32]

Food imports from the industrialized countries acted as a deterrent to investments in agriculture not only in the countries which received the food supplies, but also in food exporting developing countries. In nearly all the countries which today are highly industrialized, food exports have helped to finance their industrialization; but today the subsidized food exports from these industrialized countries, and their restrictive import policies for food, deter food exporters and potential food exporters in developing countries from investing in an expansion of their export production of those types of food which compete with food production in the industrialized countries. This reluctance is a serious handicap to development in countries at very low stages of development and with poor mineral resources.

The increasing dependence on imports of basic food in many developing countries does not only discourage local food production, it also enhances the risk of future food crises. On the export side, the world market in food is dependent upon a small number of exporters, who design the size and distribution of their food surpluses in response to pressure from farm interests and considerations of foreign policy. On the import side, world demand fluctuates widely from year to year, because of climatic changes and frequent crises in agriculture in communist countries. Poor of exporters, who design the size and distribution of their food surpluses in response to pressure from farm interests and considerations of foreign policy. On the import side, world demand fluctuates widely from year to year, because of climatic changes and frequent crises in agriculture in communist countries. Poor

32 Boserup, "Indian Agriculture from the Perspective of Western Europe," in J.S. Sarma, *Growth and Equity: Policies and Implementation in Indian Agriculture* (Washington, D.C., 1981), 55–58.

developing countries with low food stocks and small foreign exchange reserves are likely to be the losers in years in which world market demand exceeds supply. Reduction of imports and soaring food prices may result in starvation among the poor. A radical change in investment policy in favor of investments in food production to replace imports seems to be the only safe means to reduce the risk of famine in these developing countries.

The relationship between food scarcity and development is much more complicated than is assumed by Malthusian and neo-Malthusian theories. These theories focus on the negative effects of an increasing man-land ratio on food supply, but they have overlooked or underestimated the positive effects which increasing population may have on infrastructural investment and technological levels.

We have shown, on the one hand, that human societies with easy conditions of food supply remained at primitive stages of technological and intellectual development because their populations were too small and scattered for them to create the infrastructure necessary for the application of higher levels of technology, and because their populations were small enough to be able to feed themselves with primitive systems of food supply. On the other hand, we have seen examples in early and recent history of populations which imported or invented new technologies of food supply that only became applicable when these populations became larger and the change in man-land ratio made the use of new methods both necessary and possible. Such peoples entered a period—sometimes a very long one—in which technological improvements promoted further population growth and further population growth promoted further technological improvements in a beneficial upward spiral, instead of the vicious downward spiral on which the Malthusian school focused its attention.

Not everybody would be well supplied with food in a developing society which experienced a beneficial upward spiral in its population and income growth. Rapid urban development in Europe in the last centuries before the Industrial Revolution resulted in increasingly severe food crises in which the poor faced starvation. The advantages of technological change are never shared equally by all population groups, and both rapid urban and rapid agricultural development are likely to result in a deterioration of food supplies for some population groups. Also in many developing countries today the rapid growth of population and the rapid growth of average per capita income go together with malnutrition and sometimes starvation among the poor. But this does not necessarily arrest development, as long as the decision makers and the population groups which employ the new technologies benefit from the technological changes.

Nevin S. Scrimshaw

Functional Consequences of Malnutrition for Human Populations: A Comment

Nutritionists view the problem of hunger not only as the consequence of a deficit in food energy relative to need, but also as an inadequate intake of any essential nutrient, including amino acids as the building blocks of protein, vitamins, essential fatty acids, and at least a dozen minerals. Much of this hunger is hidden, and the individual is unaware of it. However, the functional consequences of hidden hunger in the development of human societies have probably been at least as important as those of overt hunger or famine.

When food intakes fall chronically below the amounts required for physiological energy balance, tissue wasting is inevitable and eventually death must ensue, as it frequently has in the past and as it is today in some countries as a result of war and civil disturbances. But far more hunger, including most due to inadequate food energy, is hidden. Whole populations are consuming an average of 10 to 20 percent fewer calories than their requirements, as estimated by the Food and Agriculture Organization and the World Health Organization (FAO/WHO), and for many individuals the intake is far less than this average. Yet these populations are not wasting away and dying of starvation. They have adapted physiologically, mainly by reducing their physical activity, and are in overall energy balance but at a social cost. Because work activities must be maintained for survival, it is discretionary activities that are the first to be sacrificed. Yet it is these activities that are needed for the development of the social infrastructure and the community, for home improvement, and for ancillary economic activities. The stereotype of the lazy peasant sleeping in the shade is all too often descriptive of a survival mechanism. For children this adaptation means less interaction with their environment at a critical age and, as a consequence,

Nevin S. Scrimshaw is Institute Professor at The Massachusetts Institute of Technology and Director of the United Nations University Sub-Program on Food, Nutrition, and Poverty. For further details see his article on 529 of this issue.

permanent cognitive deficiencies. In another kind of nutritional effect on physical capacity and work performance, a seemingly lazy and stupid peasant may be iron-deficient and will change his whole pattern of behavior after only a few days of supplementary iron.

There is currently much confusion about the number of those who are malnourished. An expert consultation by the FAO/WHO in 1975 pointed out that very sedentary individuals could survive at levels averaging only 50 percent above their basal metabolic rate, although this type of existence does not allow for either work or discretionary activities. It covers the amount of dietary energy required if an individual were to do nothing but sleep (the basal metabolic rate [BMR]), dress, eat, attend to personal hygiene, digest food, and do little else.

FAO statisticians reasoned that, if the coefficient of variation of BMR was 10 percent, as assumed in the expert committee reports, the absolute minimum for all but 2.5 percent of individuals would be 1.5 minus 20 percent (the mean minus 2 SD), or 1.2 × BMR. They then applied this figure to national food intake data to calculate the number of severely undernourished persons on the assumption that nearly all individuals below this figure would be beyond the limits of adaptation. However, this figure gives an underestimate of insufficient nutrition. There will be a statistically large and predictable proportion of individuals with intakes above 1.2 × BMR who are also beyond the limits of their capacity to adapt. It should also be clear that even 1.5 times basal metabolic rate is not sufficient either for productive economic activity or for long-term maintenance of health. The application of such a standard falls short of indicating the economic and social consequences of the reduced activity associated with low food intakes caused by poverty.

The above discussion illustrates the problems associated with evaluating even protein-calorie malnutrition with contemporary data. Clearly, the problems of trying to do so with historical data are even greater, especially when other nutrient deficiencies are taken into consideration. Boserup has started us on an exploration of the historical relationships among food intake, human survival, productivity, and welfare.[1]

---

1 Ester Boserup, "The Impact of Scarcity and Plenty on Development," in this issue.

We must also consider the synergistic interactions between social factors and the consequences of nutrition. These factors and consequences operate in both directions. The agricultural revolution, the industrial revolution, and other technological developments have had profound effects on human nutrition and its functional consequences that are rewarding topics for historical exploration. Conversely, as McKeown brings out in his article, the demographic characteristics of these periods were largely determined by the nutritional status of all of the people. Moreover, population growth and population density are not limited to the quantity of people, but must be viewed for their effects on the quality of a people. Thus, indicators of nutritional status such as physical growth and development, physical capacity, work output, cognitive performance, morbidity and mortality from infectious disease, and energy available for social development should be part of the judgment of the significance of food consumption patterns in any society at any period of time.[2]

2   Thomas McKeown, "Food, Infection, and Population," in this issue.

Julian L. Simon

The Effects of Population on Nutrition and Economic Well-Being

Why has there not been increased famine and poorer nourishment on average as the world's population has increased? Malthusian theory, with its elements of fixed land and diminishing returns to additional labor, provides no explanation. One escape route from the Malthusian trap is an increase in the supposedly fixed supply of land, and this has been the most important avenue of total food increase throughout history. But without an accompanying change in technology (including transportation), increases in the land supply must surely lead eventually to a lower standard of welfare, due both to the additional time and effort necessary to make smaller plots of land produce a living, and also due to the poorer harvest thereby produced. And it must be more and more difficult to increase the effective supply of land within given geographical bounds.[1]

Thomas Malthus therefore introduced a deus ex machina—the spontaneous invention of new farming practices which increase the possible food supply until consequent increases in population literally eat up the additional produce. This Malthusian device has led many writers to think that food and population growth have historically run a race in which the racing forces were independent. It has only been lucky chance, they have thought, that has kept food supply mostly in the lead.

This article develops the quite different theoretical scheme that food production and the way food is produced are very much affected by the demand for food, whereas effective demand depends mainly upon the size and the economic level of the population. This scheme suggests that an increased demand for food eventually leads to a more plentiful supply than would have resulted had demand remained at a lower level. But the long-run

Julian L. Simon is Professor of Economics at the University of Illinois, Urbana-Champaign and is now teaching at the University of Maryland. He is the author of *The Ultimate Resource* (Princeton, 1981) and *The Economics of Population Growth* (Princeton, 1977).

1 Thomas R. Malthus, *An Essay on the Principle of Population* (London, 1798; reprinted 1970).

benign trend should not obscure the short-run scarcities that have occurred in history before agricultural economies could respond to the increased demand.

This article does not present a systematic survey of the complex web of relationships through which population affects food supply (Figure 1), but rather presents data on the strands in Figure 1 marked with Roman numerals, corresponding to sections of the article. In addition, Section VI speculates about the effect of the loosening connection between land and nourishment upon conflict among nations.

I POPULATION AND ADOPTION OF INNOVATIONS IN SUBSISTENCE AGRICULTURE   The idea that the demand for food influences the *choice* of agricultural technique—either the choice among already used techniques, or the choice about whether to adopt an available technique for the first time—constitutes a challenge to the Malthusian system and conclusions. Malthus implicitly assumed that inventions are adopted immediately upon their discovery, a sequence which may be diagrammed as in Figure 2a.

Von Thunen pointed out, however, that the type of agricultural technology in use in a particular location depends upon the distance to the nearest city and therefore upon the population density. Engels argued, on the basis of Justus von Liebig's research, that, because of the possibilities of technical advance, mankind was not doomed by fixity of resources to live near subsistence level between population-increasing improvements in agriculture. But such views did not enter economic theory. Anthropologists, in their turn, have found considerable evidence that population density influences the mode of agricultural technique in use in primitive societies. But it was Boserup who fully developed the idea that, ceteris paribus, the length of fallow and the associated techniques and labor input depend upon population density, and that population growth leads to a shift to more labor-intensive techniques which are already known but are not in use at the time, and to a shortening of fallow.[2]

2 Johann H. von Thunen, *The Isolated State* (New York, 1966; orig. pub. 1826); Friedrich Engels, "The Myth of Overpopulation," from *Outlines of a Critique of Political Economy*, reprinted in Ronald L. Meek (ed.), *Marx and Engels on Malthus* (London, 1953); Brian Spooner (ed.), *Population Growth: Anthropological Implications* (Cambridge, Mass., 1972); Mark Nathan Cohen, *The Food Crisis in Prehistory* (New Haven, 1977); Ester Boserup, *The Conditions of Agricultural Growth* (London, 1965).

Fig. 1 Some of the Relationships between Population and Food

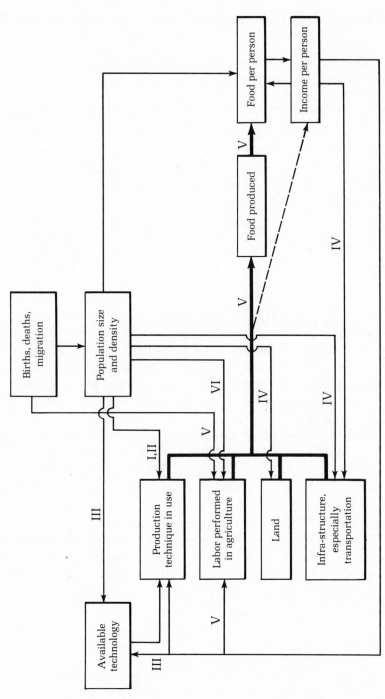

NOTE: Roman numerals indicate relationships discussed in the numbered sections of this article. Education, because it is not crucial in this context, has been omitted from this diagram to avoid complication. Imports and exports are omitted for similar reasons.

Fig. 2a Population-Push Process for a Subsistence Agriculture Community in the Presence of Unused Technological Knowledge

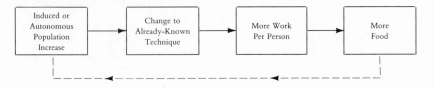

Fig. 2b Invention-Pull Malthusian Process for a Subsistence Agriculture Community

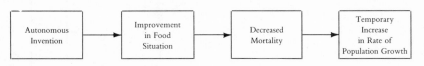

    Boserup deals only with techniques that, at the time of invention, require additional labor to produce additional output, and therefore must usually await an increase in population density for adoption. Different crop rotations are the prime example. This view, diagrammed in Figure 2b, we may call the "population push" hypothesis.

    Although there clearly are techniques (such as more intensive crop rotations) that fit the population-push hypothesis, there also are some other inventions (such as a better calendar) that save labor immediately, or that immediately increase output with the same labor, and for which there is accordingly no bar to immediate adoption. These latter inventions fit nicely with a Malthusian or "invention-pull" view of population growth and technical change. In earlier work I showed important instances of both in economic history. Earlier articles also showed the microeconomics of the adoption of these two different classes of techniques.[3]

3 Simon, "An Integration of the Invention-Pull and Population-Push Theories of Economic-Demographic History," in *idem* (ed.), *Research in Population Economics* (Greenwich, Conn., 1978), I; *idem, The Economics of Population Growth* (Princeton, 1977).

The upshot is that both Malthus and Boserup tell part of the total story. The inventions that immediately save labor are adopted as soon as people recognize them for what they are, and they lead to a spurt in population. Those inventions that require more labor for more output under existing conditions are only adopted later when population increase forces such adoptions by making them economical. Together the population-push and invention-pull theories provide a more sound and comprehensive view of demographic-economic history than does either above. Together they are consistent with a situation in which population growth increases misery by decreasing each person's share of an inelastic supply of food, but also with a situation in which the supply of food expands sharply to provide for more people.

II POPULATION AND ADOPTION OF INNOVATIONS IN MARKET AGRI-CULTURE   Boserup's population-push technique change operates because of an inability of the semi-fixed quantity of land to produce the increased amount of food necessary to meet the new demand with the old technology. In such a context of subsistence agriculture there is no market wage to fall with increased population. Nor is there new movable capital being purchased; this last point is the most important distinguishing characteristic for our purposes between subsistence agriculture and an industrial economy.

In contrast, in an industrial economy the technical change decision that follows a ceteris paribus increase in population and demand is *not* whether simply to expend (or hire) more labor to work together with the existing capital in order to increase production to the new profit-maximizing point. Rather, the decision is whether to buy new (and different) machinery, and this decision is affected by the cost of labor (and raw materials).

The common view seems to be that an increase or plentitude of workers retards the adoption of new devices by making it more profitable to use additional workers than to buy new capital. This is the converse of the view that a shortage of workers leads to the adoption of new technology by way of an increase in the price of labor, with consequent substitution of capital (embodying new technology) in place of workers.

The contemporary source of this view is the writing of Habakkuk with respect to different degrees of labor scarcity in, for example, the United States and Great Britain during the nineteenth century. Habakkuk traces this view to the nineteenth-century writers themselves, and then to Rothbarth. A chain of inference runs reasonably straightforwardly from the idea that labor scarcity induces innovation, to the idea that slower population growth, with concomitantly fewer persons of working age in the current cohort compared to the prior cohort, induces relatively faster innovation than does faster population growth.[4]

This theory fits with the United States, a land of high wages by almost any measure, which has developed and adopted much labor-saving technology in advance of other nations (although cross-national comparison is treacherous ground from which to infer an answer to the question posed here). This theory, however, does not fit the history of Europe before and after the fourteenth century. The period from 1000A.D. to 1300 A.D. was a time both of rapid population growth and of great advances in agricultural (and construction) techniques. After the Black Death (although perhaps beginning with the preceding great famine or earlier), when population ceased to grow and then declined, whereupon wages rose, advances in technique also slackened or ceased. This theory also does not fit the data showing that since World War II the less developed countries—where population growth has been rapid by any measure—have increased productivity proportionally as fast or faster than more developed countries.[5]

There is, however, another force at work. An increase in total labor supply increases total output, which is roughly the same as an increase in total demand for goods. And an increase in demand, all else equal, is likely to lead to additional investments in productive capital.[6]

4 H. John Habakkuk, *American and British Technology in the Nineteenth Century* (Cambridge, 1962), esp. 6–9.
5 Jean Gimpel, *The Medieval Machine* (New York, 1977); David Morawetz, *Twenty-Five Years of Economic Development: 1950–1975* (Baltimore, 1978).
6 This proposition is related to the argument advanced by Losch, Kuznets, and Easterlin that population growth, especially in the form of immigration, leads to an increase in total investment, especially investments in housing. August Losch, "Population Cycles as a Cause of Business Cycles," *Quarterly Journal of Economics,* LI (1937), 649–662; Simon Kuznets, "Long Swings in the Growth of Population and in Related Economic Variables," *Proceedings of the American Philosophical Society,* CII (1958), 25–52; Richard A. Easterlin, *Population, Labor Force, and Long Swings in Economic Growth* (New York, 1968).

In another article I show geometrically what may happen when the two opposing forces are both at work. Under reasonable assumptions, either effect can dominate. But the outcome of the geometry is easy to understand and accept intuitively. Population growth *can* lead to the faster adoption of new technology even though it also leads to a decline in wages. Whereas the wage change has a depressing effect upon the adoption of innovations, the demand change has a stimulative effect. But the analysis does not imply that under *all* conditions population growth *will* lead to faster adoption of new technology, just as it contradicts the clear negative effect on innovation assumed by those who have focused only on the wage effect. Rather, the outcome of population growth is indeterminate, and depends upon the parameters of the demand function and of the cost function.[7]

For the purpose of this article as a whole, the important implication is that population growth does not necessarily slow down the adoption of new agricultural innovations, and may actually speed such adoption.

III POPULATION AND THE ADVANCEMENT OF TECHNOLOGY   This section discusses the relationship between population and the invention of agricultural (and other) techniques, in contradistinction to the previous sections which discussed the *adoption* of inventions. The context is urban or modern society rather than subsistence agriculture.

Population size can affect technology through the supply of potential inventors, which in turn affects the supply of inventions. The idea that a larger population would produce more knowledge than a smaller society because of a larger number of potential inventions goes back at least to Petty:

> As for the Arts of Delight and Ornament, they are best promoted by the greatest number of emulators. And it is more likely that one ingenious curious man may rather be found among 4 million than 400 persons . . . And for the propagation and improvement of useful learning, the same may be said concerning it as above-said concerning . . . the Arts of Delight and Ornaments . . .[8]

7 Simon, "Some Theory of Population Growth's Effect on Technical Change in an Industrial Context," unpub. ms. (1982).
8 William Petty (ed. Charles Henry Hull), *The Economic Writings of Sir William Petty* (Cambridge, 1899), 2v.

This point was expressed more recently by Kuznets, and it was implicitly formalized by Phelps in his discussion of research and development.[9]

Population can also affect technology through the demand for goods. The idea that more people increase the flow of productivity-boosting inventions through the stimulating effect of increased industry volume is implicit in the cross-national analyses of productivity first done by Rostas, as well as in the learning-by-doing studies of Wright, Alchian, and Arrow. But these writers do not draw attention to the role of population size in influencing the size of industry.[10]

Exploring the theoretical ramifications of these ideas, Steinmann and I have found satisfactorily rich formulations that embody both supply-side and demand-side effects and fulfill the desire of economic theorists for mathematical tractability and steady-state properties. These analyses yield conclusions quite the opposite of the main body of economic growth theory, which expresses Malthus' central idea dynamically and reaches the same conclusions as does his static analysis.[11]

Because inventions are more often recorded, historical data are more readily available for discoveries than for adoptions. Because a long span is necessary when one is searching for a possible relationship, analyses of the relationship of population to technological discovery must reach far back in history; population changes too slowly for a mere few decades to suffice.[12]

9 Kuznets, "Population Change and Aggregate Output," in Ansley Coale (ed.), *Demographic and Economic Change in Developed Countries* (Princeton, 1960), 324–340; Edmund S. Phelps, "The Golden Rule of Procreation," in *idem, Golden Rules of Economic Growth* (New York, 1966), 176–183.

10 Leo Rostas, *Comparative Productivity in British and American Industry* (Cambridge, Mass., 1948); T. P. Wright, "Factors Affecting the Cost of Airframes," *Journal of the Aeronautical Sciences*, III (1936), 112–118; Armen A. Alchian, "Reliability of Progress Curves in Airframe Production," *Econometrica*, XXXI (1963), 679–693; Kenneth J. Arrow, "The Economic Implications of Learning by Doing," *Review of Economic Studies*, XXIX (1962), 155–173.

11 Simon, *Population Growth*, 108–136; Gunter Steinmann and Simon, "Phelps' Technical Progress Model Generalized," *Economic Letters*, V (1981), 177–182; Simon and Steinmann, "Population Growth and Phelps' Technical Progress Model," in Simon and Peter Lindert (eds.), *Research in Population Economics* (1981), III 239–254.

12 Available studies of contemporary adoptions by farmers do not throw light on the issue of the relationship of population to adoptions.

The case of Greece has special interest. Many have argued that ancient Greece's small population and great accomplishments prove that a relatively large population is not necessarily conducive to a relatively fast increase in knowledge. Figure 3 graphs the total number of "discoveries" in each period as a function of the population size in each period, and also computes the rate of population growth in the last period. From only one rise-and-fall event, one can draw little statistical assurance of a connection, but this single event certainly is consistent with the hypothesis of a positive relationship between population size and discovery rate.

A similar display for Rome in Figure 4 shows much the same results as for Greece, which should bolster our confidence that there is indeed a relationship.

Fig. 3   Population and Scientific Discoveries in Ancient Greece

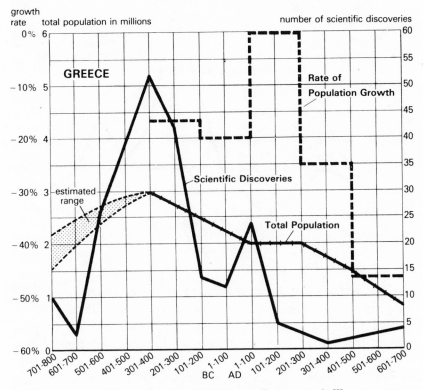

SOURCE: Pitirim Sorokin, *Social and Cultural Dynamics* (Boston, 1937), III.

Fig. 4 Population and Scientific Discoveries in Ancient Rome

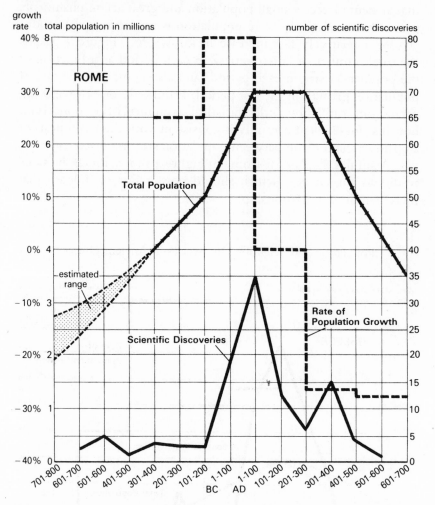

Work done jointly with Richard Sullivan, which is still at a very early stage, relates books published on agricultural production methods in England from 1500 to 1850, and agricultural patents from 1611 to 1841, to population size and agricultural prices. Our main measure of books published is a bibliography by Perkins, because it covers the longest period; we also have a bibliography by Fussell and one for the Goldsmiths' collection.

The three bibliographies are in general agreement on ups and downs with each other and with the patent series.[13]

Our most representative analysis is a regression with the logarithm of the number of titles of books published in each ten-year period in the Perkins bibliography (LPBKS) as the dependent variable, and as the independent variables, the logarithm of population in England and Wales (LPOP), the logarithm of the cumulative number of books published up until that time (plus a constant; LSM), the percentage rate of change in grain prices (PCFPI), and the percentage rate of change in nominal wages (PCWI).[14]

$$\text{LPBKS}_t = -2.3909 + \underset{\substack{(t = 2.01) \\ [\text{beta} = .372]}}{1.12 \text{ LPOP}_t} + \underset{\substack{(t = 3.2) \\ [\text{beta} = .600]}}{.70 \text{ LSM}_t}$$

$$\underset{\substack{(t = 1.36) \\ [\text{beta} = .103]}}{.007 \text{ PCFPI}_t} - \underset{\substack{(t = 1.4) \\ [\text{beta} = -.065]}}{.008 \text{ PCWI}_t,} \qquad R^2 = .87$$

The results accord with the idea that a larger population implies a larger supply of book writers, a larger stock of knowledge increases the supply of new knowledge, and higher food prices increase the demand for new knowledge about agriculture. The coefficient for wages has several possible interpretations, and its sign may be different during different sub-periods of the analysis. The results are plotted in Figure 5, which compares the observed numbers of titles and the fitted regression.

IV DENSITIES OF POPULATION AND OF TRANSPORTATION NETWORKS
Students of agricultural development agree that access to markets for inputs and outputs is all-important in the development of agriculture beyond the subsistence stage. Farm villages that are more than a mile or two from a road (especially an all-weather

13 Frank W. Perkins, *British and Irish Writers on Agriculture* (Lymington, 1932); G. E. Fussell, *Old English Farming Books, 1523–1730* (London, 1947); Margaret Canney and David Knott, *Catalogue of the Goldsmiths' Library of Economic Literature* (Cambridge, 1970).
14 Eventually we will use data from E. Anthony Wrigley and Roger S. Schofield, *The Population History of England, 1541–1871* (Cambridge, Mass., 1981).

Fig. 5 Actual and Fitted Values for Book Titles Published per Decade on Agricultural Production Methods, England, 1541–1850.

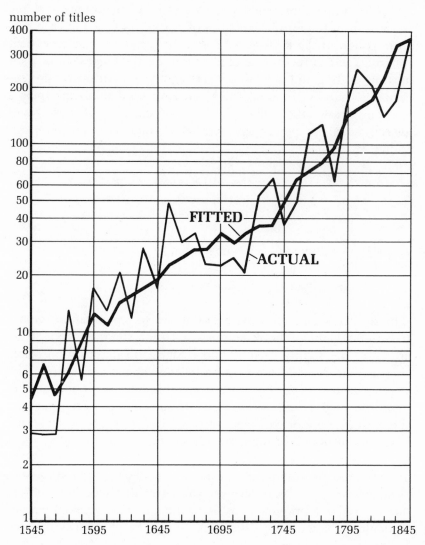

number of titles

road) will seldom find it profitable to produce beyond subsistence, and are unlikely to use modern methods.

Roads are a classic public good in the sense that the incremental cost for additional users is very low. The average cost per user is proportionately lower where there are more potential users, and it is therefore more likely that a densely populated community will find that benefits of a road exceed costs than will a sparsely populated community.

Glover and I tested this hypothesis in a comparison across nations. Figure 6 shows that even for the poorest countries the relationship is strong, and the pattern is even more consistent in similar graphs for each of the four other sets of countries grouped by income.[15]

A regression in double logarithmic form for 113 nations in 1968 gives the following results:

$$\log \left(\frac{TOT_{i,1969}}{LND_{i,1969}} \right) = -.380 + \underset{\substack{(t = 18.1) \\ (beta = .704)}}{.726 \log} \left(\frac{POP_{i,1969}}{LND_{i,1969}} \right)$$

$$+ \underset{\substack{(t = 12.4) \\ (beta = .483)}}{.657 \log} \left(\frac{Y_{i,1969}}{POP_{i,1969}} \right), \qquad R^2 = .83$$

where TOT = total miles of all roads, LND = square miles of land, POP = population, Y = national income, and i = country index.

These results seem impressive. The R^2 of .83 is exceptionally high for a cross-national regression, especially in view of the fact that only two independent variables are used; an R^2 this high suggests that one need not search further for additional independent variables to explain the variation in the independent variables. The elasticity of .73 of road density with respect to population density—that is, a 1 percent increase in population causes a .73 percent increase in road density, or as population doubles, roads increase 1.5 times—indicates that the relationship must be even stronger because the estimate is biased downward due to measurement error.

A cross-sectional sample of the countries' experiences over time was also examined, with this result:

15 Donald R. Glover and Simon, "The Effect of Population Density on Infrastructure: The Case of Road Building," *Economic Development and Cultural Change*, XXIII (1975), 453–468.

$$\left(\frac{TOT_{i,1969}-TOT_{i,1957}}{TOT_{i,1957}}\right) = .066 + \underset{\substack{(t = 3.9)\cdot \\ (beta = .448)}}{.985} \left(\frac{POP_{i,1969}-POP_{i,1957}}{POP_{i,1957}}\right)$$

$$+ \underset{\substack{(t = 1.3) \\ (beta = .151)}}{.0006} \left(\frac{Y_{i,1969}-Y_{i,1957}}{Y_{i,1957}}\right), \quad R^2 = .22$$

This method is inherently free of many of the trend problems and other defects of simple time-series regressions. Multicollinearity is observed to be very low (.04). The coefficients in this linear regression may be read immediately as elasticities. Population density shows a very significant elasticity of almost unity, whereas per person income's effect is small and not significant.[16]

Fig. 6 Relationship between Population Density and Road Density for Countries with Per-Person Income of 40–120 U.S. $

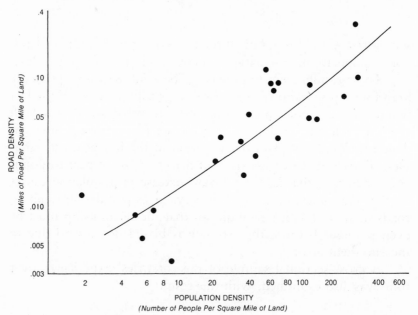

n.b. The graphs are quite similar for other income quintiles.
source: Reproduced from Glover and Simon, "Effect of Population Density," 457.

16 Simon, "The Demand for Liquor in the U.S., and a Simple Method of Determination," *Econometrica*, XXXIV (1966), 193–205.

Investigations with paved roads and other variations confirm the general conclusion that population density has a strong positive effect on the building of social capital in the form of roads that serve agricultural regions and are a crucial element in the development of agriculture beyond subsistence farming. A recent study along the same lines by Frederiksen shows a similar pattern for electrical power supply in the Philippines. A like effect is obvious for radio and television and other communications networks in developed countries.[17]

In brief, increased population density improves the infrastructure which supports and thereby increases agricultural production. Road networks also are the key factor in preventing famine by making possible the transfer of food from areas of plenty to areas of need.

V CAN FOOD PRODUCTION FORGE AHEAD OF POPULATION?　　The words "forge ahead" in the above title are colorful in order to avoid precision, because this question is not easy to state precisely. Until now the aim of this article has been to show that technical change in agriculture is, to a considerable extent, endogenous; although increased population puts an added strain on agricultural output, it also increases agricultural productivity. But the increased production from technological change might either exceed the increased demand or fall behind population growth.

A crucial point is that in the past farmers have produced only as much food as they could eat and market, and markets often were inaccessible. The amount produced, therefore, was not a clearcut measure of capacity to produce; to suppose so has led many persons to worry unnecessarily that additional food could not be produced to feed additional mouths.

Various measures suggest that people have been progressively better off as population has grown. First, for the years for which we have data since the 1930s, per person production of food has gone up, except during World War II (see Figure 7). Second, Johnson's research into famine deaths suggests that "both the percentage of the world's population afflicted by famine in

17   Peter C. Fredericksen, "Further Evidence on the Relationship between Population Density and Infrastructure: The Philippines and Electrification," *Economic Development and Cultural Change*, XXIX (1981), 749–758.

Fig. 7   World Grain and Food Production per Person

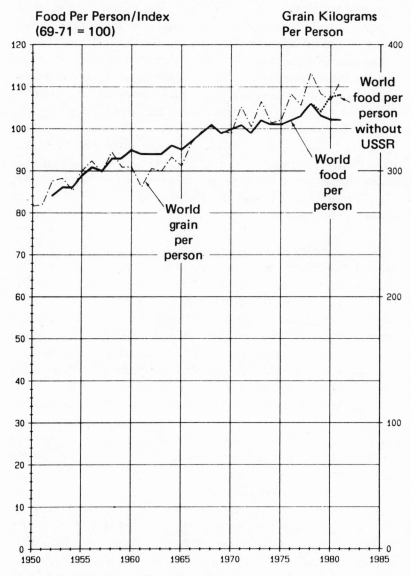

SOURCE: William J. Hudson, personal communication. Figure prepared from various USDA sources. The food index includes all food commodities—including grains, pulses, oilseeds, vegetables, and fruit. The index excludes the PRC.

recent decades and the absolute numbers have been relatively
small compared with those occurring in those earlier periods of
history of which we have reasonably reliable estimates of famine
deaths." Third, in the long run, food prices have declined. Figure
8 shows the nominal price of wheat deflated by wages in the
United States, an excellent measure for the United States and
developed countries though not applicable to the rest of the world.
Figure 9 shows the nominal price of wheat deflated by the price
index of consumer goods; because the world as a whole has
increased its purchasing power of consumer goods over the years
due to increased efficiency in producing all goods, this is a very
strong test, the results of which show decreasing cost and increasing availability of food for the world as a whole at least over the
last two centuries.[18]

Fig. 8   The Price of Wheat Relative to Wages in the United States

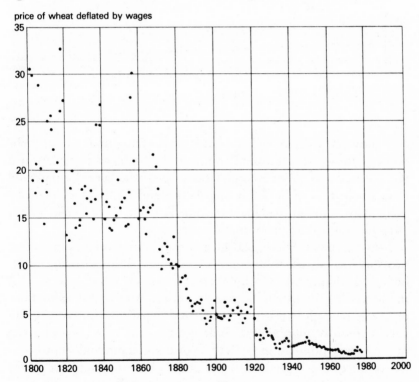

price of wheat deflated by wages

18   D. Gale Johnson, "Population, Food, and Economic Adjustment," *American Statisti-
cian,* XXVIII (1974), 89–93.

Fig. 9   The Price of Wheat Relative to the Consumer Price Index

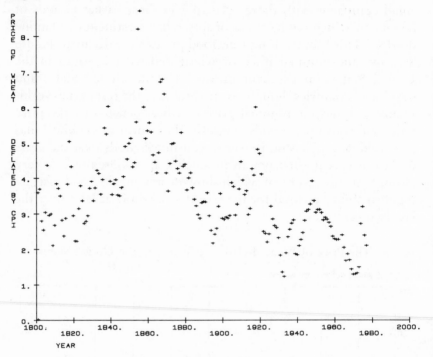

Between output and the most important input—new techniques—there are additional connections that need exploration if we are to have a better understanding of the world's past and future relationship between population and food. One such element is the course that the agricultural labor force (ALF) follows over time and with economic development.

At the heart of the Malthusian trap is increased "population pressure" on agricultural land. The scenario has increasing numbers of agriculturists working on a fixed supply of land so that the amount of land per farmer decreases. Although the quantity of arable land clearly is not fixed, land expansion cannot prevent such a trend of increasing population pressure in a very long run of increasing population growth. Nor does technological progress that reduces the *proportion* of the population in agriculture imply an escape from the trap; the proportion of the ALF to the total labor force may decrease but the *absolute* ALF may still increase.

Yet in developed areas such as North America, Western Europe, and Japan, the absolute ALF has been declining, even as population has grown. This decline is not because of food imports; many of these same countries are major food exporters. So there is a curious phenomenon to be understood.

An article by Simon, Reisler, and Gobin theorizes as follows: a faster rate of population growth leads to a faster rate of growth of the ALF, through both the supply of labor and the demand for nourishment. Higher income per person leads to a lower or negative rate of growth of ALF when the effect of income through population growth is held constant, because higher income implies greater demand for labor in other sectors of the economy. We know from a mass of other material that the effect of income on population growth is negative in the long run but may be positive in the short run.[19]

Empirical work with cross sections of countries from 1950 to 1960 and from 1960 to 1970 confirms the theory with these regressions:

$$\dot{ALF}_{1950-1960} = .76 - .31 \log y + .07 \dot{POP} - .05 \log \frac{POP}{LND} \qquad R^2 = .73$$
$$\beta = -.57 \qquad \beta = .38 \qquad \beta = -.15 \qquad n = 52$$
$$t = -6.7 \qquad t = 4.1 \qquad t = -1.8$$

$$\dot{ALF}_{1960-1970} = .48 - .21 \log y + .06 \dot{POP} - .04 \log \frac{POP}{LND} \qquad R^2 = .50$$
$$\beta = -.53 \qquad \beta = .24 \qquad \beta = 0-.12 \qquad n = 115$$
$$t = -6.9 \qquad t = 3.0 \qquad t = -1.75$$

where y = income per person, POP = population, LND = land area, $\dot{}$ = rate of change of a variable with respect to itself.

This investigation of the effect of population growth upon the total agricultural labor force and of "population pressure upon the land," showing that at some point in a nation's economic development the total agricultural labor force begins to decline even as population is increasing, confirms the trend data on food prices and output per person. It suggests that food can be provided with increasing rather than decreasing ease as population and income grow.

19 Simon, William Reisler, and Roy Gobin, "Population Pressure on the Land: Analysis of Trends Past and Future," in *World Development,* forthcoming.

VI POPULATION, FOOD, AND LAND   It is an open question to what extent wars are caused by the economic desire to acquire land and other resources. Wright discusses the matter at length, and concludes that the influence is relatively small. I examine this subject in more detail elsewhere; here I consider only the extent to which that motive is likely to strengthen or weaken in the future.[20]

We must distinguish two situations in which nations have wanted more land. First, nations have wanted to conquer new agricultural lands in order to settle their own people, or to exploit mines or other natural resources. This was the case with the Israelites and the Canaanites. It also was the notion underlying Adolph Hitler's *Mein Kampf* (New York, 1939); Hitler wrote about the lands to the east as if they were empty, or to be emptied. Second, nations have also wanted new lands *along with* their existing populations *because* of their existing populations, to increase national size for greater power, and/or for increased markets. The logic in the second case is a derivative of the logic in the first case, and if the first case no longer makes sense, the second will not make much sense either.

Would even a gift of additional land on its borders or elsewhere really benefit an industrialized nation by providing increased agricultural opportunities? If we were to consider the United States as a prototype of developed nations, there certainly would be some benefit if it suddenly had a strip of empty land fifty miles wide in what is now Mexico or Canada. This land would be additional "capital" which some Americans could use in addition to their present land and other capital. It would expand some Americans' incomes somewhat and thereby increase the average income of the United States as a whole, besides increasing its capacity to export food profitably.

But would there be much benefit in this addition to the United States? The surprising answer is "no." Even with its present vast agricultural area, less than 3 percent of the United

---

20 Quincy Wright, *A Study of War* (Chicago, 1942); Simon, "Lebensraum: An Essay on Peace in the Future or, Population Growth May Eventually End Wars," unpub. ms. (1982).

States work force is employed on farms.[21] Hence an increase in land area—even if it were to double the size of the United States—would change the occupational lives of less than 3 percent of the population. Furthermore, people in agriculture do not derive much higher (perhaps actually lower) incomes from farming than do the average of other Americans from their occupations (although this amount would be difficult to calculate on a per-hour basis). Therefore, people who would otherwise not live on farms but would till the new land would not gain much by such an increment to United States agricultural land.

We could present the question in another, more precise fashion. How much would all United States agricultural land be worth if a foreign buyer were to make a fair offer for it, or how much would it cost if we were to consider buying an equivalent amount of land from another country (miraculously no further from us, so transportation costs could be ignored)?

The calculation may be done as follows. In 1978, 2.76 percent of gross national product (GNP) came from farms, and 3.10 percent of GNP came from farms, forests, and fisheries. One of the great ratios in economics (deriving from Clark) is that throughout time and in all places—the ancient world, India now, Australia at the beginning of the century, and so on—the market value of a piece of agricultural land is roughly four times the value of a year's output. (Not relevant here is the value of urban land, and the value of farmland for tax purposes or for speculation on development and inflation, factors which now greatly affect the price of some farmland in the United States.) About 11 percent of one year's national income is all that the United States' farmland is worth to us as a nation. The amount that the nation spends in two years for recreation plus one year's expenditure on tobacco (without even including expenditures on liquor) would cover the whole bill. It is clear, then, that as land—and even as improved

---

21 This is written in awareness that some industrial workers make inputs to farming. But these workers do not affect the argument, because they could continue as they are, selling their wares to "foreign" owners of the farmland. This estimate of something less than 3% (2.7% in 1980: U.S. Department of Commerce, 1981) is, in fact, an overestimate because almost half of the persons classified as farm operators work off the farm too, most of them for 200 days a year or more: *U.S. Statistical Abstract* (1980), 689.

farmland, not just as virgin land, which is worth only a fraction of improved land—the United States' farmland would not be worth fighting even a minor war for, let alone a major war. Two years' peacetime expenditures on defense would pay the whole bill.[22]

Another way to evaluate the land is by Schultz's method of using the estimate that "20 percent of the cost of producing farm products is net rent." According to this formula, .20 × .031 (the proportion of GNP arising in farms, forests, and fishing) = 0.6 percent of each year's GNP. Capitalizing this 0.6 percent by a factor of about twenty yields something close to the estimate of 11 percent of one year's GNP as the value of the land in agriculture.[23]

According to this analysis, it would be foolish for a developed country to go to war just for agricultural land, even to obtain as much land as the United States has. And less developed countries are not in a position to start major wars without coopting allies from among the developed countries. Oil wells may still be valuable enough to fight for, but in the future, when (as I believe) energy costs will again have fallen to a very small part of GNP for developed nations, even oil will not be a causus belli.[24]

What is the history-reversing process that leads to this changing view of war and peace? The combination of increased income per person and the accompanying decline in the proportion of persons working in agriculture is the promixate cause. If only 3 percent of the income of a nation and less than 3 percent of its labor force is in agriculture—the state of even as agriculturally a developed country as the U.S.—then the quantity of agricultural land is not important enough from an economic point of view to fight about. To understand the mechanism, however, we must go deeper. Paradoxically, the long-run cause of this process is population growth. Additional people lead to actual or expected shortages and increased economic burdens in the short run. But in a fashion described earlier, these economic problems eventually lead to increases in technology, by way of both the "demand side"

22   Colin Clark, *Conditions of Economic Progress* (New York, 1957; 3rd ed.).
23   Theodore W. Schultz, "The Declining Economic Importance of Land," *Economic Journal*, LXI (1951), 725–740.
24   Simon, *The Ultimate Resource* (Princeton, 1981).

increase in payoff to invention as well as from the "supply side" increase in potential inventors in the larger population. There is no reason to expect this process not to continue indefinitely.

Nor is there physical limit upon capacity. If the need should arise, processes such as hydroponics can produce incredible amounts of food in tiny spaces, even without soil. Israel, for example, developed successful experimental hydroponic agriculture, because in the early days of that nation its planners worried about the capacity of its small territory to be selfsufficient in food. But that line of development was not pursued, simply because the rapidly increasing productivity of its farms—using conventional agricultural methods—resolved the food problem for the foreseeable future.

Difficulty would arise only if these new land-saving agricultural processes were to require labor from a relatively large proportion of the population. But we have seen that the trend has gone the other way. Nor is there convincing reason to believe that the trend will reverse in the future.

In the long run, land becomes relatively less important to farming, as Schultz pointed out in a more limited context several decades ago, and as Liebig and Friedrich Engels discussed from more technological points of view more than a century ago. All natural resources become less important for production as technology increases, because of our remarkable ability to substitute one material for another in production processes, as with aluminum in place of copper in electrical wiring, space satellites in place of copper telephone wires, and plastic shoes instead of leather.[25]

The mechanisms and trends described in this article point in an optimistic direction with respect to humankind's ability to feed itself, despite—or, more likely, because of—population growth. People expand the areas of arable by opening up new lands, plant more intensively, and invent and adopt new food-producing techniques in response to perceived need and opportunity. Roads, communications, and other infrastructures result from sufficiently

---

25 Schultz, "Importance of Land." See H. E. Goeller and Alvin M. Weinberg, "The Age of Substitutability," *Science,* CMXMI (1978), 683–689, for a full statement on the ability to substitute.

high income and sufficiently dense population settlements. From these mechanisms flow long-run increases in productivity that overcome short-run scarcities and produce historical trends toward cheaper food, with less famine and higher consumption per person in the world. In the developed countries, this increased food for more people is produced by a smaller number of farmers; the same reduction in the total number of farmers may be expected in the now poor countries as they get richer.

The attentive reader will likely ask why, if this view of history is correct, has there so often been great hunger. First, famines have largely been local, especially in Europe, and have often occurred when food was plentiful not too far away. But the costs of transportation were prohibitively high because of poor roads, and poor people could not afford to pay the scarcity prices for the food that was available locally. Second, and of probably greater consequence in terms of the numbers of persons affected, the food-increasing mechanisms described in this article do not come into play immediately when scarcity increases, and hence a pinch may be felt for many years after its onset, even to the extent of a rise in mortality according to the Malthusian model. Even in the present time, it is taking decades to grapple successfully with a price rise in oil and energy; hundreds or thousands of years ago it took much much longer than it does now to overcome a resource shortage. When food became scarce, for example in Europe during the first centuries AD, after 1300 AD, or after 1650 AD, people were slow to invent, hear about, and then adopt new methods of farming. The long lag probably was partially the result of insufficient information on population growth to convince people that the scarcity was not just a random series of bad years. But probably the more important cause was that conventional practices were deeply entrenched among poorly-educated, traditional farmers. Change in farming habits involves effort and risk, neither of which is inherently attractive.

Food production in Southeast Asia during the last 100 years presents a different story. First, contrary to popular belief, food production per person has been increasing in that region in recent decades. Second, diseases that hamper food-producing work have been more of a problem there than in Europe. Third, for a variety of reasons, which certainly include the degree of openness to market economics and to change in general, China and India did not get involved in what Kuznets called "modern economic growth" (which he dates as beginning in 1750 in Europe) until much more recently. As a result, their rapid modern population growth was in advance of their economic growth, in contrast to Europe. This is no longer the case, however, judging by the experience in recent decades.

The conclusion of this article remains optimistic. A key aspect of a modern economy is its ability to deal quickly with newly arising problems. There will be temporary increases in food scarcity in the future, just as there have been in the past, due to increases in population, political errors, and perhaps war. But with modern transportation systems, the modern organized system of agricultural research, libraries of unused technology, and modern economic flexibility, we can prevail against these scarcities relatively rapidly. Usually we will find ourselves to be better off than we were before the scarcity arose, because of the continuing good effects of the solutions to the vanquished problems. Such is the hope, based on the experience of the past.

Roderick C. Floud

Economics and Population Growth:

A Comment   Most discussions of historical demography start, continue, and finish with Thomas Malthus. This is not only because Malthus has the advantage, among historical and economic demographers, of having effectively been first in the field— a distinction to which historians naturally and rightly attach importance—but also because the Malthusian schema is extremely simple, so simple in fact that it immediately invites any self-respecting intellectual to complicate it. The three articles to which this comment is addressed thus stand in an honorable tradition; each, in its way, modifies the Malthusian schema and each complicates those early insights.

To Etienne van de Walle and Susan Watkins, Malthus' weak point lies in the assumed relationships among nutrition, morbidity, and mortality, the means by which the positive check stemming from a diminished food supply in relation to population was thought by Malthus to achieve an equilibrium, at the subsistence wage, between agricultural supply and population demand. To Thomas McKeown, the required modification to Malthus lies in the need to alter the implicit assumption of a fixed technology of agricultural supply, around which population pressure fluctuates in response to the positive check of mortality and to the preventive check of fertility control. Whereas McKeown implicitly accepts, however, another concept central to Malthus, that of diminishing returns to increased inputs of labor in agriculture, Julian Simon overturns even that. An increasing population and even, he argues, an increasing agricultural labor force, can be sustained by the existence of endogenous and continuous technological change which leads overall to increasing rather than decreasing returns to population growth. (Strictly, diminishing

Roderick C. Floud is Professor of Modern History at Birkbeck College, London. He is the author of *An Introduction to Quantitative Methods for Historians* (London; 2nd ed. 1979).

returns still exist within an individual technology, but lead inevitably to a change in that technology.)

All three articles, therefore, implicitly or explicitly reject the notion of long-run equilibrium in the relationship between resources and population, although they differ somewhat in their ideas as to whether such a Malthusian equilibrium has ever existed; van de Walle and Watkins deny it altogether, but McKeown is prepared to accept that it existed until the agricultural and industrial revolutions of the eighteenth and early nineteenth centuries. Simon rejects the pessimistic Malthusian equilibrium in favor of an optimistic version; the pressure of population will, he believes, automatically produce technological changes which will bring new resources into use to supply the needs of that growing population.

The articles of McKeown and Simon discuss, in their different ways, one of the most complex issues of modern economics and economic history, that of the sources of technological change. As McKeown clearly states here and in his previous writings, technological change is the means by which mankind escaped, during the period of industrialization, from the Malthusian trap. As McKeown puts it in his article, it was "advances in agriculture and transportation" which increased the average nutritional level sufficiently to enable populations to overcome infection and abstain from infanticide, which are for him the two main causes of high mortality in pre-industrial societies. Thus technological change enabled the European populations to avoid the need either for the positive or for the preventive check. McKeown is content to take those advances in agricultural and transportation technology for granted; he does not try to explain either why they occurred at all or why they occurred in particular in the British economy of the eighteenth century. He is content to see technological change as a gift from God and to concentrate his attention on the consequences which stem from it.

McKeown's attitude on this point is shared, perforce, by almost all economists and economic historians. Every student economist is taught that a farmer or industrialist constantly, or at least frequently, decides how to carry out his productive task by choosing that technique which will enable him to maximize his profits. His choice is constrained, however, by the range of techniques which are available to carry out that task and by the cost of the different inputs, such as labor and capital, which are needed by those techniques. Simple logic leads to the conclusion that a fall in the cost of machines (capital equipment) relative to the cost of laborers is likely to persuade an employer to use more machines and less labor, and so to change to the particular technique which minimizes costs at that moment in time. Such a change is known to economists as a change along an existing production function; it is clearly determined by the movement of costs in the economy as a whole and can be thought of without difficulty as being endogenous to the economic system, for the mix of inputs changes in response to the relative costs of the different elements in the mix.

Change of this kind, however, has a simple, see-saw character: more capital, less labor or more labor, less capital. It does not accommodate changes which enable an employer to use both less labor and less capital, thus saving both resources rather than economizing on one at the expense of the other. Such changes do not simply imply adjustments within a particular technique or range of techniques, but rather the invention and adoption of a completely new range of techniques, a change known to economists as a move to a new production function. This latter type of change is what most historians think of when they speak of changing technology or the march of invention. Yet the simple economic theory or logic which is adequate to explain adjustments to changing input costs does not explain at all well why such change should occur. Put simply, it always pays one to do something which saves money; it is therefore extremely difficult to specify why a particular money-saving change should arise at one moment in time rather than another, or why it should be particularly directed at saving labor or some other input. Whether the relative cost of labor rises or falls, it still pays to use less labor if you can find a way to do it. It is impossible, therefore, to specify the historical conditions which will produce a new invention or, in other words, to make invention endogenous to the economic system.

Simon, however, is brave enough to try. First in his book, *The Economics of Population Growth* (Princeton, 1977), and now in his article he attributes the advances in agriculture and transportation, which to McKeown and others are best seen as gifts from God, directly to the impact of increasing population. The argu-

ment is developed in a number of ways. In section I of his article
Simon challenges the conventional view that population growth
will retard the spread of innovation. This view rests on the belief
that a growing population will lead to a falling real wage and
hence to the lack of any incentive to save labor or to innovate by
the use of more machinery, since it is assumed that the cost of
labor is falling relative to the cost of capital. Simon challenges
this approach by arguing that, in certain circumstances, the increase in demand which stems from the existence of more consumers will itself expand output and hence the labor force and
thus reverse the fall in relative labor costs; it will therefore restore
the incentive to save labor and to introduce machinery in its place.
As expounded, the argument is too restricted to have great explanatory power, principally because it assumes that the cost of
capital goods remains fixed in the long-run, even though labor
costs (which presumably have some impact on the costs of capital
goods made with labor) change substantially. More important,
Simon's argument relates only to movements along an existing
production function—shifts in the mix of labor and capital—and
not to the stimuli to move to a new production function. Invention, in other words, is still exogenous to the system in section I
of Simon's article.

Simon is, in section I, approaching the question of technological change from the demand side, describing the possible
effects of a change in the number of consumers on the choice of
technique. He then, by contrast, moves to the supply side and
explores the relationship of population change to the supply of
knowledge and to transportation. He attempts to show that technological change, in the sense of a move to a new production
function, is endogenous. The method is the same—regression
analysis in which the pressure of population acts as an explanatory
variable in the model—and the model seems to serve well.

Unfortunately, serious questions arise both about the nature
of the evidence which is used to test the model and about the
specification of the model itself. For example, in Simon's discussion of invention in Greece and Rome, not only are the underlying
data for numbers of the population and numbers of inventions
largely speculative, but Figures 3 and 4 suggest that in Greece
scientific discoveries led population change, whereas in Rome
they lagged behind.

The British data are better, but there are other problems. First, the form of the regression equation which links book output to population change and food prices implies that the effects of population change are independent of the movement in food prices, which is difficult to justify; it is almost axiomatic that population growth will cause an increase in food prices, at least in the short-run, ten-year periods which are used as the time unit of analysis. If the hypothesized link between population and invention operates at least partially *through* food prices, rather than separately from movements in food prices which are independently caused, then the regression coefficients will be unreliable. In addition, the lack of any lag in the hypothesized relationship between population change and the supply of books is worrying in view of the findings of other studies that there are typically long delays in the process of innovation. There is, finally, an inherent difficulty in using an index of books to represent increments to knowledge, since much old and perhaps erroneous knowledge may be being repeated, whereas much new and potentially useful knowledge may not be printed.

Similar problems of measurement and the direction of causation arise in Simon's discussion of the effects of population on the supply of transportation. Does the causal chain run, for example, from more population and income to more roads, or from more roads to more economic growth? Simon believes the former, but the logic of McKeown's argument, and that of many historians who see transportation networks as built ahead of demand, suggests the latter. Only an investigation over a longer time-span and within national economies can really decide the issue, so that the cross-sectional data which are used by Simon are not conclusive.

Simon's work is a brave attempt to demonstrate the endogeneity of technical change, but it is a brave failure. Why should this be so? Perhaps the answer lies in the aggregative approach which he and many others have adopted. Although it must be true that aggregate changes, such as those in the size of the population, influence the conditions of economic progress, the countries, regions, and industries where technical change actually occurs differ over space and time in their institutions, in their structures of property rights, in their factor endowments, and in many other ways; hence they differ in the structures of incentives for inventors and innovators. Aggregative analysis based on single-sector and essentially monocausal models cannot begin to capture this diversity. If we begin, however, with the impeccable position that people invent and innovate because it pays them to do so, but link that with an appreciation of the constraints and incentives peculiar to each place, industry, and moment in time, then we may gain some insight, from the bottom up, of the nature of technical change. Within that, population change certainly has a part to play, but the part is surely neither as exiguous as McKeown would have us believe nor as all-important as Simon suggests.

Robert W. Fogel, Stanley L. Engerman, Roderick Floud, Gerald Friedman, Robert A. Margo, Kenneth Sokoloff, Richard H. Steckel, T. James Trussell, Georgia Villaflor, and Kenneth W. Wachter

Secular Changes in American and British Stature and Nutrition

This article reports on a collaborative project which is investigating the usefulness of data on height for the analysis of the impact of long-term changes in nutritional status and health on economic, social, and demographic behavior. In this project, measures of height are used for two related purposes. First, mean height at specific ages is used as a measure of the standard of living. When used in this way, data on height supplement other evidence, such as indexes of real wages, estimates of per capita income, and measures of food consumption. One

Robert W. Fogel is Director of the Center for Population Economics at the University of Chicago and of the Program on the Development of the American Economy of the National Bureau of Economic Research (NBER). He and the other nine authors of this article are the principal collaborators in the nutrition project described below.

The project of which this article is a part is sponsored by the NBER and the Center for Population Economics of the University of Chicago, and is called "Secular Trends in Nutrition, Labor Productivity, and Labor Welfare." Parts of the research reported here have been supported by grants from the National Science Foundation; the Social Science Research Council, London; the British Academy; the Exxon Educational Foundation; Harvard University; Ohio State University; Stanford University; the University of California, Berkeley; and the University of Rochester. The findings are tentative and subject to change. Statements made in this report do not necessarily reflect the views of the NBER or any of the other cooperating institutions or funding agencies. The research reported here is part of the NBER's program in Development of the American Economy.

This article is a revised and shortened version of the one presented at Bellagio. To meet space requirements, two sections of the original paper and some of the documentation have been deleted. The original paper is available as a preprint in the NBER Working Paper series (No. 890, May 1980). For a more extensive treatment of some of the findings summarized here, see the articles in the special issue of *Social Science History*, VI (1982), as well as James Trussell and Richard Steckel, "The Age of Slaves at Menarche and Their First Birth," *Journal of Interdisciplinary History*, VIII (1978), 477–505; Steckel, "Slave Height From Coastwise Manifests," *Explorations in Economic History*, XVI (1979), 363–380; Lars G. Sandberg and Steckel, "Soldier, Soldier, What Made You Grow So Tall?" *Economy and History*, XXIII (1980), 91–105; Steckel, "Height and Per Capita Income," *Historical Methods*, XV (Winter, 1982), 1–7.

advantage of height data is their abundance and wide coverage of socioeconomic groups. Consequently, it is possible to develop continuous series for a wide range of geographical areas, as well as for quite refined occupational categories. It is also possible to develop far more refined measures of the extent to which particular classes and areas were affected by changes in economic fortunes than has so far been possible through the use of either real wage indexes or measures of per capita income. Although it is unlikely that large bodies of height-by-age data will be uncovered for periods before 1700, the data are abundant from 1700 on, adding more than a century to most of the current series on per capita income. The wide geographical and occupational coverage offers the possibility that aggregate indexes constructed from them will be more representative of national trends than are long-term wage indexes, which are composed of narrow, discontinuous series.[1]

Second, height is being used to investigate the effects of improvements in nutrition on social and economic behavior, especially on labor productivity, the selection of individuals for particular occupations, and the decline in mortality. The search for data capable of illuminating the desired relationships has been a major aspect of this line of research. Data have been located in

---

1 Time series on height may be more reliable indicators of long-term changes in the welfare of the laboring classes than are the currently available indexes of real wages. Critics of the real wage indexes that have been computed for the eighteenth and nineteenth centuries, in both the U.S. and Great Britain, have noted the problems that beset the existing time series of nominal wages as well as the price deflators. The nominal wages for particular localities and particular occupations often remain relatively fixed over many years, sometimes even during periods of sharp fluctuations in the level of prices, so that the trend in real wages depends heavily on the choice of price indexes. Price deflators are generally lacking in information on the cost of shelter, which, in the more rapidly growing cities, may have accounted for more than one quarter of the income of laborers. Efforts to turn wage indexes of particular occupations and localities into general regional or national wage indexes have produced nominal wage indexes, the movements of which are dominated for long periods of time by changes in a few occupations or localities and by discontinuities in underlying series. Von Tunzelmann's recent examination of the real wage series for England revealed that different reasonable ways of combining the individual series of nominal wage rates and the choice of different price deflators could imply either a rise of 250% in the national average of real wages between 1750 and 1850 or no rise at all. G. N. Von Tunzelmann, "Trends in Real Wages, 1750–1850, Revisited," *Economic History Review*, XXXII (1979), 33–49. Data on height by occupation are more complete in their geographical scope than the wage data, especially for the lower-wage occupations, and do not need to be deflated by price indexes.

military records, censuses, and household surveys which allow the analysis of the effect of height on days of illness and on the incidence of specific diseases. One of the bodies of data permits analysis at the household level of the impact of both height and weight on labor productivity, using wage rates as the measure of this factor. Work has recently been initiated which introduces height as a variable in production functions estimated for agriculture and manufacturing but has not yet progressed far enough to warrant a report. However, the third section of this article does report an investigation of the relationship between height and the productivity of United States slaves (as measured by their value) and the effect of height on mortality rates in Trinidad.

PRINCIPAL SAMPLES AND PROCEDURES   The project is based on a set of thirteen samples of data containing information on height-by-age and various socioeconomic variables which cover the period from 1750 through 1937 for the United States, Trinidad, Great Britain, and Sweden. Six of the samples are from U.S. military records for the period from 1750 to 1910. The other three U.S. samples contain information on both sexes: the sample of coastwise manifests provides information about slaves who boarded coastwise vessels between 1810 and 1863; the Fall River survey covers working children of school age during 1906–07; the cost of living survey covers all family members in a sample of households from 1934 to 1937. The Trinidad data set consists of complete censuses of the slaves on the island in 1813, with updates in 1814 and 1815, and then every three years until 1834.

One of the British samples is composed of poor boys from various parts of Great Britain, especially London, taken in by the Marine Society, a charitable organization, from 1750 to 1910; the other is drawn from military recruitment records compiled between 1750 and 1910. The Swedish sample is drawn from muster rolls of army reserves who served from 1765 to 1885. Cooperative arrangements will be undertaken to obtain comparable data for other nations, including Germany and France, from which the U.S. population is derived. The data in these samples are being linked with data available in both manuscript and published sources. Such linking increases both the range of variables that can be brought into the analysis and the complexity of the interrelationships between height, nutritional status, and economic and social behavior that we can investigate. As of early 1982, information had been collected on about 300,000 individuals, which is about 60 percent of the anticipated final number.

Measures of height are employed as the principal index of nutritional status. Both laboratory experiments on animal populations and observational studies of human populations have led physiologists and nutritionists to conclude that anthropometric measurements are reliable indexes of the extent of malnutrition among the socioeconomic classes of particular populations. Measures of height and weight at given ages, the age at which growth of stature terminates, attained final height, and especially the rate of change in height or weight during the growing ages "reflect accurately the state of a nation's public health and the average nutritional status of its citizens." Consequently, these measures are now widely used by the World Health Organization and other agencies to assess the nutritional status of the populations of underdeveloped nations.[2]

The use of anthropometric measures as measures of nutrition rests on a well-defined pattern of human growth between childhood and maturity. The average annual increase in height (velocity) is greatest during infancy, falls sharply up to age three, and then falls more slowly throughout the remaining pre-adolescent years. During adolescence, velocity rises sharply to a peak that is approximately one half of the velocity achieved during infancy, then falls sharply and reaches zero at maturity. In girls the adolescent growth spurt begins about two years earlier, and the magnitude of the spurt is slightly smaller than in boys.

This growth pattern reflects the interaction of genetic, environmental, and socioeconomic factors during the period of growth. According to Eveleth and Tanner:

> Such interaction may be complex. Two genotypes which produce the same adult height under optimal environmental circumstances

2 Appendix A of NBER Working Paper 890 summarizes the findings of the principal studies. For more extensive descriptions see James M. Tanner, *Fetus into Man: Physical Growth From Conception to Maturity* (Cambridge, Mass., 1978); idem, *A History of the Study of Human Growth* (Cambridge, 1981). The relationship between height per capita income and the distribution of income in modern populations is analyzed in Steckel, "Height and Per Capita Income." For a summary of the evidence on the relationship between anthropometric measures, nutrition, and health, see A. Roberto Frisancho, "Nutritional Influences on Human Growth and Maturation," *Yearbook of Physical Anthropology*, XXI (1978), 174–191. Phyllis B. Eveleth and Tanner, *Worldwide Variations in Human Growth* (London, 1976), 1.

may produce different heights under circumstances of privation. Thus two children who would be the same height in a well-off community may not only both be smaller under poor economic conditions, but one may be significantly smaller than the other . . . . If a particular environmental stimulus is lacking at a time when it is essential for the child (times known as 'sensitive periods'), then the child's development may be shunted, as it were, from one line to another.[3]

The relative importance of environmental and genetic factors in explaining individual variations in height is still a matter of some debate. For most well-fed contemporary populations, how-ever, systematic genetic influences appear to have very little im-pact on mean heights. For example, the mean heights of well-fed West Europeans, North American whites, and North American blacks are nearly identical. There are some ethnic groups in which mean final heights of well-fed persons today differ significantly from the West European or North American standard; in these cases the deviation from the European standard appears to be due to genetic factors. However, since such ethnic groups have rep-resented a miniscule proportion of American and European pop-ulations, they are irrelevant to an explanation of the observed secular trends in mean final heights in the U.S. and in the various European nations since 1750. Nor can they account for differences at various points of time between the means in the final heights of the U.S. population and the principal populations from which they were drawn. In this connection, it should be noted that today the mean final heights of well-fed males in the main African nations from which the U.S. black population is derived also fall within the narrow band designated as the West European stan-dard.[4]

---

3 *Ibid.*, 222
4 The belief that heterosis (hybrid vigor) would make Americans substantially taller than the ethnic groups from which they were drawn has not been sustained by previous anthropometric research. See Luigi Luca Cavalli-Sforza and Waber F. Bodmer, *The Ge-netics of Human Populations* (San Francisco, 1971), 602–620, for a theoretical argument as to why the effect of heterosis in human populations is small. Our investigations have failed to yield consistent signs on dummy variables for either males or females born of mixed unions. The magnitude of the positive coefficients for adults, not all of which are statistically significant, fall in the range of 0.17 to 0.66 inches. The average of all the coefficients so far estimated for adults (N = 9) is 0.19 inches. Even this small difference is not necessarily due to heterosis; it might reflect differences in treatment during the growing years. Eveleth and Tanner, *Worldwide Variations*, 21–22, 43–64, 83–104; NBER Working Paper 890, Appendix A.

Physiologists, anthropologists, and nutritionists have charted the effect of nutritional deficiencies on the human growth profile. Short periods of severe malnutrition or prolonged periods of moderate malnutrition merely delay the adolescent growth spurt; severe, prolonged malnutrition may diminish the typical growth-spurt pattern and contribute to substantial permanent stunting. If malnutrition is both prolonged and moderate, growth will continue beyond the age at which the growth of well-fed adolescents ceases. Hence, the average age at which the growth spurt peaks, the average age at which growth terminates, the mean height during adolescent ages, and the mean final height are all important indicators of mean nutritional status. Any one of these factors can be used to trace secular trends in nutrition. The more of these measures that are available, the more precise the determination of the severity and duration of periods of malnutrition.

In considering the relationship between nutrition and height, it is important to stress that height is a net rather than a gross measure of nutrition. Moreover, although changes in height during the growing years are sensitive to current levels of nutrition, mean final heights reflect the accumulated past nutritional experience stretching not only over the growing years of the individuals measured, but over the lifetimes of their mothers and perhaps of their grandmothers as well. Thus when mean final heights are used to explain differences in productivity, they reveal the effect not of current levels of nutrition on productivity, but of the net nutritional levels during the growing years of the measured individuals and, to an extent still to be established, of conditions during their mothers' and grandmothers' lives.

The measure of net nutrition represented by mean heights depends on the intake of nutrients, on the amount of nutrients available for physical growth after the necessary claims of work and other activities (including recovery from infections), and on the efficiency with which the body converts nutrients into outputs. The body's ability to generate a surplus for growth will vary with such factors as age, the climate, the nature of the available food, clothing and shelter, the disease environment, the intensity of work, and the quality of public sanitation. The same nutritional input can have varying effects, depending upon environmental conditions. The differing nutritional requirements for different intensities of work and other environmental conditions suggest that changes in the level of gross input (measured by food consumption) might not provide a full indication of changes in the nutrients available for physical growth. It is important to stress that, although mean height measures the cumulative effect of the nutrients available after allowing for physical maintenance, work, and the impact of the man-made and natural environment, it does not by itself indicate whether fluctuations in net nutrition are due to changes in the consumption of food, in the claims on the food intake, or in the efficiency with which food is converted into outputs.[5]

It cannot be assumed that there has been an invariable relationship, regardless of time and place, between height and such other important variables as occupation, wealth, literacy, ethnicity, residence, fertility, mortality, morbidity, migration, and a variety of intergenerational variables. Much attention has been devoted to determining which relationships are stable and which are not, and to the determination of the factors which have been influential in shifting relationships.

Although the findings to date are illuminating, the process of mapping the relationship between height and various socioeconomic variables is still at an early stage. Each new finding raises new questions and the answers frequently require a search for new data sets or the construction of new variables from the existing data sets. Many of the new issues point to the need to bring intergenerational variables to bear on the analysis. Some of the progress along these lines has been made in the study of the Trinidad data. Work has been initiated which links data on height in other samples with genealogies and with census data on the

---

5 It has sometimes been argued that it is impossible to separate, by statistical analyses, the effect on growth of disease and of a generally inadequate level of food intake. This argument assumes a much higher level of colinearity than actually exists. It is true that the body draws more heavily on nutritional stores when it is fighting an infection than when it is not, so that an infection may cause growth to cease during a period of infection. However, as Nevin S. Scrimshaw pointed out at the meeting in Bellagio, if a child is normally well fed, and if there is sufficient time between infectious episodes, there will usually be full catch-up when an infection ceases. Normal, well-fed children do not grow at equal daily rates, but alternate periods of growth well in excess of the daily average with periods of little or no growth, as disease and other claims on nutritional intake wax and wane. In well-fed children these lacunae in growth have no affect on final heights, because of full and rapid catch-up, but in malnourished children they contribute to permanent stunting.

households in which the persons measured were raised. When this work is completed it will be possible to investigate more fully the influence of the nutritional status of parents and grandparents on the health and productivity of their children and grandchildren.[6]

Since much of what is known about the socioeconomic determinants of height-by-age profiles is based on observations of modern populations, particularly in relatively rich nations, the usefulness of this knowledge for historical analyses is yet to be established. Because past conditions of malnourishment and health may have been far worse than those prevailing in many poor countries today, possible departures from currently known variations in the shape of the height-by-age profile are under investigation. Our work so far suggests that exceedingly severe conditions led to variations in the growth patterns that need to be carefully explored, but that, despite these qualifications, the general patterns established from the study of modern populations appear to apply to historical populations as far back as the beginning of the eighteenth century.

STATISTICAL ISSUES   Much of our effort during the past five years has been devoted to assessing the quality of the data contained in the various samples and to working out procedures for the detection and correction of biases that might distort our estimates of secular trends in height. Many of these problems relate to the fact that the oldest and most numerous bodies of information were collected by military organizations. Use of military data raises questions about the extent to which soldiers and sailors were representative of the underlying populations from which these data were drawn. The problem is more severe in volunteer than in conscript armies. Volunteer armies, especially in peacetime, are selective in their admission criteria and often have minimum height requirements. Consequently, even if information on rejectees exists, the question of the extent to which applicants are self-screened remains. In many conscript armies virtually every male of eligible age, including those who offer substitutes or are otherwise excused, are examined and measured.

6 In the case of the Civil War data set, recruits are also being linked with pension records which give pensioners' medical histories (including degrees of impairment of productivity at various ages) between 1865 and their death. This linked sample will be used to analyze the effect of childhood malnutrition on adult morbidity, labor productivity, and health.

Our procedures for the detection and correction of bias turn on a combination of theoretical considerations, empirical information, and simulation techniques. Much of the power of these techniques hinges on the fact that the distribution of final heights is well described by a normal distribution. The standard deviation of this distribution is rather tightly bounded for European, North American, and Afro-American populations. Regardless of the ethnicity or the socioeconomic conditions of the population in question, the standard deviations appear to fall in the range of 2.6 ± 0.6 inches.[7] The distribution of height at each age during growing years is not normal, but is nearly so.[8]

Sample-Selection Biases　　Use of military records to measure trends in height calls attention to a variety of sample-selection biases, the most important of these being the problem of left-tail truncation which is characteristic of both the U.S. and British peacetime armies. Before turning to this issue, two others need to be considered: the self-selection bias of volunteers, and whether persons rejected for reasons other than height are nevertheless shorter than those accepted.

There is clearly evidence of self-selection bias in volunteer armies. Persons of foreign birth and native-born laborers living in cities are overrepresented, whereas native-born individuals living in rural areas are underrepresented. Since there are significant differences in height among these groups, it is necessary to standardize for these characteristics in estimating the trend in aggregate heights. Necessary weights are available from federal censuses and other sources. Much of the interest turns on secular trends in the heights of particular groups which, even if underrepresented, are nevertheless present in sufficient numbers to permit analysis.

7　This is the case in large samples of complete populations. For smaller samples the range of the standard deviation is larger. For further evidence, see W. F. F. Kemsley, "Weight and Height of a Population in 1943," *Annals of Eugenics*, XV (1951), 161–183; Bernard D. Karpinos, "Height and Weight of Selective Service Registrants Processed for Military Service During World War II," *Human Biology*, XXX (1958), 292–321; U.S. National Center for Health Statistics, "Weight, Height, and Selected Body Dimensions of Adults: United States 1960–1962," Series 11, No. 8 (Washington, D.C., 1965), 39 (hereinafter referred to as USNCHS).

8　The standard deviation of height follows a pattern during the adolescent growth spurt that is quite similar to the velocity profile. It rises as the growth spurt approaches, reaches a peak at the peak of the growth spurt, and then declines to the level just before the onset of the spurt. Cf. Trussell and Steckel, "Age of Slaves," 502.

There is the issue of whether volunteers in particular subgroups (e.g., blue-collar urban laborers aged twenty to twenty-five) are representative of the class from which they are drawn. Our approach to this question is to compare the characteristics of the volunteers in the peacetime army with individuals of the same subgroups in wartime armies subject to conscription (World War II), or in armies in which a very high proportion of those of military age were examined (the Civil War), or in scientifically designed random samples (such as the national sample of 1960 to 1962). Most of our work to date has focused on the records of the Union Army. The Civil War involved a larger proportion of persons of military age than any other war in American history. Approximately 95 percent of white males between the ages of eighteen and twenty-five in the Union states were examined and approximately 75 percent of the examinees were inducted. The results of our investigation so far indicate that, with respect to height, volunteers from particular subgroups are representative of the subgroups from which they are drawn, although we are still at an early stage in this investigation. If subsequent research should indicate biases so far undetected, that work will also provide the desired correction factors.[9]

There remains the question of whether persons actually inducted into the army but rejected for reasons other than height were shorter than those accepted. The World War II data analyzed by Karpinos show that 41 percent of all those called for examination were rejected and that rejectees were an average of 0.22 inches shorter than those inducted. Consequently, the failure to take account of rejectees would bias the estimated mean final height of the overall population upward by 0.09 inches. Although a bias of this magnitude is statistically significant because of the large sample size, it is too small to have a significant effect on most of the points at issue in this study. The data presented by

---

9 USNCHS, 39. These figures are estimated from data in Benjamin A. Gould, *Investigations in the Military and Anthropological Statistics of American Soldiers* (Cambridge, Mass., 1869), hereinafter referred to as the *Gould Report*; Jedediah H. Baxter, *Statistics, Medical and Anthropological, of the Provost-Marshal-General's Bureau, Derived from Records of the Examination for Military Service in the Armies of the United States During the Late War of the Rebellion of Over a Million Recruits, Drafted Men, Substitutes, and Enrolled Men* (Washington, D.C., 1875), I, ii–iii (hereinafter referred to as the *Baxter Report*); U.S. Provost-Marshal-General, "Final Report 1863–1866" (U.S. House of Representatives, Exec. Doc. No. 1, 39th Cong. 1st Sess.), Ser. Nos. 1251, 1252, I, 2–163.

Baxter indicate that the bias arising from the non-measurement of persons rejected because of disease in the Union army introduces an upward bias of 0.03 inches in the estimated final height of the overall population.[10]

Measurement Biases   These are a series of issues regarding the reliability of measures pertaining to the height-by-age schedule. Some relate to the accuracy of the age information, some to the accuracy of the height information. Issues regarding age include whether ages were heaped, were reported to the nearest or the last birthday, or were arbitrarily assigned on the basis of height. Issues regarding height include whether there was heaping on even heights, whether heights were rounded to the nearest inch (or fraction of an inch) rather than to the last full inch (or fraction thereof), and whether individuals were measured with or without shoes.

Accuracy in age has little bearing on the determination of the secular trend in final heights, since it is of little importance whether a person classified as thirty is actually twenty-eight or thirty-two. Such heaping is of some importance during the growing years. There is evidence of age heaping at ages ten and twenty, and at the minimum age for recruitment into military organizations. Although such heaping will add perturbation to the height-velocity profile, it does not usually affect the determination of the age at which the profile peaks. A more serious issue arises in the case of the coastwise manifests, where it has been suggested that ages were arbitrarily assigned on the basis of height. If that were true, however, the standard deviation of height would not, as it does, have the characteristic pattern of increasing and then decreasing as the peak of the growth spurt is approached and surpassed.[11]

Heaping on even inches is evident even when the measurement is conducted by qualified personnel (as in the national sample of 1960 to 1962). In military organizations with minimum height

10 Karpinos, "Height and Weight," 294, 302, 311. The bias in height is computed from *Baxter Report*, II, Table 16, by fitting normal curves to the data on the distribution of the heights of rejectees and recruits. The drawing of a sample of rejectees from the Union Army records has recently been completed. This sample will make it possible to press the analysis of the characteristics of rejectees further than is possible from published data, but the work on it is still at too early a stage to report here.
11 Trussell and Steckel, "Age of Slaves," 502.

requirements, there is further evidence of heaping at the inch just above the cutoff. Simulation models indicate that even-number heaping does not introduce a systematic bias. Although it may affect the accuracy of estimates of mean height, even with large amounts of heaping (in the range of 15 to 30 percent), the error will be in the neighborhood of one tenth of an inch. With respect to rounding, from the earliest date for which military records are available, the standard practice was to round to the nearest inch or fraction of an inch. A study of actual practice in World War II revealed a slight tendency to round downward, which introduced an average error of 0.2 inches. There is no reason to assume that this tendency has changed over time. Our analysis of the data in the Union Army records indicates that the bias may be due mainly to a tendency to round the heights of tall persons who should have been measured at fractional inches downward to the nearest inch. In any case, the magnitude of this error will not seriously distort secular trends, nor should it significantly affect the cross-sectional analysis of the relationship between height and economic or demographic factors.[12]

In the case of the coastwise manifests and the colonial muster rolls, the question arises as to whether individuals were measured with or without shoes. To resolve this question, we have turned to data on people recruited into the Union Army or the regular army where individuals are known to have been measured without shoes. The Gould report contains a sample of black recruits born in the slave states who were aged twenty-five and over (N = 13,653). The mean height in this sample, 67.2 inches, is virtually identical with the mean height (67.1 inches) computed for the same category in the coastwise manifests. Similarly, those recruited into the regular U.S. Army who were born between 1771 and 1790 averaged 68.3 inches (N = 611), which exceeds the mean height in the Revolutionary sample of 0.2 inches. When the collection of data from the regular army is extended back to 1790, the test can be repeated not merely with birth cohorts adjacent to those in the Revolutionary Army but with cohorts that overlap those of the Revolutionary Army.[13]

12   USNCHS, 39; Karpinos, "Height and Weight," 297.
13   *Gould Report*, 147. The Baxter sample was limited to military units where men were measured without shoes. Baxter (I, 14–15) conjectured that the recruits in some of the

Methods of Estimating Mean Height from Truncated Distributions
For many of our files, the possibility of obtaining useful information from the height-by-age data depends on solving the problem of selection bias due to truncation or shortfall in the height distribution, particularly for lower heights. Various distortions of the true underlying distribution of heights in the population contributing soldiers and sailors are to be expected in military height distributions, including heaping on whole or even numbers of inches, oversampling in the center of the distribution, and occasional undersampling of high heights. Although some distortions are apparent in all our bodies of data, the problem of undersampling of small heights is particularly acute for the regular armed forces of Britain and the United States. These organizations set minimum height limits at different times, varying with military needs, sometimes shifting frequently, and sometimes ranging as high as 67 inches. Minimum height standards were flexibly enforced so that very sharp cutoffs are not usually apparent in the data. It appears that in some cases 30 or 40 percent of the small heights in the underlying distribution may be missing. Such undersampling could vitiate the information content of the data unless reliable statistical procedures are employed to correct for the problem.

An important aspect of our project has been the development of statistical estimators that perform reliably in the presence of undersampling of small heights. These estimators must also cope with the other distortions that we suspect in the observed distributions. The multiple distortions make our problem more complicated than most undersampling problems treated in the statistical literature, even though some ideas presented in the literature may be capable of extension.[14]

---

units in the Gould sample were measured with shoes. However, for the ages shown in Table 1 below, the Baxter and Gould samples yield mean heights that differ from each other by less than one tenth of an inch. This finding indicates that the proportion of the men in the Union Army that may have been measured with shoes was too small to affect the analysis.

14 See, for example, A. C. Cohen, "Estimating the Mean and Variances of Normal Populations from Singly Truncated and Doubly Truncated Samples," *Annals of Mathematical Statistics,* XXI (1950), 557–569; H. Leon Harter and Albert H. Moore, "Iterative Maximum-Likelihood Estimation of the Parameters of Normal Populations from Singly and Doubly Censored Samples," *Biometrika,* LIII (1966), 205–213; Dale J. Poirier, "The Use of the Box-Cox Transformation in Limited Dependent Variable Models," *Journal of the American Statistical Association,* LXIII (1978), 284–287.

Our problem occurs at two levels. The first is the estimation of average height of an underlying distribution for men old enough to attain their terminal heights. A normal distribution for terminal heights is both well established for contemporary data and consistent with preliminary examination of our files, and the assumption of normality for the underlying distribution places our problem into a well-defined parametric framework. We are also faced with the problem of how to estimate the mean of a distribution of height at a given age during the ages of growth. Modern data indicate that the underlying distributions during adolescence are at first skewed to the right, as early maturers attain peak growth velocity, and then skewed to the left, when only late maturers still await their growth spurt.

Our two principal methods for correcting left-tail censoring, the quantile bend method (QQ) and the maximum likelihood method (RSMLE) are described in two recent papers. Extension of the RSMLE method to regression analysis is reported in a third paper. These methods have been tested extensively both by Monte Carlo techniques and by simulation techniques on actual distributions of heights; the tests have shown both to be generally reliable.[15]

One of the tests, for example, was performed on a sample of the heights of London school children for 1965. The data consist of complete (i.e. nontruncated) distributions at each age during the growth spurt. Sample sizes varied from 801 to 2,493; the absolute value of the coefficient of skewness (γ_1) varied from 0.031 to −0.201. Our procedure was to use our estimators to infer the true mean of the distribution under conditions of increasing truncation. The truncation was allowed to range from 0 to 80 percent of the distribution (truncating from the lower end). The particular point at issue was whether techniques devised to cope with truncation of normal distributions would be reliable when applied in an estimation of distributions of height at growing ages, which are positively skewed during the rising portion

15 Kenneth W. Wachter, "Graphical Estimation of Military Heights," *Historical Methods,* XIV (1981), 31–42; *idem* and Trussell, "Estimating Historical Heights," *Journal of the American Statistical Association,* LXXVII (1982), 279–303; Trussell and Wachter, "Estimating the Covariance of Height in Truncated Samples," unpub. ms. (1982).

of the growth spurt and negatively skewed during the declining portion. This effect was first discovered by Boas in 1892 and was documented by Tanner using London County Council data for 1955. The degree of skewing is statistically significant but small enough so that the distribution is treated as normal in the estimation of the centiles that demarcate the bounds for normal adolescent development. Nevertheless, it was necessary to determine whether even such moderate skewing would mislead our estimators in situations in which such skewing is combined with truncation.[16]

The estimators achieved nearly perfect results before truncation, demonstrating that skewing was too small to require the abandonment of the normal approximation in this case.[17] The estimators generally continued to behave well even with truncation of up to 50 percent of the original distribution. The RSMLE estimator performed very well with both continuous and grouped data. At levels of truncation below 50 percent it consistently produced estimates close to the true mean, although there was a tendency to over-correct, i.e., to produce estimates slightly below the true mean. The accuracy of the RSMLE estimator decreased with truncation above the modal value. The QQ estimator was generally correct even with truncation above 50 percent.

The "Basketball" Problem   It has been argued that one cannot assume, merely from the fact that a military distribution appears to be closely approximated by a normal or a truncated normal distribution, that the mean of the distribution may be taken as a reasonable estimate of the mean final height of males in civilian life. The issue raised here goes beyond biases of the type already considered. Persons rejected for reasons other than height, as we have seen, are only slightly shorter than those accepted (less than one tenth of an inch in the Civil War case) and

16 Tanner, "Boas' Contributions to Knowledge of Human Growth and Form," *Memoirs of the American Anthropological Association*, LXXXIX (1959), 76–111. Tanner cites several of Franz Boas' works in the bibliography, *ibid.,* 108.
17 A conclusion previously reached in Tanner, R. H. Whitehouse and M. Takaishi, "Standards From Birth to Maturity for Height, Weight, Height Velocity, and Weight Velocity: British Children, 1965," *Archives of Disease in Childhood*, XLI (1966), 454–471, 613–635.

the self-selection biases served to favor particular socioeconomic subgroups rather than to distort the height distribution of these subgroups.

What is at issue in the "basketball" problem is the possibility that the sampling criteria of the military organizations might produce distributions of height which, although normal, have a much higher mean height than that of the general population of adult males. In this connection, it is argued that one cannot use the normality of a given distribution as evidence of its representativeness. It is further suggested that if procedures such as those that we have developed were applied to the height distribution of players in the National Basketball Association (NBA), we would discover that this distribution was also normal, so that careless application of our procedures could lead to the erroneous conclusion that the mean height of American males was 78 inches.

Clearly, one cannot use the mere normality of a military distribution as evidence that it represents the overall adult civilian distribution—among other reasons, because the height distribution of each of the major socioeconomic subgroups in the population is also normal, although their means are significantly different. The power of the QQ procedure lies in what it tells us about height distributions that depart from normality. The distortions in such distributions are clues which, when carefully analyzed, suggest the nature of the selection or self-selection criteria that produced the distortions.[18]

The usefulness of our procedures is well illustrated by applying them to the distribution of heights in the NBA. Figure 1 shows the QQ plot for the NBA. If the distribution of heights were normal, the plot should form a straight line with the mean of the distribution given by the intersection of the plot with the zero ordinate. As can be seen in Part A of Figure 1, the plot of the NBA distribution is irregular, unlike the Civil War distribution of heights in Part C. Upon inspection, it appears that the NBA distribution

18 Theoretically, if the heights of each of the subgroups of a population are normally distributed but have different means, the overall population cannot be normally distributed and have the same standard deviation as the subpopulations. Nevertheless, the normal distribution gives a good fit to the overall distribution in such data sets as the Union Army, as well as to each of the major subgroups, and the standard deviations are generally quite similar.

Fig. 1 Application of the QQ Procedure to the Basketball Problem.

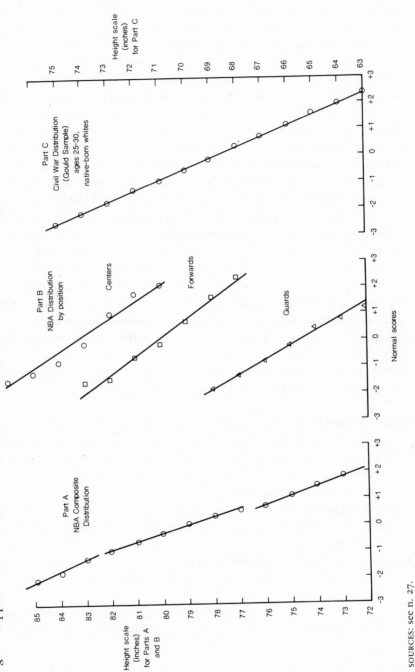

SOURCES: see n. 27.

might actually consist of at least two, and possibly three, straight-line segments. In other words, the plot in Part A suggests that the NBA distribution of heights might actually be the result of a composite of three normal distributions. Indeed, when separate distributions are computed for guards, centers, and forwards, we obtain three single-peaked distributions that appear to be censored normals, with means at 74.4, 80.2, and 83.4 inches (see Part B of Figure 1). Thus it appears that the managers of teams in the NBA have target heights for each position. Target heights may yield normal distributions even if the underlying population from which the sample is being drawn is highly skewed (as is the extreme right-hand tail of the distribution of adult heights).[19]

It follows that when working with military data one should take into account the sampling strategy of particular military units. In the case of the U.S. Army, official orders that established the standard for recruiting in different units have been published. In the British case, the standards are described in unpublished orders. The most common procedure was to have a minimum height requirement which shifted up or down depending on the demand for and supply of recruits. Some units, such as the cavalry and the navy, had both minimum and maximum requirements. Only a few parade companies had target heights, which were their ideal but which they did not always achieve.

PRELIMINARY FINDINGS   Although the major portion of the work over the past five years has been devoted to solving problems of data retrieval and management and the development of appropriate statistical procedures, preliminary analyses of the data have yielded striking findings regarding secular trends in heights, in nutrition and health, and in the welfare implications of these trends. The secular pattern of native-born U.S. whites prior to 1910 appears to be substantially different from that of most European populations. Similarly, the experience of U.S. blacks diverged from that of blacks born in the Caribbean or in Africa.

The Early Achievement of Modern Stature and Improved Nutrition in the United States   By the time of the American Revolution,

19   Zander Hollander (ed.), *The Complete Handbook of Pro Basketball* (New York, 1979; 6th ed.); the plot in Part C is based on data in the *Gould Report*, 96, 101.

Table 1 Mean Final Heights of U.S. Native-Born White Males in Three Wars

	AGE CATEGORY	SAMPLE SIZE	SAMPLE MEAN (INCHES)	STANDARD ERROR (INCHES)
American Revolution	24–35	968	68.1	0.08
Civil War				
Gould sample	25–30	123,472	68.2	0.01
Baxter sample	25–34	54,931	68.2	—
World War II	20–24	119,443	68.2	0.01

NOTE: Computed from data in colonial muster rolls, *Gould Report, Baxter Report,* and Karpinos, "Height and Weight." The Revolutionary, Gould, and Baxter samples are based on inductees. The World War II sample includes rejectees. Maximum mean height in the World War II sample falls in the 20–24 age category. The data in Baxter's summary do not permit the calculation of the standard error of the mean. Data presented by Karpinos indicate that inductees were about 0.09 inches taller than examinees. Data presented by Baxter indicate that inductees were 0.03 inches taller than examinees. Only the Revolutionary sample has been corrected for truncation bias. Preliminary analyses indicate that such corrections would not reduce the figures shown for the Civil War and World War II samples by more than 0.2 inches.

native-born whites appear to have achieved nearly modern final heights. The analysis of a sample of recruits from the Revolutionary Army (1775–1783) indicates that the final height of native-born white males between the ages of twenty-four and thirty-five averaged 68.1 inches. This figure is not only one to four inches greater than the final height of European males reported for several nations during the late seventeenth and early eighteenth centuries, but is also virtually identical with final heights in the Union Army during the Civil War and in the U.S. Army during World War II (see Table 1). Extending the analysis to a sample of recruits during the French and Indian War (1756–1763) indicates that final heights were increasing during the middle of the eighteenth century. After controlling for place of birth, place of residence, and occupation, cohorts born between 1740 and 1765 were 0.4 inches taller (t = 2.4) than those born between 1715 and 1739. Since cohorts born before 1740 still attained final heights that averaged above 67.5 inches, it appears likely that improvements in nutrition began early and were quite rapid in America.[20]

20 The evidence on adult heights in Europe during the eighteenth and early nineteenth centuries have not generally been analyzed for secular trends and in some cases have not yet been adequately analyzed for truncation bias. The principal studies of European heights

This inference is supported by data on food consumption in Massachusetts discovered by McMahon. Wills deposited in Middlesex county between 1654 and 1830 indicate a sharp rise in the average amount of meat annually allotted to widows for their consumption. Between c. 1675 and c. 1750 the average allotment increased from approximately eighty to approximately 165 pounds per annum. Over the next seventy-five years allotments rose more gradually, reaching 200 pounds at the end of the first quarter of the nineteenth century. The evidence both on stature and on food allotments suggests that Americans achieved an average level of meat consumption by the middle of the eighteenth century that was not achieved in Europe until well into the twentieth century. [21]

Cycles in Height   The estimated mean final heights of males for the three wars reported in Table 1 do not necessarily imply a perfectly flat secular trend between c. 1778 and c. 1943. Contrary to the popular impression that there have been continuous increases in height and secular improvements in nutrition, the evidence thus far analyzed in this project indicates that there may actually have been cycles in height of both native-born whites and blacks residing (but not necessarily born) in the United States.

Analysis of information contained in the coastwise manifests indicates that the final heights of slaves born in the early 1790s were approximately one half inch less than those of slaves born in the late 1770s (see Figure 2). The final heights of cohorts born after 1790 increased for approximately twenty years, so that cohorts born after 1815 were slightly taller than cohorts born during the late 1770s and 1780s. Thereafter final heights remained fairly steady at approximately 67.3 inches for cohorts born through the early 1830s. The data in the manifests now available are too sparse to carry the analysis of this time trend beyond cohorts born in

---

during this period are cited in NBER Working Paper 890, Appendix A. Only the series for Norway (V. Kiil, *Stature and Growth of Norwegian Men During the Last 200 Years* [Oslo, 1939], 175) and the sample of Swedish heights recently retrieved and analyzed by Sandberg and Steckel in "Soldier, Soldier," provide continuous series that reach back to the first half of the eighteenth century.

21 Sarah F. McMahon, "Provisions Laid Up for the Family," unpub. ms. (1980). George K. Holmes, "Meat Supply and Surplus," *U.S. Bureau of Statistics Bulletin*, 55 (1907), 87–98.

Fig. 2   Time Profile of Height of Slave Men Aged 23–49.

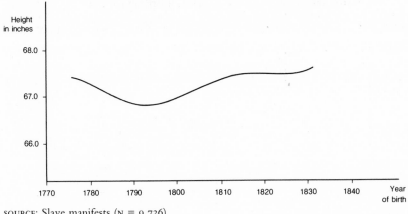

SOURCE: Slave manifests (N = 9,726)

the early 1830s. But the data on blacks taken from the Union Army muster rolls, which mesh quite well with the results from slave manifests for overlapping cohorts, indicate that cohorts born in the late 1830s and early 1840s may have experienced a decline in final heights that was even sharper than that experienced by cohorts born between 1780 and 1795.[22]

The time trend in the final height of northern, native-born whites is somewhat different from that of U.S. slaves. The rising trend observed for cohorts born before the Revolution levels off and appears to have remained fairly steady for cohorts born between the Revolution and the end of the 1790s. The regular army data needed to continue the trend from 1800 to 1819 have not yet been processed, but the preliminary analysis of a subsample (N = 773) of Union Army records bearing on this period, which covers only the last few years of the teens, suggests that cohorts born during the first two decades may have experienced increasing final heights. It also appears that their upward trend leveled during

22   Analyses of trends in heights of adolescent slaves confirm the general pattern revealed by adult heights, except that the amplitude of the cycles in adolescent heights are even greater than they are in final heights (Steckel, "Slave Height"). Taken together, the evidence on adolescents and adults suggests that there were periods of deterioration in the nutritional status and health of slaves that substantially retarded their rate of development during adolescence, but that this loss in tempo was partly compensated by a longer period of growth that permitted some "catching up."

Fig. 3 An Index of the Trend in the Mean Final Heights of U.S. Native-Born Whites, by Birth Cohort, 1819–1836

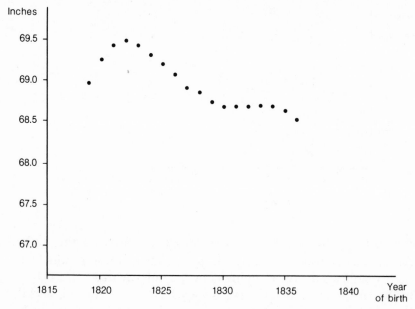

SOURCE: Preliminary sample of Union Army muster rolls (N = 533). Estimated from data on recruits into the Union Army who were between ages 25 and 44 at the time of measurement.

the 1820s and then declined (see Figure 3). Over a period of fifteen years the decline in the final heights of native-born whites appears to have been about one inch.

There is evidence of a cycle in stature between the Civil War and World War II. Table 2 shows that final height increased at a rate of 1.2 inches per generation between the cohorts born c.1906 and c.1921; between the c.1921 and c.1931 cohorts, the rate was 2.7 inches per generation. Obviously, even the 1.2 inch rate could not have extended back to the Civil War. That would require the final height of c.1863 to have been approximately two inches below the level indicated by the Gould and Baxter samples. Indeed, since the final height of the c.1906 cohort is about one half inch below the final height shown in the Civil War data, sometime between c.1863 and c.1926 (1906 + 20), final height declined.

Preliminary analysis of the British data has been focused on the trend in heights in London of adolescent boys from poor

Table 2 Twentieth-Century Growth Rates in Mean Final Height of U.S. Males (estimated from cohorts measured in c.1943 and c.1961)

Part A: Mean Final Heights Arranged by Cohorts

AGE CATEGORY WHEN MEASURED	SAMPLE SIZE	MIDPOINT OF THE INTERVAL IN WHICH COHORT WAS BORN	MEAN HEIGHT AT TIME OF MEASUREMENT
From U.S.D.H.E.W. (1965)			
1. 25–34	10,281	1931	69.11
2. 35–44	11,373	1921	68.22
From Karpinos			
3. 20–24	141,803	1921	6815
4. 25–29	99,786	1916	68.06
5. 30–34	96,704	1911	67.81
6. 35–37	53,624	1906.5	67.58

Part B: Growth Rates Per Generation Between Cohorts

INTERVAL OVER WHICH GROWTH RATE IS CALCULATED, BY BIRTH OF COHORT	GROWTH RATES (IN INCHES PER 30 YEARS)
1921–1931	2.7
1906.5–1921	1.2

NOTE: Data from longitudinal studies of stature indicate that shrinkage does not usually begin before age 50 (Tanner, privately communicated). If taller individuals were more likely to survive to a given age, the estimated growth rates would be biased downward, but the size of the bias would be small. If, for example, those who died between ages 30 and 40 were one inch shorter on average than those who survived to age 40, then (using the applicable life table in Samuel H. Preston, Nathan Keyfitz, and Robert Schoen, *Causes of Death: Life Tables for National Populations* [New York, 1972]) one would have to reduce the height of the c.1921 cohort by 0.03 inches before computing the 1921–1931 growth rate. This change would increase the 1921–1931 growth rate from 2.70 to 2.77 inches per generation.

SOURCES: Karpinos, "Height and Weight," 296, 302; USNCHS, 39.

families over the period from 1770 to 1870. This analysis reveals that the mean height of boys between the ages of fourteen and sixteen from families of laboring classes was relatively steady from c.1775 to c.1790 and then declined for two decades, the lowest point coming somewhere near 1810. The extent of the decline was about 1.5 inches. From c.1810 to c.1838 mean heights increased rapidly, at a rate of two inches per decade, so that the maximum previous mean was exceeded by 1820. After c.1838 heights again appear to have declined, but the new rate of decline was only about 0.2 inches over a period of twenty years, after standardizing for socioeconomic characteristics.

The exact timing of the sharp rise in height following the close of the Napoleonic wars is still under investigation. Although future work on statistical issues might lead to an expansion or compression of the period of rapid increases in heights, it is clear that poor adolescent boys in London were about four inches taller after 1838 than their counterparts had been before 1790. Indeed, the adolescent poor of London in the late eighteenth century were so short that only two of the eighty-one ethnic groups for which modern height data are available record lower adolescent heights. These are the Lumi and Bundi of New Guinea—two exceedingly impoverished populations. Even after the period of rapid increase, poor London boys were still short by modern British standards; at age fourteen, they were about five inches shorter than British boys of the same age today—a gap that is due partly to the slow rate of physical maturation and partly to malnutrition, probably early in life, that shifted the whole growth profile downward.

The Influence of Economic and Social Factors on Height   Multivariate regression analysis has been applied to several of the samples under study in order to relate final heights to such economic characteristics as occupation, migration experience, urban birth or residence, race, and place of birth. At the present time, with a few exceptions, the analyses have been limited to the information about each individual contained in the records on height. However, work is now underway to link information on the individuals and their families in the manuscript schedules of censuses, in probate and tax lists, and in other records. For example, the individuals included in the sample from the muster rolls of the Union Army are now being linked with information on their households contained in the manuscript schedules of the 1850, 1860, and 1870 censuses and with the pension records on these individuals and their heirs, usually filed late in their life or shortly after their death. In this way it is possible to obtain relevant information on the individuals, not only at the age of enlistment, but also during their growing years and in their later life. Such linking also allows an analysis of the effect of intergenerational factors (such as the ethnicity, wealth, and social status of parents and grandparents) on the development of children and grandchildren. Where such interrelationships cannot be established through direct linking at the household level, it is possible to use cross-sectional regression techniques, with counties or similar geographical divisions as the unit of observation, to analyze the nexus between height and relevant social and economic variables.

The regressions so far performed on the muster rolls of the French and Indian War, the Revolutionary War, the regular army during the early national period, and the Civil War show that in all four periods (1756–1763, 1775–1783, 1815–1820, and 1861–1865), persons of foreign birth were about an inch or more shorter than those of native birth. There was a significant shift over time in the impact of urban-rural residence on the final heights of the native born. Beginning with final heights virtually identical with native-born persons of urban birth, native-born persons of rural birth gained an advantage of 0.5 inches by the second decade of the nineteenth century, and this gap continued, if not widened, down to the time of the Civil War. There were also significant shifts over time in the relationship between occupation and stature. From only minor discrepancies in final heights between farmers and other occupational groups during the colonial period, significant differences had emerged by the time of the Civil War. Blue-collar recruits are nearly 0.8 inches shorter than farmers, after adjusting for urban/rural and nativity status. In all four time periods, the cross-sectional regressions yielded statistically significant coefficients on region of birth, race, and migratory experience.

Because ex-slaves in the Union Army were geographically concentrated, the sample already in hand is large enough to experiment with cross-sectional analysis at the county level. The analysis of final heights was performed on a sample of 913 ex-slaves who were between the ages of twelve and seventeen at the time of the 1850 census. On average, ex-slaves were about one inch shorter than were native-born whites. Moreover, slaves from the deep-South states that specialized in cotton and rice were shorter than those from border states engaged in tobacco and general farming. These state differentials appear to be explained by the positive correlation of height with per capita corn production, a negative correlation with the median size of the slave plantation, and a negative correlation with urbanization.[23]

In the case of the London boys there is abundant information on their socioeconomic characteristics before they entered the Marine Society which may be relevant in explaining variations in heights. However, an analysis of this information is retarded by the limited range of differences in the occupational categories, by variations in the minimum height standard, and by the rapid pace of change. Two characteristics which do appear as significant determinants of height so far are addresses outside London (associated with taller boys) and the designation "destitute" (with shortness).[24]

The Influence of Height on Social and Economic Behavior　One of the bodies of data recently analyzed bears on the impact of height on the productivity of manual laborers. Some commanders of the Union Army treated runaway slaves as contraband of war, and so, in addition to recording some of the usual information found in muster rolls, they also included information on the value of the slaves. One such contraband list, discovered in records for Mississippi, has recently been analyzed. The mean height of the 523 adult males in this sample was 67.4 inches, with a standard deviation of 2.8 inches—almost identical to the corresponding figures for Mississippi recruits obtained in the main sample of black companies.[25]

23 Since corn was mainly a feed crop, corn per capita may be viewed as a proxy for meat per capita.
24 The Marine Society, the source of the height data on the London boys, was a charitable organization which received indigent or otherwise poor boys and prepared them for careers in the merchant marine or the Royal Navy.
25 These Mississippi records were discovered by Armstead Robinson. The estimates of value appear to have been made by bona fide slave appraisers. The contraband sample is exceptional not only because of the information on value, but also because it is a rare instance, for the early and mid-nineteenth century, when data are available for both height and weight. The Mississippi slaves had a mean weight of 2.3 pounds per inch of height, when measured at mean height. Corresponding figures for samples of adults aged 30–34 are 2.2 pounds per inch for whites in the Union Army, 2.3 pounds per inch for white registrants in World War II, and 2.3 pounds per inch for black registrants in World War II. These weight-for-height figures indicate that Mississippi slaves were slightly heavier, for given stature, than the whites in the Union Army, but about the same as registrants for selective service in World War II. The Union Army figure was computed by fitting a linear regression to the data in the *Gould Report,* 426–428; the World War II figures are from Karpinos, "Height and Weight," 305–308.

Regression analysis revealed that the value of slaves was positively associated with both height and weight. A slave of average weight for his height who was one standard deviation taller than the mean height was worth 7.7 percent more than a slave who was one standard deviation shorter than the mean height. Some part of this increment in value may be because tall slaves were, on average, stronger, healthier, and more capable of intense labor than were short slaves. But two other factors, which could not be entered into the regression because of the absence of information on them in the contraband sample, are probably reflected in the differential in value which was associated with stature. It is probable that healthy slaves had a longer life expectation than unhealthy ones. It is also possible that slaves in the more highly skilled jobs were taller than were those engaged in field work. Thus the increase in productivity implied by the height differential in value could have taken several forms: one is greater intensity of labor per day at a given task and for a fixed expectation of life and labor; a second is unchanged intensity of daily labor at a given task with an increased expectation of life and labor; and a third is unchanged intensity of daily labor and life expectation, but employment in occupations requiring greater skill than ordinary field work.

Analysis of the data in the Trinidad sample bears on these possibilities. Height was a factor in the selection of slaves for particular occupations in Trinidad. Among adult males, craftsmen were on average one half inch taller and drivers (the foremen of field gangs) a full inch taller than fieldhands, whereas domestics were an inch shorter than fieldhands. Since slaves were not usually chosen for craft occupations until their twenties, and since regression analysis revealed no relationship between the occupation of the parents and the height of the children, it appears that the final height of children was not affected by their position, but that owners or overseers used height as a criterion for determining which slaves would be assigned to particular occupations.

The most important result to emerge from the study of the Trinidad data thus far is that death did not choose slaves at random. Short slaves at every age during the life cycle were more likely to die than were tall ones. After standardizing for age, the annual death rate for the shortest quintile of males (47 per 1,000) over a twenty-month period extending from 1813 to 1815 was more than twice as great as that of the tallest quintile of males

(21 per 1,000). Among females the standardized death rates for the lowest and highest quintiles of height were 43 and 29 per 1,000, which suggests that female death rates were less sensitive to nutritional circumstances than were male rates. One implication of this finding is that the combination of the exceedingly high death rates in Trinidad and the large impact of height on the probability of dying makes the observed height-by-age profile rise more rapidly than would have been so in a less severe environment in which a larger proportion of short slaves would have survived to adult ages. Alternative simulations suggest that a 50 percent reduction in the death rate, with other factors held constant, might have reduced the observed final heights of males by approximately one inch.

SOME ECONOMIC AND DEMOGRAPHIC ISSUES   The apparent downward shift in the U.S. height profile for native-born whites during the last several decades of the antebellum era does not imply that the profile of every subpopulation declined: the decline might have been heavily concentrated within the urban population. The rate of urbanization accelerated sharply after 1820, and conditions of life in the larger cities apparently deteriorated. There is evidence in several northeastern cities of an upward trend in the mortality rates. Another possibility is that the decline was the consequence of an increased flow of immigrants; experiments on animals indicate that malnutrition in one generation affects the size of subsequent generations. The patterns observed in the height-by-age data are consistent with evidence that the period between 1820 and 1860 was marked by an increase in the inequality of income distribution, with the heights and wages of common laborers falling relative to those of other groups.[26]

The two cycles in height discovered for U.S. slaves probably have somewhat different explanations. Since the coastwise manifests did not distinguish between foreign- and native-born slaves, and given the three-inch differential between the heights of U.S.

26 Yasukichi Yasuba, *Birth Rates of the White Population in the United States, 1800–1860* (Baltimore, 1962); Ranjit K. Chandra, "Antibody Formation in First and Second Generation Offspring of Nutritionally Deprived Rats," *Science*, CXC (1975), 289–290; Peter H. Lindert and Jeffrey G. Williamson, "Three Centuries of American Inequality," in Paul Uselding (ed.), *Research in Economic History* (Greenwich, Conn., 1976), I, 69–123.

and African-born slaves in Trinidad indicated by the data, an increase from 15 to 30 percent in the proportion of the African-born slaves listed in the manifests could account for about three quarters of the first decline in slave heights. Since the years between the end of the Revolution and the close of the international slave trade witnessed a sharp increase in slave imports, such an explanation is plausible. Some part of the second height decline (that of slaves born in the late 1830s and the 1840s) might be due to ethnic mix, but it is unlikely that the share so attributed could exceed one quarter of the estimated decline. The Trinidad data indicate that the first generation of native-born males in non-sugar production were about 1.5 inches taller than the African-born males, which suggests that about half of the height gap was made up in one generation. Moreover, it is probable that close to half of the persons descended from Africans imported into the U.S. between 1783 and 1808 and born between 1835 and 1845 were not children but grandchildren or great-grandchildren of Africans. It seems likely, therefore, that most of the second decline was due to a rise in the intensity of labor, a decline in meat consumption, a rise in morbidity, or some combination of all of these factors.[27]

The changing levels of nutrition and health over time implied by the height data have substantial implications for the study of the U.S. mortality experience. The evidently high level of nutrition in America at the time of the Revolution may well provide a partial explanation for the low mortality rates, relative to Europe, which characterized the early U.S. demographic experience.

27 Steckel, "Slave Mortality: Analysis of Evidence from Plantation Records," *Social Science History*, III (1979), 86–114. The estimated effects of ethnic mix on the cycles in slave heights should be considered upper bounds for two reasons. First, to the extent that imported slaves were West Indian creoles, the effect of changes in the ethnic mix on mean height would be diminished. Curtin's investigations suggest that about 90% of all slaves imported into the U.S. between 1701 and 1810 were born in Africa. Second, since the proportion of African-born slaves in the U.S. slave population between 1780 and 1810 appears to have varied in a relatively narrow range (18 to 22%), a doubling of the proportion of African slaves among those born between 1775 and 1795 suggests sharp changes in the age structure of African imports, with the share of children rising more rapidly and reaching higher levels than has hitherto been supposed. Philip D. Curtin, *The Atlantic Slave Trade: A Census* (Madison, 1969), 142–145; Fogel and Engerman, *Time on the Cross* (Boston, 1974), I, 23; David Galenson, "The Atlantic Slave Trade and the Barbados Market, 1673–1723," *Journal of Economic History*, XLII (1982), 491–511.

Since the consumption of food is a major component of the standard of living in preindustrial societies, the advantage in height also provides strong evidence of the superior material conditions enjoyed by the average American during the period. However, despite an apparently close correlation between changes in heights and in mortality during the years between 1730 and 1850, a substantial portion of the pre-1850 decline in national mortality rates appears to be explained by other factors besides changes in nutrition.[28]

The late eighteenth and early nineteenth centuries were characterized by the narrowing of interregional differences in mortality rates between New England and the South. Crude mortality rates in Massachusetts appear to have remained in the fifteen to twenty-five per 1,000 range throughout this period, while the rates for whites in the South declined from about fifty per 1,000 to about twenty-five per 1,000. The higher mean final height found for the South than for the North during this period tends to dispel the notion that the southern mortality rates were linked to lower levels of nutrition in that area. It now seems more likely that superior nutritional circumstances operated to close the gap between regional death rates by counteracting factors that increased mortality in the South (disease pool, climate, etc.). Frag-

28 The height data will also be used to test the hypothesis that nutrition affected U.S. fertility rates. Recent summaries of evidence bearing on the link between nutrition, fecundity (reproductive capacity), and fertility (actual reproduction) are John Bongaarts, "Does Malnutrition Affect Fecundity? A Summary of the Evidence," *Science*, CCVIII (1980), 564–569; Jane Menken, Trussell, and Susan Watkins, "The Nutrition Fertility Link: An Evaluation of the Evidence," *Journal of Interdisciplinary History*, XI (1981), 425–444. Both articles stress that moderate chronic malnutrition has only "a minor effect on fecundity" and that the effect on fertility "is very small" (Bongaarts, 568). However, famine and severe chronic malnutrition can substantially reduce fertility. It is not clear how much of the reduction associated with famine and severe chronic malnutrition is due to a decline in fecundity (although amenorrhea and reduction in sperm motility and longevity are involved) and how much is due to such indirect factors as loss of libido, increased separation of spouses (because of search for work or food), and, especially for societies during the eighteenth and nineteenth centuries, increases in deaths which lead to a premature ending of childbearing or to increased birth intervals (because widowhood reduces sexual intercourse). Cf. Rose E. Frisch, "Population, Food Intake, and Fertility," *Science*, CXCIX (1978), 22–30. NBER, "Report on the Program of the National Bureau of Economic Research on Long-term Factors in American Economic Development," unpub. ms. (1980).

mentary evidence suggests that southerners were heavy consumers of meat in the late colonial and early national eras.[29]

Nevertheless, it is possible that some part of the height advantage of the South was due to the Trinidad effect. Although death rates were far less severe in the South between 1750 and 1860 than in Trinidad c.1813, the higher probability of death for shorter persons would have inflated southern heights relative to northern ones, over and above the direct nutritional effect. Consequently there appears to be not only a direct nutritional effect but also (holding nutrition constant) a mortality effect and an interaction effect. The magnitudes of these separate effects are yet to be determined.[30]

We are, as previously indicated, studying the relationship between mortality and nutrition in the United States (using height as an index of nutrition), and we are also introducing measures of nutritional status into production functions for both the agricultural and manufacturing sectors. The results of the latter procedure may not be unambiguous, since the intensification of labor that enhanced productivity and accompanied the growth of the manufacturing sector could have led to an increase in the per capita energy output relative to the consumption of calories and nutrients among adolescent laborers, and this may have produced a decline in stature.

29 Maris A. Vinovskis, "Mortality Rates and Trends in Massachusetts Before 1860," *Journal of Economic History*, XXXII (1972), 184–214; Fogel et al., "The Economics of Mortality in North America, 1650–1910: A Description of a Research Project," *Historical Methods*, XI (1978), 75–108. Sokoloff and Villaflor, "The Early Achievement of Modern Stature in America," *Social Science History*, VI (1982), 453–481; Lewis C. Gray, *History of Agriculture in the Southern United States to 1860* (Washington, D.C., 1933), 2v. In 1901, the earliest year for which systematic surveys of food consumption by region are available, the per capita consumption of beef and pork was about 4% greater in the South than in the North. The food survey is from U.S. Bureau of Labor, *Eighteenth Annual Report of the Commissioner of Labor* (Washington, D.C., 1903), 647–648. The North is an average of the North Atlantic and North Central regions and the South is an average of the South Atlantic and South Central regions, using the regional populations as weights.

30 The Trinidad effect might also have contributed to the decline in white heights after the mid-1820s shown in Figure 3, since persons from the earlier birth cohorts who survived to be mustered into the Union Army would be taller than those from later birth cohorts, even if the mean height of each cohort at a specified age (such as 30) was the same. Given the prevailing mortality schedules, however, and the age span involved (25–45), the Trinidad effect could account for only about one tenth of the drop after the mid-1820s shown in Figure 3, and it could not explain the preceding rise in heights.

It cannot be assumed, therefore, that a decrease in the final heights of native-born whites after 1825 necessarily implies a reduction in per capita food consumption. It might seem unlikely that the stature of whites, who were free and who experienced most of their growth by age twenty, would be much influenced by changes in labor organization. During the nineteenth century, however, especially before 1850, boys commonly entered the labor force before age sixteen, which generally preceded the peak of the adolescent growth spurt. Consequently, a decline in height could have resulted because there was an increase in the per capita energy output of these young workers without a corresponding increase in the per capita consumption of calories and nutrients. British investigations of child labor in factories during the nineteenth century support this hypothesis. Children of a given socioeconomic class who worked in factories were substantially shorter at each age than children of the same class who were not so employed.[31]

Still, it is possible that the food consumption of the urban laboring classes did decline between 1825 and 1860. This possibility cannot be ruled out either because of the slight downward trend in food prices or because of the upward trend in some of the currently available indexes of real wages. Part of the problem with the wage indexes, as previously noted, is that the series on money wages may confound urban with rural wage rates and is not adequately standardized for locational and occupational mix. Another part of the problem is that the current measures of consumer prices do not include data on the cost of shelter, which may have accounted for a quarter or more of the total expenditures of urban laborers during this period. There is considerable evidence that the rapid growth of the urban population between 1820 and 1860 led to severe shortages in urban housing, and hence probably to a sharp rise in the price of shelter. The decline in the availability of wood and the shift from wood to coal as a fuel source may also have contributed to the rising cost of shelter.

Consequently, it is entirely possible that an index of consumer prices that included the cost of shelter would show a decline

---

31 Great Britain, "Report of the Factory Commissioners of 1883," *Parliamentary Papers,* XX (1833); British Association for the Advancement of Science, "Final Report of the Anthropometric Committee," *Report of the 53rd Meeting* (London, 1884), 296–299.

in the real wages of urban laborers between 1825 and 1860. Moreover, if the income and price elasticities of the demand for shelter
by urban laborers (at the relatively meager incomes of the time)
were sufficiently low, sharp rises in the cost of shelter could have
led to decreases in the amount of food consumed, particularly in
the consumption of such relatively expensive foods as meat and
fish, even in the face of constant or declining food prices.

In the English case, we have been able to make a comparison
between a series on heights and a widely used series on real wages
for London artisans. Although Von Tunzelmann has demonstrated that nation-wide indexes of real wages are unreliable because of the implicit shifts in the weights brought about by the
splicing together of diverse series, the question remains as to
whether indexes for particular localities and classes of labor are
reliable. Also at issue is the assumption that trends in the real
wages of artisans mirror those of common laborers. Tucker's
series on the real wages of London artisans benefits from the
restriction of its geographical scope to one locality. When one
compares the mean height of boys between the ages of fourteen
and sixteen from families of common laborers in the London area,
over the years between 1775 and 1865, with Tucker's series, a
certain degree of conformity is evident (see Figure 4). The heights
of the boys will reflect their cumulative nutritional experience
over their lifetime, and especially the experience of the years
immediately preceding and during the growth spurt. Accord-
ingly, the height series is related to the wage series lagged five
years, although longer lags (ten and thirteen years) provide similar
results.[32]

The two series generally move together during both rising
and declining phases, except for the last two decades. The correlation suggests that, for most of the century, the real wages of
artisans and of the poorest sections of the London working class
tended to move together. However, the elasticity of height with
respect to Tucker's wage index is not constant, and the preliminary regression analysis of the relationship between the height of
boys in the Marine Society and the occupational strata within the

---

32 Each observation is an average of 10 years centered at the indicated date. Von
Tunzelmann, "Trends in Real Wages," 48–49. See also Tucker, "Real Wages of Artisans,"
21–35.

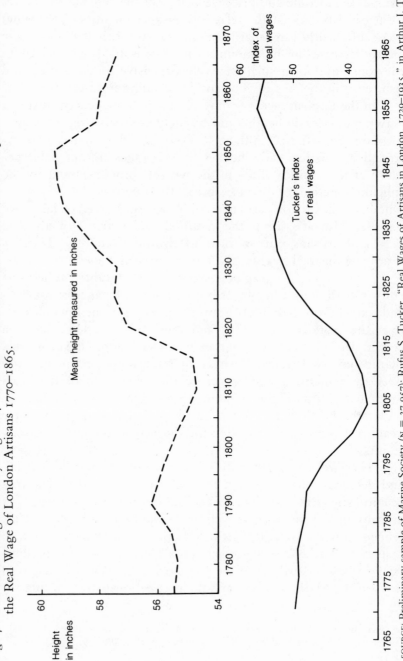

Fig. 4 The Mean Height of Boys Aged 14–16 from Families of London Laborers Compared with Tucker's Index of the Real Wage of London Artisans 1770–1865.

Height in inches

60

58

56

54

Mean height measured in inches

1780 1785 1790 1795 1800 1805 1810 1815 1820 1825 1830 1835 1840 1845 1850 1860 1870

Index of real wages

60

50

40

Tucker's index of real wages

1765 1775 1785 1795 1805 1815 1825 1835 1845 1855 1865

SOURCE: Preliminary sample of Marine Society (N = 37,957); Rufus S. Tucker, "Real Wages of Artisans in London, 1729–1935," in Arthur J. Taylor (ed.), *The Standard of Living in the Industrial Revolution* (London, 1975), 28–30.

laboring classes changed over time. These findings raise the possibility of a changing relationship between the wages of common laborers and of artisans even prior to 1840, and illustrate the problem of generalizing from the experience of one group of a population (or the average) to those of other groups.

During the past half century economic and social historians have developed new measures, such as per capita income and indexes of real wages, that have shed much light on the course of economic development and on the degree to which various socioeconomic classes have shared in the benefits of that development. Use of these measures has helped to correct misimpressions that were based on isolated scraps of evidence, but such use has also raised new questions that reveal the limitation of these measures. For many countries reliable per capita income estimates could not be pushed back much further than the mid-nineteenth century and then could only be constructed for decadal intervals. Consequently, national income accounts have shed relatively little light on the evolution of cyclical phenomena or on how and when differences in per capita income among nations, which were already large by 1850 or 1860, came into being. Similar problems have arisen with long-term series of real wages which are often spliced together from a variety of short series in the hope that shifting from one occupation to another, or one locality to another, would not undermine the comparability of the observations in the series.

Efforts to fill existing gaps in knowledge have taken many directions, and the exploration of the uses of data on height is one of them. That data on height contain much information on economic and social well being is one of the oldest propositions in the social sciences. Such distinguished figures of the past two centuries as Louis René Villermé in France, Adolphe Quetelet in Belgium, Edwin Chadwick and Francis Galton in England, and Benjamin A. Gould and Franz Boas in the United States have used this body of information to investigate economic and social behavior. Recent efforts are, therefore, not breaking with scientific tradition but are returning to a fruitful line of research with larger and richer data sets, improved statistical techniques, and the expanded capacity to handle large data sets which has been made possible by high-speed computers.

The preliminary findings of the new work are promising, but the tentative nature of the findings should be emphasized. The most secure generalization to emerge so far is that patterns of improvement in nutrition and health after 1700 were more varied and complex than is usually appreciated. Although heights and nutrition appear to have improved markedly in the United States (and the colonies that preceded it) during the eighteenth century, so that modern heights were reached by the time of the American Revolution, similar developments in Western Europe were delayed by as much as a century. England appears to have been at least a half century into its Industrial Revolution before witnessing a marked improvement in the heights or nutrition of its laboring classes. Down to the end of the Napoleonic wars the nutritional levels of poor London adolescents were worse than they are today in all but a few of the most impoverished populations of the underdeveloped world.

Nutritional advances during the nineteenth century were uneven both among different classes within particular nations and across the nations of the North Atlantic community. In the United States the height differentials between socioeconomic classes were markedly greater during the Civil War than they had been during the Revolution. In England, however, the growth profile of the London poor shifted upward so rapidly that half of the gap with modern teenage heights was closed in just two or three decades. Increases in average height were not as continuous as has often been supposed in either Europe or America, but were interrupted by substantial periods of decline. In the American case, average heights of both whites and blacks began to decline with cohorts born during the late 1820s or early 1830s and continued to do so past the Civil War. Rapid and sustained increases in height probably resumed with cohorts born sometime before World War I and proceeded, at rates outstripping previous experience, for half a century.

What is at issue now is the explanation for these patterns of change in heights and nutrition. Among the factors that might be involved are changes in the ethnic composition of the native-born population, increased claims on food intake as a consequence of increased intensity of labor or a deteriorating disease environment, and shifts in the urban-rural composition of the population. The life-cycle and intergenerational data sets which are now being linked to the height-by-age data should help to differentiate among these possibilities as well as to determine the effects of changes in nutrition during the growing ages on labor productivity, morbidity, and mortality at later stages of the life cycle.

Carl E. Taylor

Synergy among Mass Infections, Famines, and

Poverty   A recurrent theme through the pages of human history has been a presumed relationship between epidemics and famines. But, does a relationship exist, or have historical records exaggerated coincidental occurrences of the two events, since both are so dramatic? Observed associations may not have a true causal relationship; both may have been the result of social forces such as wars, migrations, and political disruptions. In addition, can we say anything about the commonly observed and continuing synergism between mass infections and chronic malnutrition and their demographic impact in selectively weeding out the poor and socially deprived? If so, it may help us to understand how such events occurred in the past.

It has also become important to measure and discuss openly sex selection in health care and mortality. Hopes for a shift toward new roles and rights for women have to be recognized as a deviation from past patterns in which high female mortality was an important mechanism for maintaining demographic balance. Historically, a principal means of limiting population growth has been discrimination against the poor and against females. However, it is increasingly evident that a better balance between birth and death rates can most effectively be achieved by providing special care to these two groups. If this hypothesis can be scientifically validated, we will be fortunate that goals which we perceive to be morally right would also be the most reasonable way to help resolve three of our most serious world dilemmas—the population problem, discrimination against the poor in health care, and improving the role and status of women.

Carl E. Taylor is Professor of International Health at the Johns Hopkins University. He is the principal editor of *Child and Maternal Health Services in Rural India: The Narangwal Experiment,* forthcoming.

CONGRUENCE OF EPIDEMICS AND FAMINES   Famines and epidemics have been consistently linked in historical records, and, although no systematic analysis of quantitative data is possible because they are so sketchy, the apparent association has, nevertheless, become generally accepted and has influenced scholars through the years. A quotation from Hippocrates illustrates the way that epidemics, general disruptions of food supplies, and famines have been recorded: "So great a plague and mortality was never yet known, in the memory of man. . . . The bringing of provisions from the country to the city was an additional grievance, and equally affected those who came with them into the city."[1]

The question can probably never be answered as to whether the reported associations were due to a true synergism or whether both famines and epidemics were caused by other social forces. Aycock and Lutman, and also Schneider, pointed out that the suspected relationships between disease and malnutrition were accepted more because of reiteration than because of firm evidence. Sigerist concluded that the most salient initiating factor of such synergistic interactions—general social dislocation due to wars, migrations, and political disruption—was a common cause for both epidemics and famines.[2]

Evidence might be found by focusing on Europe after 1850, which was a period which saw a major drop in the number of epidemics and famines. Zinsser concluded that "It is not easy to account for the decline." He listed as possible factors: "cyclic change in the character of prevalent diseases. . . . the fact that wars, during this period, were of short duration and operations were within relatively circumscribed areas. . . . the safeguard against famine provided by the development of intensive agriculture and the perfection of railroad transportation. . . . [and] the rise of modern medicine, rational approaches to prevention, and

1 Nevin S. Scrimshaw, Taylor, and John E. Gordon, *The Interactions of Nutrition and Infection* (Geneva, 1968). Hippocrates (trans. Francis Clifton), *Upon Air, Water and Situations* (London, 1752), 95–100.
2 W. Lloyd Aycock and Grace E. Lutman, "Vitamin Deficiency as an Epidemiologic Principle," *American Journal of Medical Science*, CCVIII (1944), 389–406. Howard A. Schneider, "Nutrition and Resistance to Infection: The Strategic Situations," in Robert S. Harris and Kenneth V. Thimann (eds.), *Vitamins and Hormones* (New York, 1946), IV, 35–70. Henry E. Sigerist, *Civilization and Disease* (Ithaca, 1943), 9.

the organization of health supervision which gradually extended into all ramifications of community life." In short, a strictly historical approach has given only limited insight into the relationships.[3]

DEMOGRAPHIC IMPACT ON THE POOR   Do famines and epidemics produce a selective demographic impact on the poor? Reports from contemporary observers make sobering reading as they describe conditions during the epidemic era in Europe. Abundant evidence shows that synergism between malnutrition and common infections normally occurred most frequently among the poor, and it is only reasonable that this effect became much more evident in times of great deprivation. As trade and travel reached levels that encouraged the easy spread of epidemics, it became increasingly apparent that unrestrained commercial greed placed the poor in particular jeopardy. Epidemics mainly affected urban slums. Economic conditions may have been even worse in the rural areas from which people were migrating, but the relative isolation of these population groups shielded them from the greatest impact of such diseases.

The sanitary conditions in the cities seemed to have been designed to favor disease, with slops and toilet pots being dumped unceremoniously out of upstairs bedroom windows into the streets below. Vermin flourished, especially because of the conviction in Europe that one of the most unhealthy things one could do was to take a bath. When an epidemic started in the slums, the wealthy escaped to their estates and châteaus in the country until it burned itself out. The massive mortality caused by epidemics and famines selectively eliminated the bottom of the economic pyramid.

An example from historical writings concerning a specific disease is the following description of relapsing fever. Scott reviewed the known outbreaks up to 1880 and found that there was no consistent association with climate, weather, season, soil, etc. He noted that "privation was thought also to be causative and the name 'famine fever' and . . . 'starvation typhus' evidence this

3   Hans Zinsser, *Rats, Lice and History* (Boston, 1950), 292.

idea." But Scott concluded that epidemics did not generally co-incide with famine. The most significant factors seemed to be "Housing defects, slums and dirty environment, with overcrowding and bad hygiene . . . and relapsing fever is almost entirely . . . a *morbus pauperum,* as Engel calls it . . . 'The untaxed pay their tax in disease.' This has been noted often in temperate climates, but examples are seen also in warmer countries."[4]

During the decline of the epidemic era in Europe and America, what happened to nutrition and population growth patterns among the various social classes? McKeown's view that the economic advances which accompanied the industrial revolution eventually led to better nutrition, and that this progressively contributed to a reduction in the prevalence of infections, is epidemiologically sound. During the transition period, those economic benefits from free-wheeling entrepreneurship that did trickle down eventually ensured a better nutritional status for individuals at the bottom of the economic scale. But reports, such as those of Chadwick and Shattuck, record dramatically higher mortality for the poor than for those better off economically during the transition period.[5]

CURRENT PATTERNS OF SYNERGISM AROUND THE WORLD   Since we will probably never be able to determine the precise causal links between epidemics and famines from historical data, it may help to consider evidence based on what we know now of biological relationships. Epidemics and famines have declined as major demographic forces. The impact of the synergism between malnutrition and infections, however, continues almost unrestrained because epidemics and famines were only the tip of a very large iceberg. Synergism between common infections and malnutrition probably accounts for more mortality, morbidity, and reduced growth and development than any other combination of factors.

4 H. Harold Scott, *A History of Tropical Medicine* (Baltimore, 1942), II, 785.
5 Thomas McKeown, *The Modern Rise of Population* (New York, 1976). Edwin Chadwick, "Report on an Inquiry into the Sanitary Conditions of the Labouring Population of Great Britain (London 1882)," in Benjamin Ward Richardson (ed.), *The Health of Nations: A Review of the Works of Edwin Chadwick* (London, 1887), II, 7–318; Lemuel Shattuck, *Report of the Sanitary Commission of Massachusetts* (Cambridge, Mass., 1850; repub. 1948).

Infections such as diarrhea and measles, which would be self-limited in normally nourished children, continue to be major causes of mortality in children who are malnourished.[6] In addition, common infections precipitate overt malnutrition where nutritional status is borderline. Even today the downward spiral caused by the interaction of these factors represents one of the principal challenges to health care in developing countries.

When evidence on synergism first attracted scientific attention it came from two directions. Nutrition research workers conducting experiments on laboratory animals complained repeatedly that infections selectively killed off their malnourished animals. Similarly, experiments on infections in humans were ruined when malnutrition intervened. Morley, Bicknell, and Woodland observed that epidemics of kwashiorkor followed epidemics of measles. The relationship became most evident in clinical research when improved nutritional support resulted in remarkable improvements for patients suffering from tuberculosis and typhoid. A major justification for nutritional programs became the fact that they could help control infections. Infectious disease specialists also claimed that their programs would improve nutritional status. From such experiences the realization emerged that research on both problems must be brought together.[7]

The effects of the synergism between nutrition and disease is highly correlated with socioeconomic status and sex. Data from all countries show that most of the children who die are from poor families and also that in many cultures the mortality of female children is greater than that of males. In India, regular censuses have been carried out for more than a century. During this time a distinct gradient has been found in the ratios of males to females in different regions. At birth in most developed countries there are about 105 males to 100 females, but the higher survival rates of females then leads to a ratio in the general population of less than 100. However, in North India, the sex ratio has consistently been over 110 and it declines as one goes south.

---

6 But see Ann G. Carmichael, "Infection, Hidden Hunger, and History," in this issue.

7 David C. Morley, Joan Bicknell, and Margaret Woodland, "Factors Influencing the Growth and Nutritional Status of Infants and Young Children in a Nigerian Village," *Transactions of the Royal Society of Tropical Medicine and Hygiene,* LV (1968), 164.

Table 1 Sex Ratios in India, 1901–1971

STATE	1901	1911	1921	1931	1941	1951	1961	1971
Kerala	99.6	99.2	98.9	97.9	97.4	97.3	97.9	98.4
Punjab	120.2	128.2	125.2	122.7	119.6	118.5	117.2	115.6
(Reorganized)								
All India	102.9	103.8	104.7	105.3	105.8	105.7	106.3	107.4

SOURCE: Pravin M. Visaria, "The Sex Ratio of the Population of India," *Census of India, 1961* (New Delhi, 1971), I.

For example, in the 1971 census the sex ratio in the Punjab was 115 but in Kerala it was 98 (Table 1).[8]

More careful analyses have shown that these differences are caused mainly by relatively greater female mortality in infancy, childhood, and during child-bearing years. Kelly's calculations show that the greater female mortality observed in the Punjab is responsible for approximately an 8 percent reduction in the population growth rate. This differential mortality is not only cultural but also relates to economic opportunities for women. Rosenzweig and Schultz, in careful econometric analyses of household data from various parts of India, have shown that differential mortality between male and female children in the various states is correlated with different employment opportunities for men and women and is also directly influenced by marked variations in intrafamily resource distribution.[9]

High female mortality is most clearly related to son preference in North India, Pakistan, and Iran, but in many developing countries this phenomenon is also present, although less overt. Markle demonstrated the potential demographic impact on the population of the United States that would result if couples could

8 Pravin M. Visaria, "The Sex Ratio of the Population of India," *Census of India, 1961* (New Delhi, 1971), I. Mohamed A. El-Badry, "Higher Female than Male Mortality in some Countries of South Asia: A Digest," *Journal of the American Statistical Association,* LXIV (1969), 1234–1244.
9 Narindar Uberoi Kelly, "Some Socio-Cultural Correlates of Indian Sex Ratios: Case Studies of Punjab and Kerala," unpub. Ph.D. diss. (Univ. of Pennsylvania, 1975). Mark R. Rosenzweig and T. Paul Schultz, "Market Opportunities, Genetic Endowments, and Intrafamily Resource Distribution: Child Survival in Rural India," *American Economic Review,* LXXII (1982), 803–815.

in fact have the number of sons that, in surveys, they had indicated they desired. The time in which the population would double given the current sex ratio at birth of 105 would be 118 years; for a sex ratio of 113, doubling time would be 157 years; and for a sex ratio of 116, it would be 178 years. The family surveys had indicated male preference levels that would have produced sex ratios of between 113 and 116. Similarly, it has been postulated that female infanticide in medieval Europe contributed to the limitation of population growth.[10]

SYNERGISM IN CURRENT PROGRAMS FOR HEALTH, NUTRITION, AND FAMILY PLANNING   In assessing the current situation, I will turn from historical records to present the results of our own research. It is one example of many studies conducted around the world which can provide insights useful for interpreting past patterns of health, nutrition, and population growth. Over a period of many years, at the Narangwal Rural Health Research Center in India, a series of analyses were done under field conditions. They demonstrated that there can be a synergism of programs as well as of problems. In four clusters of villages, services were provided to measure the impact of infection control, nutrition, an integrated package of both, and a control group. The results showed that infection control and nutritional improvement applied together is more effective and can be provided at lower cost and with greater equity than could either program alone.[11]

The relation between nutritional status and child mortality was especially dramatic and illustrates the importance of looking not only at famines but also at hidden hunger (Fig. 1). Perinatal mortality was reduced most when the diet of mothers was supplemented, particularly with iron and folic acid. Infection control had about half as much effect on perinatal mortality, mainly due

10   Gerald E. Markle, "Sex Ratio at Birth: Values, Variance, and some Determinants," *Demography*, XI (1974), 131–142. Emily R. Coleman, "L'Infanticide dans le Haut Moyen Age," *Annales*, XXIX (1974), 315–335. Steven Polgar (ed.), *Culture and Population: A Collection of Current Studies* (Chapel Hill, 1971).
11   Department of International Health, Johns Hopkins University, "Integration of Family Planning and Health Services: The Narangwal Experience," *Indian Journal of Medical Research* (New Delhi, 1983). Arnfried A. Kielmann et al., *Malnutrition, Infection, Growth and Development: The Narangwal Experience*, forthcoming.

Fig. 1 Probability of Death Between 1- and 36-Month-Old Infants according to Nutritional Status.

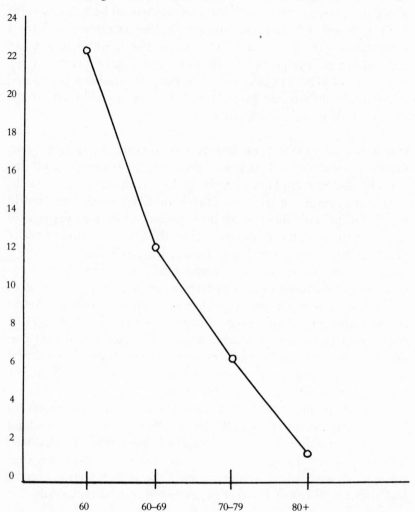

SOURCE: Figs. 1–6, 9, and 10 have been adapted from data in Arnfried Kielmann et al., *Malnutrition, Infection, Growth and Development: The Narangwal Experience*, forthcoming.

to the reduction of neonatal tetanus by immunization of mothers and to improved delivery practices of traditional birth attendants. Infant mortality was reduced most by infection control and less by improved nutrition. Mortality in children between the ages of one and three was reduced by both.

Morbidity duration for the twelve most common illnesses was reduced by about two days from an average of a little over a week, primarily by increased surveillance of illnesses to ensure early diagnosis and treatment by family health workers. Growth improved significantly as a result of nutrition surveillance and supplementation; major changes in weight were evident at fourteen months and in height at twenty-one months (Figs. 2 and 3). Psychomotor scores also increased significantly, especially in the combined-care village (Fig. 4).

A direct correlation was found between socioeconomic status and sex, on the one hand, and weight and height, on the other (Figs. 5 and 6). Each of the three variables of caste, sex, and nutrition services was associated with an increase in weight of about one half kilogram and in height of two centimeters in children who were three years of age; at thirty-six months, a high caste male from a nutrition-intervention village proved to be two

Fig. 2 Effects of Various Factors on Average Weight (Kg.) of All Children in Study Villages at Ages 0–36 Months Compared with Control Villages[a]

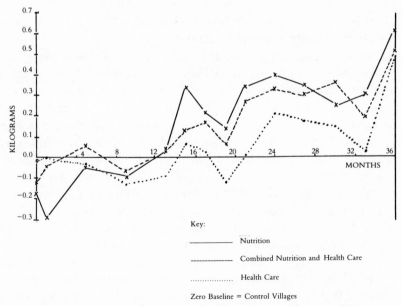

Key:

———————— Nutrition

– – – – – – – – Combined Nutrition and Health Care

.... Health Care

Zero Baseline = Control Villages

a   Adjusted for sex, birth order, mother's age, caste, year, and season of observation.

Fig. 3 Effects of Various Factors on Average Height (Cm.) of All Children in Study Villages at Ages 0–36 Months Compared with Control Villages[a]

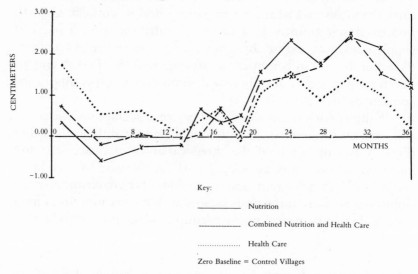

Key:

——————— Nutrition

- - - - - - - - - Combined Nutrition and Health Care

· · · · · · · · · · · Health Care

Zero Baseline = Control Villages

a Adjusted for sex, birth order, mother's age, caste, year, and season of observation.

kilograms heavier and six centimeters taller than a low caste female child from a control village.

In most cases, the integrated-care villages did only as well as the best of the single-service villages. The combined-care villages enjoyed improved mortality and morbidity equal to those achieved in the health-care villages. In addition, the growth and development benefits in these combined-care villages were similar to those of the nutrition villages, and all of these benefits were gained at a cost equivalent to the price of nutrution care alone. These effects were achieved for only $2 per capita per year in villages receiving either the combined program or only nutrition care. In the infection-control villages the cost was about half as much, but the nutritional benefits were not obtained.

A parallel population project was also conducted at Narangwal in which five clusters of villages received the following: family planning education alone, family planning and women's services, family planning and child care, all three services, and a control group. The purpose was to measure how much maternal

Fig. 4   Means and Standard Errors (S.E.M.) of "Average" Psychomotor
Index in Experimental Villages[a]

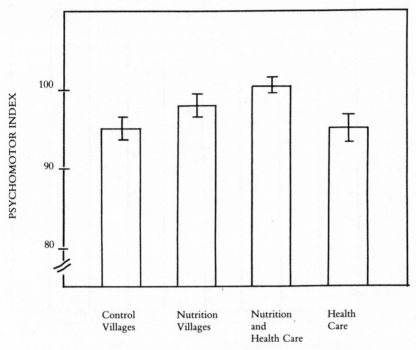

a   Adjusted for socioeconomic, demographic, and morbidity variables.

care and child care, separately and together, contributed to family
planning use. This project was terminated by political events
before we could determine the final levels at which family planning curves would plateau.[12]

The advantage of integrating family planning with either
women's services or combined services is evident both in acceptance figures and in current practice rates adjusted for the demographic impact of the contraceptive methods used in the various
groups according to a calculation that we called "effective-user
rates" (Figs. 7 and 8). The plateaus in curves representing data
from the Family Planning Alone and Family Planning and Child
Care villages are evident.

12   Taylor et al., "Integrated Family Planning and Health Care," in *idem, Child and
Maternal Health Services in Rural India: The Narangwal Experiment,* forthcoming.

Fig. 5   Mean Weight at 17 Months by Caste and Sex[a]

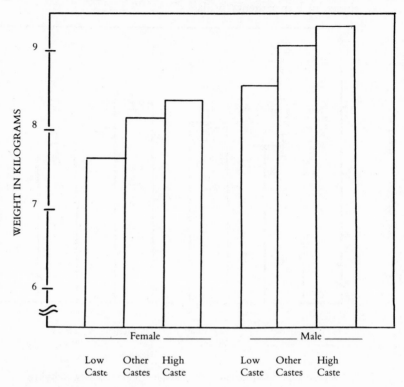

a Adjusted for service input group, birth order, maternal age, season, and year of observation.

One objective of the study was to test the hypothesis that acceptance of family planning is greater when parents believe that their existing children will survive. Definitive data were not obtained, which was expected because, according to our original assumptions, we had projected a lag of about five years before the long-term impact of child survival on attitudes would become evident. However, those parents who came to believe during the project that more children were surviving than had thirty years ago used children's services almost twice as much as those parents who did not believe that to be so (Fig. 9). The parents who felt that more children were surviving also were more apt to use family planning services (Fig. 10). Of particular interest are analyses based on detailed calculations which show the relative impact on family planning of specific components of integrated services.

Fig. 6 Mean Height at 17 Months by Caste and Sex[a]

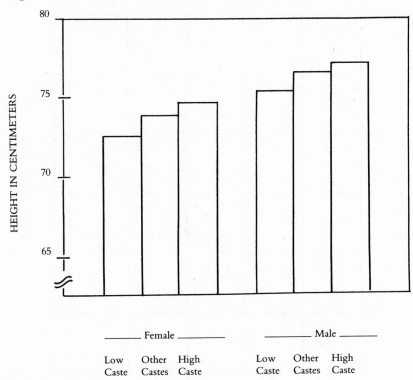

a Adjusted for service input group, birth order, maternal age, season, and year of observation.

Users of women's preventive care, children's illness care, and children's preventive care practiced family planning 50 percent of the time; in comparison with about 15 percent for non-users. The difference between those who did and did not use women's illness care was somewhat less (Fig. 11).

Cost-effectiveness analyses showed the greater efficiency of integrated services (Table 2). These figures are estimates based on work sampling studies of the total services. An average unit cost for each type of service was allocated and the impact on family planning in each study group was then calculated. Where combined services were provided, the costs were distributed and a relevant proportion was allocated to family planning using a detailed analysis of the service activity. Costs were five to ten times lower in combined care villages. This result applied equally to

Fig. 7 Cumulative Rates of New Accepters in Experimental Groups

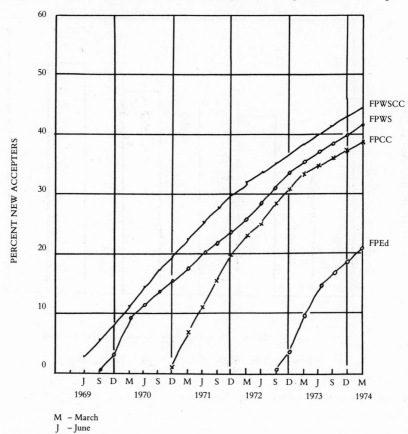

M – March
J – June
S – September
D – December

SOURCE: Figs. 7, 8, and 11 adapted from data in Taylor et al., "Integrated Family Planning and Health Care," in *idem, Child and Maternal Health Services in Rural India: The Narangwal Experiment,* forthcoming.

costs per user, to costs for contraceptive protection for the first two years of services, and to cost per birth averted. A feature of integrated services was that the impact depended largely on concurrent use of services.

In the past, most analyses of factors influencing demographic trends have accepted as given the assumption that, because fertility tended to fall first among the affluent and educated, we would have to wait until general development improved the quality of

Fig. 8 Trends in Effective-User Rates in Experimental Groups

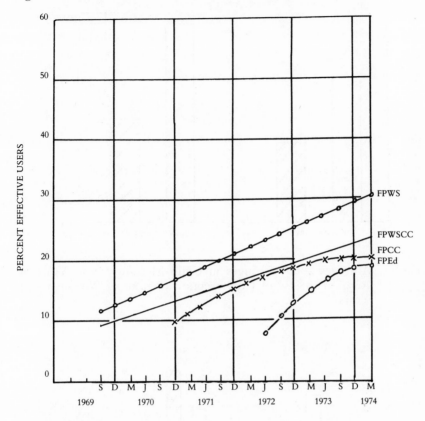

M – March
J – June
S – September
D – December

life of an entire population before fertility would fall. From past historical data it has been difficult to determine the relative impact of particular components of development. Recent studies show that economic growth is not as important as equitable distribution in producing demographic changes. The variables that have shown the greatest association with declining fertility have been education (especially of women), health care, a decline in child mortality, and a poorly defined set of conditions relating to the role of women. To accelerate the process of balancing demo-

Fig. 9   Changes in Attitudes concerning Beliefs about Child Deaths

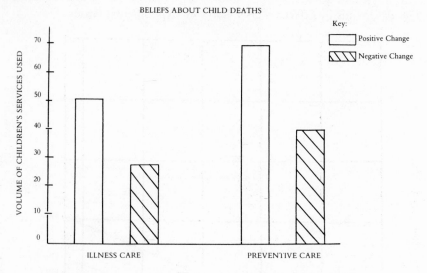

BELIEFS ABOUT CHILD DEATHS

Fig. 10   Attitudes about Changes in Child Mortality in 30 Years in Relation to Use of Contraception (Percent of Women 15–45 Years)

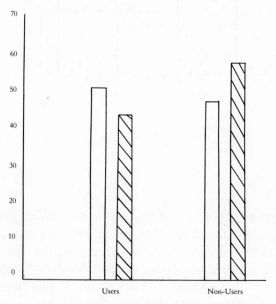

Less children die now than before (n = 390)

More children die now than before (n = 340)

$X^2 = 4.45$, p = .04

Fig. 11 Relationship between Use of Health Service Programs and Acceptance of Family Planning

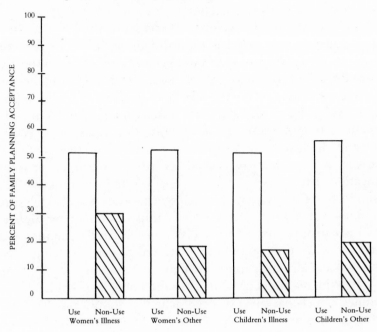

Table 2 Estimated Cost per Family Planning Accepter per Year of Protection in Experimental Groups at Narangwal (in Rupees)

	INTEGRATED FAMILY PLANNING AND WOMEN AND CHILDREN'S HEALTH CARE	FAMILY PLANNING AND WOMEN'S SERVICES	FAMILY PLANNING AND CHILD CARE	FAMILY PLANNING ALONE
Cost per Accepter	5.0	9.0	15.0	50.0
Cost per year of protection for first two years of services	23.0	45.0	66.0	142.0
Cost per birth averted	49	111	162	349

SOURCE: adapted from data in Taylor et al., "Integrated Family Planning and Health Care," in *idem*, *Child and Maternal Health Services in Rural India: The Narangwal Experiment*, forthcoming.

graphic and socioeconomic development it would obviously be desirable to identify more specifically those factors which selectively facilitate birth rate decline.[13]

Of various social development factors, it is probable that the integrated program that has the most direct influence is a combination of health, family planning, and nutritional support organized to reach those in greatest need. At Narangwal, care was targeted according to the prevalence of health and nutrition problems, and services therefore did reach those who would most benefit. The program equalized utilization rates by selectively focusing on low caste families, not because of their caste, but because they were most in need according to criteria for service allocation that were generally accepted in the community. Table 3 shows that this integrated package of services was able to correct previous imbalances in the use of family planning by high and low caste groups. Initially, the difference in family planning practice rates was 13 percent in low caste and 21 percent in high caste. This was equalized to approximately 46 percent for both groups.

It is increasingly evident that the control of epidemics and famines which has already been achieved should not be seen as being in competition with efforts to limit population growth. Long-range, steady development of services to obtain complete coverage will be greatly facilitated if all resources and efforts can

Table 3 Percent of Family Planning by Caste

	PERCENT USING MODERN METHODS		
CASTE	BEFORE PROJECT	DURING PROJECT	INCREASE
High	21	46	+25
Low	13	47	+34

SOURCE: adapted from data in Taylor et al., "Integrated Family Planning and Health Care," in *idem, Child and Maternal Health Services in Rural India: The Narangwal Experiment,* forthcoming.

13 James P. Grant, *The State of the World's Children, 1981–82* (New York, 1981); Margaret Wolfson, *Changing Approaches to Population Problems* (Paris, 1978); The World Bank, *World Development Report, 1980* (New York, 1980).

be brought together through rationalized integration as part of primary health care.

In attempting to interpret past historical events by extrapolating from current experience, caution needs to be exercised in making judgments about social and political factors because of their intrinsic variability in different time periods and places. This concern does not, however, hold with the same force in relation to biological factors. For instance, relationships between malnutrition and infection can be interpreted with the expectation that findings will apply through various historical periods, even though specific diseases and types of malnutrition will vary in their prevalence and distribution in populations depending upon local epidemiological circumstances and environmental conditions.

Events that were documented in historical records have tended to be dramatic disasters that affected large numbers of people in short periods of time, especially epidemics and famines. Of much greater overall significance, however, was the epidemiological impact of conditions such as hyperendemic malaria or hidden hunger which had a continuing demographic influence on the distribution and number of people. In this kind of relationship it is likely that extrapolating backward from present findings will be especially valuable in interpreting the past.

Finally, findings from current field research solidly support the reasonable prospect that it is no longer necessary to rely on spontaneous interactions between the natural forces that influence birth and death rates to maintain a demographic balance. Current evidence provides an increasingly solid scientific basis for achieving such a balance by emphasizing goals of equity and social justice in the implementation of programs that integrate nutrition, health care, and family planning.

The Relationship of Nutrition, Disease, and Social Conditions: A Graphical Presentation

The charts which follow were drawn up in order to clarify the relationships among nutrition, disease, and social conditions that were identified by participants at the Bellagio conference. These graphic summaries of complex interactions served both as a point of reference and as a means of representing the central issues under discussion. Specific concerns and relationships could thus be placed within the context of the overall connections among these major determinants of human well-being.

Figure 1 is a model of the dynamic linkages that unite agricultural, social, nutritional, and physical activities. The model posits a progression from the first to the last, affected at each stage by technological (including medical) developments, and then a reciprocal influence from the health, energy, and productivity of a population to its agriculture. A society's prospects are determined first by its resources and the ratio of its population to productive land. These, in turn, are subject to the effects of technology and the health and capacity of the people, and, along with technology, help determine the political, social, and economic structures that promote technological advance and also the distribution of food and hence of nutrients. Whether the diet leads to good nutrition, though, is determined not only by its nutritional quality, as modified by technology, but also the level of physical activity and the effects of disease. Nutrition and disease are strongly affected by a reciprocal influence, referred to as "synergy." Finally, the level of nutrition, combined with the effects of such disease as may be present, establishes the health, capacity, and productivity of a population. At that point the linkages return to the society's resources.

All infections, regardless of the infectious agent responsible and including those that are not apparent, are capable of worsening nutritional status by the following mechanisms:

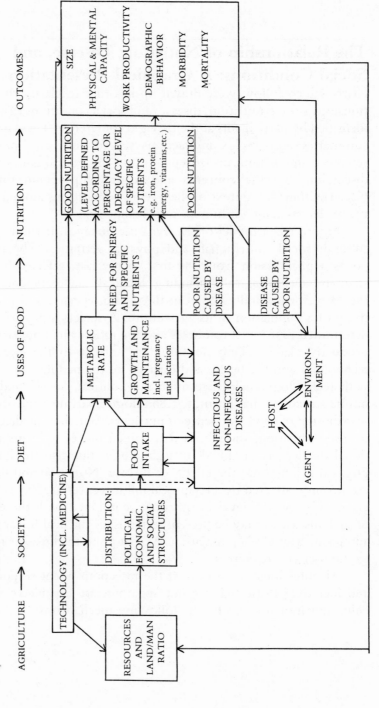

Fig. 1 A Holistic Approach to Human Food and Nutrition

AGRICULTURE → SOCIETY → DIET → USES OF FOOD → NUTRITION → OUTCOMES

1. Reduced appetite
2. Poorer quality of diet ingested
3. Increased metabolic loss of nutrients
4. Increased metabolic needs and internal diversion and sequestration
5. Decreased absorption when gastrointestinal tract is affected.

Conversely, nutritional deficiencies are capable of reducing resistance to infection and thereby increasing the prevalence and severity of many infections through a variety of mechanisms including:

1. Reduced production of humoral antibodies
2. Impaired cell-mediated immunity
3. Less effective phagocytosis
4. Weakened epithelial barriers
5. Lower lysozyme production
6. Various other non-specific effects[1]

Although all infections influence nutrition, the reverse is not true. As illustrated in Figure 2, some infections are so virulent

Fig. 2 Nutrition and Infection

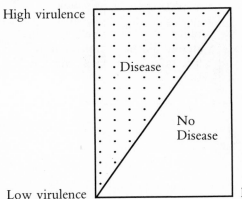

---

1 Phagocytes engulf microorganisms and form particles. Epithelial barriers are a protective covering on internal and external surfaces. A lysozyme is a basic protein in body fluids that functions as an antibacterial enzyme.

that they produce disease regardless of differences in resistance; others are so avirulent that disease will occur only in very debilitated subjects. With intermediate degrees of virulence, however, nutritional status can often be the determining factor. Figure 3 lists some diseases that are known definitely to be influenced by nutritional status under some circumstances and others on which the influence of nutrition is minimal. In between are infectious diseases in which nutritional influences are variable or equivocal.

These schematizations are intended merely as general guides, not as definitive descriptions of particular situations. They were intended to establish the larger context within which studies of the relationship between nutrition and disease, or between both of these conditions and social change, could be pursued.

Fig. 3 Nutritional Influence on Outcomes[a] of Infections

DEFINITE	EQUIVOCAL OR VARIABLE	MINIMAL

Measles
Diarrheas
Tuberculosis
Most Respiratory
   Infections
Pertussis
Most Intestinal Parasites
Cholera
Leprosy
Herpes
	Typhus
	Diphtheria
	Staphylococcus
	Streptococcus
	Influenza
	Syphilis
	Systemic Worm
	   Infections
		Smallpox
		Malaria
		Plague
		Typhoid
		Tetanus
		Yellow Fever
		Encephalitis
		Poliomyelitis

a   Morbidity or mortality

Gretel H. Pelto and Pertti J. Pelto

Diet and Delocalization:
Dietary Changes since 1750   During the past two centuries virtually all of the populations in the world have experienced dramatic changes in their dietary patterns. In the industrialized countries changes in food patterns have been associated with improved levels of nutrition and public health, although some nutrition-related diseases are increasing. Similar processes of change in the less industrialized nations, however, have often had serious negative effects. We examine here some of the primary processes of change in food resources and distribution over the past 250 years, focusing on three main transformations that have had profound effects on global eating patterns. Our primary thesis is:

First, the general direction of transformations in food use throughout the world in the past two or three centuries has involved an increasingly rapid "delocalization" of food production and distribution. By "delocalization" (discussed more fully below) we refer to processes in which food varieties, production methods, and consumption patterns are disseminated throughout the world in an ever-increasing and intensifying network of socioeconomic and political interdependency. From the point of view of individuals and families at any one place on the globe, delocalization means that an increasing portion of the daily diet comes from distant places usually through commercial channels.

Second, in the industrialized nations, delocalization has been associated with an increase in the diversity of available foods and the quantity of food imports, and, therefore, with improved diets. In earlier periods this improvement of diet, especially through diversification, primarily benefited the upper social classes, but

Gretel H. Pelto is Associate Professor of Nutritional Sciences at the University of Connecticut. Pertti J. Pelto is Professor of Anthropology and Community Medicine at the University of Connecticut. They are co-authors of *Anthropological Research: The Structure of Inquiry* (Cambridge, 1978) and co-editors of *Medical Anthropology*.

during the twentieth century the effects have diffused to a wide spectrum of people in the "developed" world.

Third, in the less industrialized countries of the world, the same processes of delocalization have tended to produce opposite effects on dietary quality, except for the elite. Until recent times many peoples in the Third World have been primarily dependent on locally produced food supplies, which remained largely outside the networks of commerce. As these populations have been drawn more and more into full commercial participation, economic and political forces have encouraged concentration on one or two main cash crops, with an accompanying deterioration of food diversity, as well as a loss of local control over the distribution system. Thus, world-wide food distribution and food-use transformations have occurred at the expense of economically marginal populations.

These general ideas about changes in food availability and dietary patterns have been discussed for a number of years. Here we present them in a manner that is intended to encourage historical research on these associations. To date there has been relatively little careful empirical investigation of the relationships among social change, dietary change, and nutritional status and health. Research questions need to be framed in a manner that permits hypothesis-testing and a refinement of the general model.[1]

THREE MAJOR PROCESSES OF DIETARY CHANGE   The dramatic transformations in dietary patterns that have taken place in the past two and a half centuries are one key aspect of the much larger picture of massive social and economic change that has affected all parts of the world. The specific dimensions have varied widely in relation to particular historical, political, and ecological conditions, but the basic food-use changes of interest to us have largely come about as a result of three fundamental developments:

1. A world-wide dissemination of domesticated plant and animal varieties.

2. The rise of increasingly complex, international food distribution networks, and the growth of food-processing industries.

1 Cf. Alan Berg, *The Nutrition Factor* (Washington, D.C., 1973); Frances Moore Lappé and Joseph Collins, *Food First* (Boston, 1977).

3. The migration of people from rural to urban centers, and from one continent to another, on a hitherto unprecedented scale, with a resulting exchange of culinary and dietary techniques and preferences.

Each of these processes has been powerfully influenced by national and international politico-economic forces, cultural and religious movements, and other factors. One fundamental sector of great importance has been the development of new technologies; in particular, transportation and communications technologies have played major roles.

Our rationale for focusing on the three processes listed above rests on a view of the basic elements of delocalization as they affect the behavior of particular local communities. That is, if we picture the dietary possibilities of people in a French rural commune, a small valley in Mexico, or an island in Polynesia, their food selections will change if:

a. New plant and animal varieties are introduced to the community for local production, or locally produced foods are removed from the community for sale elsewhere.

b. New foods are made available through commercial or governmental channels.

c. The people themselves move to a new area, or they receive immigrants from elsewhere, resulting in cultural exchange of culinary/dietary preferences.

Changes may also occur because of purely local developments of new food production or preparation techniques, but such occurrences are generally much less frequent.

Throughout our discussion of dietary change we confront the philosophical question of basic causes. Attempting to isolate clear, necessary and sufficient causes may have some utility in relatively simple systems. However, human behavior is more understandable if we conceptualize a system of complex, interconnected forces (including biological, psychological, economic, political, technological, and other factors), so that a focus on one component as a prime mover rests more on philosophical or stylistic preference rather than on demonstrable, empirical evidence. Understanding the developments in human food use patterns of the past 250 years depends, first of all, on sorting out the primary (descriptive) trends and processes, leaving for the future the search for the more or less clear prime movers.

THE CONCEPT OF DELOCALIZATION   The concept of delocalization, which is central to our analysis of changes in human dietary patterns, is one major aspect of all the historical changes to which people give various labels such as modernization, development, progress, acculturation, and so on. In using the term delocalization we are focusing attention on one fundamental, apparently undirectional tendency in human history, particularly of more recent centuries. Delocalization has many different facets, but there are two that are most important for our discussion here.

First, there is the delocalization that results in the reduction of local autonomy of energy resources, due to dependence on gasoline-driven equipment for transportation, local industry, and other essential processes. In recent times this loss of local energy autonomy has been quite striking in the remoter areas of the globe where motor-driven boats, snowmobiles, and other equipment have been widely adopted.

Second, in more complex urban centers, delocalization is evidenced in the increased sensitivity (of prices, costs, etc.) to political fluctuations in any sector of the world energy and food network, as can be seen, for example, in the world-wide impact of Soviet grain purchasing policies, OPEC price manipulations, coffee and sugar production levels, and the beef consumption demands of the international fast-food industry.

DELOCALIZATION AND FOOD SYSTEMS   One way to gain an understanding of delocalization in matters of human food use is to consider the opposite—local autonomy. In small-scale hunting and gathering societies, such as those of the Inuit (Eskimo) and the San peoples of the Kalahari, or among our ancestors of pre-agricultural times, the great bulk of food supplies and other energy resources had to be obtained from the immediate local environment. For that reason hunting-gathering societies have always been rather small—usually no more than 300 to 400 persons in the local group (often much less), with population densities that seldom exceeded ten persons per 100 square miles.

Among a great many small-scale cultivator peoples of central Africa, the Amazon rainforest areas, and the South Pacific, local groups have been largely dependent on their own food and energy resources, although some trading of food and other goods has been common between coastal and inland peoples, and between animal-keeping pastoralists and their more sedentary neighbors; occasionally, trade has been widespread among the various islands of the South Pacific.

Despite the presence of small-scale regional trading, human societies of earlier times were, to a considerable extent, unaffected by the state of food supplies in other areas. If crops failed or herds were decimated by disease in any particular area, famine was the usual result; there was no way to send for disaster relief.

In contrast to small-scale, semi-autonomous communities, peasant populations in Europe, Asia, and Latin America, in past centuries, have been a good deal more dependent on at least some commercial exchanges with other regions and nations. A common feature of peasant societies, however, has been the dependence on a wider marketing system for the purchase of non-food supplies and equipment, in exchange for which local peasant peoples were able to transfer their surplus food production, thus feeding not only themselves but the non-food producing people of the cities. A large proportion of the peasant family's food needs were met from their own farm, even though they were dependent on the commercial system for iron equipment, some clothing, a few luxury items, and (in recent decades) special foods such as sugar, salt, tea or coffee, and spices.

Before the fifteenth century there was a slow and gradual dissemination of certain major crops and food animals into ever-wider parts of the world. For example, the wheat, barley, and dairy food complex spread into all parts of Europe, south into Africa, and eastwards into Asia, from the presumed origins in the Far East. A similar process of diffusion occurred with the rice-growing complex in East and South Asia. These slow processes of diffusion certainly had significant effects on food systems in the world but the impact of changes precipitated by the age of discovery were dramatic and rapid.

WORLD-WIDE DISSEMINATION OF DOMESTICATED PLANTS AND ANI-MALS   Beginning with Columbus' voyages to the New World, and other fifteenth-century expeditions into hitherto unknown parts, Europeans acquired knowledge about food crops and production systems that was formerly unavailable to them. At the same time, European settlers, missionaries, and adventurers spread the knowledge (and requisite seeds and other materials) of both Old World and New World animal domesticates to other parts of the world. By the beginning of the seventeenth century the boundaries of the various plant and animal species were transformed, as the major crops and animals were introduced into different ecological zones. By 1700 maize, rice, wheat, barley, oats, and potatoes, as well as cattle and other livestock had spread throughout most of the world, whereas earlier each of these food sources had been grown by only a segment of the world's population.

The consequences of the world-wide dissemination of domesticated plants and animals were dramatic. In Europe the slow but steady adoption of maize, potatoes, and other American cultigens began to have powerful effects by the eighteenth century. The addition of potatoes to the basic subsistence economy has been seen by some researchers as a cause of major changes in demographic patterns. For example, Vanderbroek has claimed that potatoes sustained rapid population expansion in the southern Netherlands in the middle of the eighteenth century. His data indicate that potato cultivation grew rapidly in the 1740s and 1750s, returning a five times greater yield per acre than wheat, which had previously been the main crop. Rapid population increases in that part of the Netherlands contrasts, in his view, with slower population growth in areas where potatoes were not adopted at that time.[2]

In approximately the same period the potato spread to northern Europe, where in Sweden, Finland, and Russia its cultivation was seen as an important hedge against famine. Governmental and private groups propagandized on behalf of potato cultivation, and free seed potatoes were made widely available. In Finland at the end of the eighteenth century the Finnish Economics Society distributed free seed potatoes and gave monetary prizes and medals to potato growers. "A famine and epidemic in 1765 persuaded Catherine the Great of the potential importance of the tuber to

2   Christian Vanderbroek, "Aardappelteelt en Aardappelverbruik in de 17e en 18e Eeuw," *Tijdschrift voor Geschiedenis*, LXXXII (1969), 49–68.

Russia, and her government launched a campaign to encourage its cultivation. However, the potato did not become a major crop in central Russia until after the crop failures of 1838 and 1839."[3]

Some writers may have exaggerated the importance of the potato in the economics of Europe, but considerable weight may be given to the remarks of Morineau, who noted that ". . . the potato, thanks in part to its very real advantages, became the only short-term solution (to increased food needs) everywhere in Western Europe. This it remained, despite some periods of blight, as long as new granaries had not opened in other parts of the world and until, in due course, agricultural science was able to produce much higher grain yields than the traditional agriculture."[4]

Negative consequences of the role of potatoes have been noted, particularly in the great potato famines in Ireland in the nineteenth century.

Ho and other scholars consider American cultigens to have been central to the growth of ecological carrying capacity in China. Ho suggests that by the end of the eighteenth century rice cultivation areas (the wetlands) and the dry region lands of millet and wheat had neared their limits of production, so that any further expansion of Chinese population would have been at the cost of increased nutritional deficiencies and periodic famine. However, the adoption of maize and sweet potatoes significantly increased the food supply.[5]

In presenting these observations concerning the world-wide diffusion of major cultigens, we do not need to subscribe to the theory that new foods caused population expansions in various regions of the world. In fact, it would appear that the causal arrows have often been in the opposite direction, in that population pressures have triggered the intensification of food production techniques. It is plausible that both types of situations have occurred repeatedly in different human populations: at times the fortuitous importation of new food crops or production methods

---

3 Alfred W. Crosby, Jr., *The Columbian Exchange* (Westport, Conn., 1972), 184.
4 Michel Morineau, "The Potato in the Eighteenth Century," in Robert Forster and Orest Ranum (eds.), *Food and Drink in History* (Baltimore, 1979), 17–36.
5 Ping-ti Ho, *Studies on the Population of China, 1368–1953* (Cambridge, Mass., 1959). Crosby, *Columbian Exchange,* 199–200.

has occurred before population expansion; in other circumstances the reverse has happened.[6]

Europe and Asia were not the only continents that experienced large-scale changes in food production as a result of contacts with new cultigens. Africa was an early recipient of new production ideas, in part because slave traders introduced maize and other crops to West Africa in order to provision their ships. Maize was introduced so early in some parts of Africa that some researchers have argued for its aboriginal development there.[7]

In the Americas the powerful influences of wheat, barley, and other Old World crops have been overshadowed by the effects of the massive infusion of meat animals. Before the coming of the Europeans, the natives of North and South America had only turkeys, dogs, llamas, chickens, and guinea pigs as sources of meat. The meat of pigs, cattle, sheep, and other food animals were quickly included in the diet of both the European settlers and the native inhabitants.

THE RISE OF COMMERCIAL FOOD DISTRIBUTION NETWORKS   A second major process in the delocalization of food occurs with the proliferation of commercial food distribution systems, which now affect virtually all societies. Food patterns in formerly remote communities are powerfully affected by the presence of commercially distributed food.

The growth of commercial food distribution networks has been intricately related to the development of food processing technologies. Food processing involves a wide spectrum of manipulation, from relatively simple preservation, such as canning and freezing, to the preparation of cooked, ready-to-eat meals and a variety of snack foods. The great expansion in commercial food processing has taken place in the twentieth century, although

6 Ester Boserup, *The Conditions of Agricultural Growth* (Chicago, 1965). William T. Sanders, "Population, Agricultural History, and Societal Evolution in Mesoamerica," in Brian Spooner (ed.), *Population Growth: Anthropological Implications* (Cambridge, Mass., 1972), 101–153.
7 Carl O. Sauer, *Seeds, Spades, Hearths, and Herbs* (Cambridge, Mass., 1952). Cf. Michael D. Gwynne, "The Origin and Spread of Some Domestic Food Plants of Eastern Africa," in H. Neville Chittick and Robert I. Rotberg (eds.), *East Africa and the Orient: Cultural Synthesis in Pre-Colonial Times* (New York, 1975), 248–271.

important developments occurred throughout the nineteenth century. French, British, and American inventors all contributed to the development of hermetically sealed canning processes in the 1830s and 1840s, followed by the processing of condensed milk and the mechanization of biscuit making.[8]

Prior to the nineteenth century the scope and scale of commercial operations in foodstuffs were limited. The larger and more important commercial houses dealt mainly in a few specialized items—coffee, sugar, spices, tea, salt, and alcoholic beverages. Some researchers have claimed that liquor and beer were practically the only foodstuffs for which production was responsive to demand before the latter half of the nineteenth century. However exaggerated such a statement, it does serve to highlight the importance of the commercial enterprises, and the more complex food marketing, that came into existence in the middle of the last century.[9]

SUGAR: THE COMMERCIAL FOOD PAR EXCELLENCE   Sugar is one processed food item that has played a major role in dietary transformations since the eighteenth century. The history of sugar documents the growing significance of commercial food marketing over the past 200 years. Like many other food products, cane sugar was known and used for centuries in some parts of the world before it rose to prominence in European trade. Gourmets of ancient India knew sugar, and there was some cultivation of sugar cane in Arab Spain and southern France in the eighth century. However, it was a rare and costly luxury until cane production was initiated in the New World.

The special conditions of the Americas, which combined favorable growing conditions, large acreages, and the importation of relatively low-cost (slave) labor, brought about rapid increases in production. During the eighteenth century it was still a costly commodity, but as production increased there was a fairly steady drop in price, and public demand for sugar rose rapidly. The use

8   Waverly Root and Richard de Rochemont, *Eating in America* (New York, 1976), 158; James P. Johnston, *A Hundred Years of Eating: Food, Drink, and Family Diet in Britain Since the Late Nineteenth Century* (Montreal, 1977), 33.
9   Maurice Aymard, "Toward the History of Nutrition," in Forster and Ranum. *Food and Drink*, 1–16.

of by-products of the sugar cane process in the manufacture of rum contributed to the profitability of the sugar business. By the early years of the nineteenth century the average per capita consumption of sugar in the United States had risen to twelve or thirteen pounds per year. From that point the rise was relatively steady to 1929, when a peak of 109 pounds per capita per year was reached. During the Great Depression sugar intake decreased but rose again with better economic times. Patterns of consumption in England were similar, with a peak in 1960 of 112 pounds per capita per year.[10]

MIGRATION: RURAL TO URBAN AND CROSS-NATIONAL POPULATION MOVEMENTS   The processes of change discussed thus far all refer to the transfer of ideas and materials—the food products themselves—from one area to another, accompanied by mechanisms of interdependency. The third mechanism is, superficially at least, different because the basic feature is the movement of persons. Migration to urban areas from rural regions, and movements from one nation or continent to another, introduce an additional dimension—food preferences and food knowledge are transferred by the migrants themselves. The migrants may exert their influence simply as individuals (or groups of individuals) with specific food preferences, but they also introduce change by actions, such as the establishment of food stores, restaurants, or other special enterprises.

Ethnic foods were introduced by migrants in earlier centuries and especially in America in the nineteenth century. There is a dual feature to the·impact of migrant peoples on dietary practices: on the one hand, emigrés from distant places often preserved their traditional food patterns, so that, for example, Italian immigrants in major United States cities were soon able to maintain their consumption of pasta, sausages, olive oil, and other products in neighborhood cafes and restaurants, as well as in their homes; on the other hand these ethnic foods became available to non-Italians

---

10 Root and Rochement, *Eating in America*, 418; Richard O. Cummings, *The American and His Food* (Chicago, 1940); Chris Wardle, *Changing Food Habits in the U.K.* (London, 1977).

as well, and the growingly sophisticated urban-dwellers could select from a variety of different cuisines.

In most cases the old ethnic diets were not maintained in their traditional forms. Working hours—in factories, shops, and offices—soon made the old schedules (e.g. the large midday meal that is common in many European countries) difficult to continue. Even strongly held religious food patterns (e.g. among orthodox Jews) had to be modified to meet the new conditions.

One of the first ecumenical movements in ethnic food adoption was the spread of French cooking as a high prestige practice among upper-class and middle-class people around the world. Equally significant in influencing multi-cultural sophistication in food has been the spread of Chinese restaurants, which can be found in most major cities of the world today. Many of the international exchanges manifested in ethnic restaurants and grocery stores testify to the final phases of the colonial era, during which increasing numbers of families from "the colonies" established ethnic enclaves and food patterns in Europe: Indonesians in Holland, Indian restaurants and shops in England, and Morrocan and other North African coffee houses in France.

The latest phases of world-wide ecumenical sharing of cuisine (as opposed to dissemination of the raw materials) has taken the form of an accelerated development of international cooking at home. Also, visible today throughout the world is the rapid spread of multi-national, fast-food chains.

MECHANISMS OF CHANGE AND CONSUMPTION TRENDS   The three main processes outlined above have been vehicles by which long-standing dietary patterns have been more and more radically altered in practically all parts of the world. The results of these changes are reflected in consumption statistics and nutrient profiles, which show, for example, continuing increases in the percentages of sugar consumed as diets become "modernized." In the United States the consumption of flour and cereal products dropped from 680 pounds per capita per year in 1910 to 450 pounds in 1970. During the same period vegetable fat consumption increased from 20 grams per capita per day to nearly 50 grams. Viewed in terms of nutrient consumption (rather than types of foods) in the period from 1910 to 1970 iron has declined from 15.2 mg. per capita per day to 8.0 mg. while riboflavin increased from 1.86 mg. to 2.46 mg.; another eight vitamins showed similar increases during that sixty-year span.[11]

It is difficult to find adequate statistical information on dietary changes in small-scale, non-modern societies because of the paucity of careful, quantitative studies. However, some of the main dimensions of change can be inferred from recent ethnographic studies. For example, in the Alaskan Eskimo community of Napaskiak, Oswalt noted that "everyone regards certain [store foods] as absolute necessities. These include sugar, salt, flour, milk, coffee, tea, tobacco, and cooking fats. Other foods frequently purchased include various canned meats and fish, crackers, candy, carbonated beverages, canned fruits, potatoes, onions, and rice." Similarly, among the Miskito Indians of Nicaragua, store-bought foods already accounted for over 30 percent of the diet in 1969, when Nietschmann made a detailed analysis of their food system. The store purchased foods, including sugar, flour, beans, rice, and coffee, had captured two thirds of the Miskito food economy by 1973, mainly because of the depletion of the green sea turtles, which are now sold to international food companies rather than consumed locally. Since the purchased foods are quite different in nutrient content from the wild foods that they replace and are especially high in carbohydrates, the Miskito, like virtually all small-scale societies, are undergoing rapid dietary change.[12]

The Eskimo and Miskito examples are particularly illustrative because they clearly reflect two different aspects of the worldwide commercial food system: in the Miskito situation commercial food distributors have taken away a primary food resource—the sea turtles—thus forcing the local people to change their food patterns. In the North Alaskan situation the emphasis is on the increased availability of modern foods in the local stores. Even in cases where local traditional food resources are not depleted, the availability of sugar, flour, canned goods, and other store food has a powerful effect on diets.

---

11   United States Dept. of Agriculture, Report No. 138 (Washington, D.C. (1974); Willis A. Gortner, "Nutrition in the United States-1900 to 1974," *Cancer Research,* XXXV (1975), 3246–3253.

12   Wendell Oswalt, *Napaskiak: An Alaskan Eskimo Community* (Tucson, 1963), 102; Bernard Nietschmann, *Between Land and Water* (New York, 1973).

DELOCALIZATION AND THE FINNISH FOOD SYSTEM   Changes in food use brought about by delocalization are clearly revealed in Finland, which was transformed from an underdeveloped nation into an urban, industrialized society from the 1930s to 1970. Until 1940 the great majority of Finnish families were rural; the major cities, other than Helsinki, were little more than overgrown market centers. In 1950 the infant mortality rate was still 43 per 1,000; before the war it had been considerably higher. In other health and welfare statistics, as well as in its income and occupational profile, Finland contrasted sharply with the more industrialized nations of Europe and America.

The traditional Finnish dietary pattern was heavily dependent on dairy products. Finland still ranks as the leading nation in the world in per capita milk consumption, in addition to which Finns consume large amounts of butter, cheese, buttermilk, and viili, a fermented milk product, which is somewhat akin to yogurt.

Grain products made up another major portion of the diet. Rye, oats, and barley had been the most important cereals in earlier centuries, with increasing amounts of wheat in the nineteenth and twentieth centuries. Potatoes were eaten practically every day in considerable quantity, a pattern that continues today for most of the population. Meat, and to a lesser extent fish, although consumed in modest quantities, have been important sources of protein.[13]

In the pre-World War II Finnish diet a major source of vitamin C was the wild lingonberry (and other berries), gathered in large quantities and stored for use throughout the winter. Also characteristic was a lack of green vegetables and fresh fruit, other than berries. Throughout the 1950s the supplies of imported fresh fruit in Finnish grocery stores was irregular.

During the 1960s the commercial food system changed drastically, as large supermarkets were established by several cooperative associations and by private entrepreneurs. Frozen foods, food freezers in stores and in homes, and many other technological features were introduced. A rapid expansion of the network of paved roads also contributed to these developments. At the same time, Finnish nutritionists and government policy-makers

---

13   I. Talve, *Suommen Kansanomaisesta Ruokataloudesta* (Turku, 1973).

mounted extensive informational campaigns to increase the consumption of vegetables and fruit and decrease the intake of saturated fats and sugar. The nutrition information programs were fueled, in part, by the realization that Finland had, until very recently, the highest rates of cardiovascular disease in the world.[14]

Food consumption trends from 1950 to 1973 show the interesting changes that have occurred during the recent decades of delocalization (see Table 1). These changes reflect delocalization both within the Finnish economy, and in relation to world-wide markets. Much of the increase in fruit and vegetables represents greatly expanded imports from Eastern Europe and the Mediterranean countries, made possible by the expansion of the modern European trucking network equipped with refrigeration, air conditioning, and other technological features. Meanwhile producers in Finland have begun to use artificially heated greenhouses (relying on new developments in plastic sheeting) to grow cucumbers and tomatoes, which are now in great demand since the introduction of salads into the Finnish diet.

From 1940 to 1970 Finnish farm families gave up most aspects of their earlier self-sufficiency in basic foods. In short, they changed from being peasants to being commercial farmers. The highly developed system of producers' cooperatives played a major part in these changes, augmented by the growth of private

Table 1   Consumption Trends in Finland, 1950–1973 (annual per capita consumption)

	YEAR					
ITEM	1950	1955	1960	1965	1970	1973
Wheat(ks)	81.5	86	75	70	65	60
Meat	60	60	60	60	60	60
Sugar(ks)	28.3	38	40	40	45	45
Rye	48	42	39	32	25	24
Butter/margarine	22	22	22	22	22	22
Fruit/vegetables	33	48	53	52	65	81

SOURCE: *Elinolosuhteet 1950–1975* [Living Conditions 1950–1975], Central Statistical Office of Finland, 86.

14   Ancel Keys, *Seven Countries: A Multivariate Analysis of Death and Coronary Heart Disease Rates* (Cambridge, Mass., 1980).

food-producing companies. Meat animals, milk, and cereal grains are now delivered directly to the cooperatives or to private buyers. In turn, the farmers buy back selected meat products at a members' discount. Certain parts of slaughtered animals (including the blood), that were routinely used in the family food economy, are now unavailable or must be purchased in processed form from the cooperatives. Blood pancakes and bloodbread, for example, are now generally made from packaged mixes. Even butter and cheese are usually purchased from the cooperatives to which the farmers sell their raw milk, unlike the pre-war days, when families prepared a large share of their own basic foods, from barn and field to the dinner table.

The changes in utilization of home-produced food in Finnish farming households represents delocalization at the local, or micro-level. Thus delocalization refers not only to the increased availability of foods from distant lands; it also means the giving up of local community control to the regional and national food-processing systems.

Although the impact of delocalization in terms of making new foods available was more dramatic in Finland than in some other Western European countries, the general process has been much the same throughout the industrialized world. The example of Finland is instructive because the major changes have occurred largely in the past fifty years, nearly a century later than in most parts of Western Europe. There have been major differences in some aspects of delocalization, as the pattern of land tenure, differences in international trading networks, and political processes have all strongly affected the course of developments in food distribution and dietary patterns.

DELOCALIZATION IN THE THIRD WORLD   A major feature of food delocalization in the nineteenth and twentieth centuries has been the transformation of food systems in non-industrialized areas as they have become involved in supplying some of the food needs of Euro-American communities. Sugar plantations were among the first manifestations of a rapidly developing commerce in food products. A large-scale banana trade developed later, mainly in the twentieth century. Shipments of bananas, like many other fruits and vegetables, could not become major world trade commodities until the development of effective storage technologies, in addition to faster shipping times.

In countries such as Jamaica the economic livelihood of many small farmers became tied to the fluctuations in world prices of bananas (or other cash crops), as well as to government policies of encouragement or discouragement of farm production. Jamaica is highly delocalized in terms of food resources, as most of the daily diet depends on imports from North America and other sources. The significance of delocalization for the Jamaican (as an example of the effects of modernization in Third World countries) is illustrated by events in the 1970s. As analyzed in a study by Marchione in the mid-1970s, the cost of food in Jamaica (not adjusted to take account of inflation) soared as a result of the oil crisis and other factors in international markets. In the period from 1973 to 1975 the retail price of wheat flour increased 142 percent, corn meal 100 percent, salt cod 75 percent, rice 65 percent, and sugar 60 percent. Banana prices, however, paid to local, mostly small-scale producers, did not rise.[15]

Marchione studied the impact of a nutrition program in the St. James area of Jamaica during this period and found that world market forces resulted in a return to subsistence crop-growing by many farmers. The expected negative effects of highly inflationary food prices appear to have been offset by increases in home-grown foods. Instead of declining, the nutritional status of small children in the St. James area improved during this period. The research design of the evaluation study made it possible to determine that it was mainly the farmers' food production responses to market conditions, rather than the local nutrition education program, that brought about improved nutritional status in the children.

It is also important, Marchione suggests, to note that during this period the climate of commerce in food was affected by the Jamaican government's policy of striving for greater national self-sufficiency. "Jamaican government policies to ban food exports, levy taxes on foreign-owned bauxite companies, create public service jobs and redistribute or force idle land into production represent concerted efforts to gain local control of energy forms and flows; i.e. power."[16]

15 Thomas J. Marchione, "Food and Nutrition in Self-Reliant National Development," *Medical Anthropology*, I (1977), 57–79.
16 *Ibid.*, 73.

Another striking example of the negative consequences of delocalization is the widespread adoption of beef cattle production in many parts of Latin America in response to the growth of hamburger and other fast-food merchandizing in the United States. In Guatemala, beef production nearly doubled from 1960 to 1972, yet domestic per capita consumption of beef fell by approximately 20 percent during the same period. In Costa Rica during the same period total production of beef rose from 53.3 to 108 million pounds, yet the amount available for domestic consumption remained constant (34.8 million pounds), resulting in a reduction of nearly one third in beef consumption while exports climbed from 17.5 to 73.7 millions of pounds.[17]

Analyzing the impact of this large-scale shift to beef production, DeWalt found that large areas of forest in Honduras were being cut down to make room for cattle. From 1952 to 1974 the forested area in southern Honduras was reduced from approximately 74,000 to only 41,000 hectares, During the same period the land area in permanent crops actually declined. DeWalt comments that the "implications of the conversion of southern Honduras into a vast pasture for export-oriented cattle production . . . are the following: first in the long run fewer individuals will have access to land on which to produce their own subsistence crops. Employment opportunities in the local region will decline because livestock raising is less labor intensive than grain crop production. The permanent and temporary migration that these processes produce can only exacerbate the already explosive social, economic, and political situation that exists in Central America."[18]

These cases are intended to illustrate how world-wide delocalization of food production and distribution has created a complex web of interrelations, changes which place local food-producing populations in serious jeopardy, particularly if they are dependent for their livelihood on one or two principal cash crops. In the developing world, delocalization results in a loss of food resources and flexibility as productive agricultural land is put to use for cash crops in competition with land use for local food production, and national food systems become increasingly de-

---

17 Billie R. DeWalt, "The Cattle are Eating the Forest," unpub. ms. (1981).
18 *Ibid.*, 24–25.

pendent on the developed nations for shipments of grain and other basic foods.

DIETARY DIVERSITY, NUTRITIONAL STATUS, AND DELOCALIZATION
Good nutrition depends on adequate consumption of calories, protein, fats, vitamins and minerals. Whereas a sufficient intake of calories (and, to some extent, protein and fat) depends on quantity of food consumed, adequate consumption of other nutrients depends on the utilization of foods that are high in these substances. Because vitamins and minerals are differentially distributed in food, it is generally felt that more varied and diverse diets are more likely to be adequate from a nutritional perspective. A "mixed portfolio" also seems advisable on ecological grounds and may provide some protection from overexposure to mildly toxic components of foods.

When delocalization results in an expanded food supply and greater diversity of available foods, one would hypothesize that there should be an improvement in nutritional status, whereas a reduction in diversity, as well as in the quantity of available foods should be associated with a decline in nutritional status. In the industrialized world, it appears that there have generally been significant improvements in nutrition in the past century. There are several lines of evidence to support this statement. The major vitamin-deficiency diseases have now virtually disappeared in developed countries and, although mineral-deficiency diseases are still prevalent, they tend to be much less severely manifested than in developing countries. Except for anorexia nervosa, obesity rather than emaciation is the primary problem of caloric consumption.

Another indicator of improved nutrition is the secular growth trend that makes modern Europeans and North Americans seem like giants compared to the average size of people in the seventeenth and eighteenth centuries. In 1876 Charles Roberts, a doctor employed in a British factory, noted that "a factory child of the present day at the age of nine years weighs as much as one of ten years did in 1833 . . . each age has gained one year in forty." This comparison was possible because a large-scale program of measurements of children was carried out in 1833 to provide evidence for Parliament to consider the effects of child labor. "At that time, working boys aged ten years averaged 121 cm. in height compared with 140 cm. today; those aged eighteen years averaged 160 cm. compared with 175 cm. today." The recent trends in Japan from 1950 to 1970 show a nearly 3 cm. increase per decade among seven year olds, and a 5 cm. per decade increase in twelve year olds. Other factors, including improved sanitary conditions, have also played a part in these trends, but the role of nutrition seems clear.[19]

Although the secular trends in industrialized countries point to a general improvement in nutrition, it is important to note the complexities that are involved in the interpretation of data on height. The issues are ably discussed by Fogel and his colleagues, who point out the significance of "cycles of height" in the past two centuries in British and American populations. Fogel argues that these fluctuations reflect different levels of nutrition and this supports Tanner's and others' interpretation of the meaning of secular trends in height.[20]

Age at menarche is another measure frequently cited in connection with the overall improved nutrition levels of Europeans, North Americans, and other industrialized populations. Tanner has demonstrated that the average age at menarche for girls in Finland, Norway, and Sweden was between sixteen and seventeen years in the middle of the nineteenth century, from which there has been a progressive decline to the present day. Now, the averages hover around thirteen years.

Increased caloric and protein intakes throughout the nineteenth and twentieth centuries have had major impacts, but the increased diversity of available foods has also played a role. In Britain from 1950 to 1973 total fruit as a component of household consumption increased from 18 ounces to 25 ounces per week per person, while in the same period bread dropped from 56 ounces to 34 ounces. Diversification of protein resources was evident in the rise in poultry consumption.[21]

DELOCALIZATION AND FAMINE   One of the more obvious, yet infrequently noted, results of the delocalization of food products

19 J. M. Tanner, *Foetus into Man* (Cambridge, Mass., 1978), 150–151.
20 Robert W. Fogel et al., "Secular Changes in American and British Stature and Nutrition," in this issue.
21 Wardle, *Changing Food Habits*, 72.

in the industrialized world is the elimination, except during wartime, of disastrous famines. Food catastrophes, such as the Irish potato famine, or the less well-known famine between 1865 and 1867 in northeastern Europe, are no longer a threat in developed nations. Recent Soviet grain purchases and shipments of food to Poland show how modern commercial channels can redistribute food in times of serious regional shortages.

In most of the world the channels of food distribution can be expanded in response to regional shortages, although serious distribution problems still remain. Recent crises in Bangladesh, India, and parts of Africa demonstrate that in extreme situations appropriate foods cannot be transported and distributed effectively enough to the populations in need.[22]

McAlpin notes that population growth rates fluctuated widely in India well into the twentieth century because of the interrelated effects of periodic famine and disease. She points out that the development of an effective railroad network helped reduce the sharp impact of regional food shortages.[23]

Famines still occur in isolated parts of India, as they do in some other parts of Asia, but McAlpin's data indicate that "mortality from famines was not an important force in slowing India's population growth after 1921." Thus, the forces of delocalization—the spread of transportation systems and food distribution networks, plus governmental communications and food relief systems—have effectively eliminated most (but not all) of the impacts of regional crop failures and other disasters that in the past led to severe periodic famine conditions.

DEVELOPING NATIONS: SHORTAGES AND DISTORTIONS   Many of the changes that we have described for the industrialized nations have also affected parts of the Third World. The spread of diverse food resources by means of the New World-Old World exchange of cultigens and livestock has had a powerful impact on most of the world. Thus, potentially, the populations of Latin America, much of Asia, and many parts of Africa could have a greatly

22 For a discussion of entitlements, see Louise A. Tilly, "Food Entitlement, Famine, and Conflict," in this issue.
23 Michelle B. McAlpin, "Famines, Epidemics, and Population Growth: The Case of India," in this issue.

expanded diversity of foods. Despite that potential, the lack of economic purchasing power for all but a minority in the most affluent sectors means that the diets of the majority are restricted in quantity and quality.

Inequality of wealth is not the only factor that has contributed to the declines in quality and quantity of food in rural sectors of developing nations. Modern farming practices, including the widespread use of chemicals—pesticides and herbicides—may have unexpected, often unnoticed, side-effects on food use. For example, the widespread use of herbicides in the maize fields of Mexico has resulted in the elimination of a number of "weeds" that had been regular, vitamin-rich additions to the peasant diets.[24]

Global delocalization of food resources involves a number of major cost increases. A large part of the price of food items pays for the processing, packaging, advertising, and shipment of foods, as well as the profits of various entrepreneurs in the food chain. Poor people cannot afford to pay these added costs, and hence they are reduced to a narrower selection of the cheaper foods.

Although there continues to be some argument about "how to define" malnutrition, there is little disagreement that for sheer numbers, there are more millions of malnourished people in the world than ever before. The most telling and shocking statistic is the effect of malnutrition on child mortality. Berg estimates that in 1978 "malnutrition was a factor in the deaths of at least 10 million children."[25]

A discussion of all the complex factors involved in contemporary problems of malnutrition is beyond the scope of this article, but we suggest that the poorer populations in developing countries, especially in rural areas, have experienced declines in total caloric consumption (per capita) and in dietary diversity as traditional subsistence systems have been severely disrupted by the forces of modernization, especially delocalization.

Delocalization captures some of the main dimensions of change in food production and diet over the past 250 years. Historically,

24 Ellen Messer, "The Ecology of Vegetarian Diet in a Modernizing Mexican Community," in Thomas K. Fitzgerald (ed.), *Nutrition and Anthropology in Action* (Amsterdam, 1977), 117–124.
25 Berg, *Malnourished People: A Policy View* (Washington, D.C., 1981), 2.

the process appears to be unidirectional, as most regions of the world give up local autonomy to increased linkages with global food distribution networks. The example of Jamaica, however, is only one of many national policy attempts to counter delocalization through political encouragement of self-sufficiency. Although the process of delocalization is so complex as to appear to be outside the range of local political decision-making, it may not be an inevitable aspect of development.

In examining the relationship between delocalization and changes in nutrition and health status, we are not claiming that the process has been wholly positive in the industrialized countries and completely negative in the Third World. Increased obesity, problems of food sensitivities, and other, more subtle nutrition-related problems may well be related to delocalization of food patterns in the industrialized countries. At the same time, traditional food systems in developing countries are often far from ideal from a nutritional standpoint, and, in many circumstances, environmental factors severely constrain local food production.

There have been massive changes in local food systems over the past 250 years as the world community has become knit into a tightly inter-connected network of economic, social, and political relations. The effects on nutrition and dietary patterns have been powerful. World-wide food production capabilities have increased greatly. However, serious problems of maldistribution of food resources remain, and some problems are becoming worse, not better. Although a considerable proportion of the global community derives clear benefit from food delocalization, many rural and urban low-income communities are experiencing serious malnutrition.

Further analysis of delocalization of food may help to explicate historical conditions. At the same time, improved understanding of the relationship between delocalization and nutritional status may help to make nutrition planning and policy development more effective in the future.

Nevin S. Scrimshaw

The Value of Contemporary Food and Nutrition
Studies for Historians

The articles in this issue that have been written by historians provide stimulating reading for nutritionists because so much of the evidence for the effects of hunger and malnutrition in historical records are precisely reflected in contemporary differences among societies. Almost any historical pattern of interaction among food supply, food consumption, and the human condition can be identified and studied in some part of the world today, although not necessarily on the same scale or for the same duration. What this means, however, is that nutritional mechanisms and consequences that can be discerned only with great difficulty from the usually sparse and inadequate historical data can often be understood with reasonable certainty through access to detailed contemporary information and analysis. It is as if historians investigating the food and nutrition problems of the past and their consequences had been given a Rosetta stone that facilitated the interpretation of otherwise obscure written material.

Unfortunately for society, but conveniently for historians, the effects of famine, hunger, chronic energy deficiency, protein-calorie malnutrition, vitamin deficiencies, and mineral deficiencies have been meticulously described by the application of modern investigational techniques to living populations. The quantitative effects will depend on the specific situation, and their appraisal will be dependent on the limitations of historical data, but the qualitative effects of malnutrition on morbidity, mortality, work capacity and performance, cognitive ability and behavior, fertility,

Nevin S. Scrimshaw is Institute Professor at The Massachusetts Institute of Technology and Director of the United Nations University Sub-Program on Food, Nutrition, and Poverty. He is also Director of the MIT/Harvard International Food and Nutrition Planning Program. Of his many books the most recent, edited with Lincoln Chen, is *Diarrhea and Malnutrition: Interactions, Mechanisms, and Interventions* (New York, 1983).

and population dynamics are known to an extent not even suspected until relatively recently.

Modern historians thus have tools for the investigation and interpretation of nutritional effects in historical settings that have not been available to their predecessors. The results of their taking advantage of this opportunity should be rewarding. Issues that can only be dimly perceived in the light of the historical evidence alone can now be illuminated with the information available on analogous contemporary situations.

There are a number of topics worthy of special consideration by historians:

Interaction of Nutrition and Infection The profound effects of even subclinical malnutrition on morbidity and mortality from many of the common infectious diseases and, to a considerable extent, the mechanisms involved have been documented over the past two decades, and this information is a valuable tool for historians. The most significant analysis of the historical relationships among nutrition, mortality, and population growth has been made by McKeown, a pediatrician, whose views also appear in this volume. The extent to which infections, even those so mild that they are not manifest as clinical disease, adversely affect nutritional status is the other aspect of the interaction. Infections can precipitate clinical manifestations of deficiency of almost any nutrient that is already of borderline adequacy in the diet.[1]

Effects of Chronic Energy Deficiency In both the contemporary and historical world a considerable proportion of the population has consumed less dietary energy than would be the case

---

1 Scrimshaw, Carl E. Taylor, and John E. Gordon, *Interactions of Nutrition and Infection* (Geneva, 1968); Ranjit K. Chandra and Paul M. Newberne, *Nutrition, Immunity, and Infection: Mechanism of Interactions* (New York, 1977); Robert M. Suskind (ed.), *Malnutrition and the Immune Response* (New York, 1977); Lincoln Chen and Scrimshaw (eds.), *Diarrhea and Malnutrition: Interactions, Mechanisms, and Interventions* (New York, 1983); Thomas McKeown, *The Role of Medicine: Dream, Mirage, or Nemesis?* (Princeton, 1979); *idem,* "Food, Infection, and Population," in this volume; Scrimshaw, "Significance of the Interactions of Nutrition and Infection in Children," in Suskind (ed.), *Textbook of Pediatric Nutrition* (New York, 1981), 229–240; William R. Beisel, William D. Sawyer, Erich D. Ryll, and Dan Crozier, "Metabolic Effects of Intracellular Infections in Man," *Annals of Internal Medicine,* LXVII (1967), 744–779.

if it were to consume as much food as its estimated requirement, based on the intakes and activity levels of more privileged populations. Since metabolic adaptation to low energy intakes is limited, most of the necessary adaptation is a reduction in physical activity. The effect on the kinds of discretionary activities that are important for household improvement, community development, and social advance may be profound and, if sufficiently pronounced, may affect work output as well.[2]

Effects of Vitamin Deficiencies   The effects of various overt and subclinical vitamin deficiencies are now well documented, and their historical role can now be better deduced from fragmentary information about diets and clinical symptoms. Some of the vitamin deficiencies of historical importance, such as those of ascorbic acid (scurvy), niacin-tryptophan (pellagra), thiamine (beri-beri), and vitamin D deficiency (rickets), are no longer the major public health problems that they were only a few decades ago, but they were thoroughly studied in time to be well understood in modern clinical, metabolic, and epidemiological terms. In a quite different sense, much can also be learned from such volumes as Braddon's book on beri-beri and *Goldberger on Pellagra,* and from other studies carried out before it was known that these diseases were due to nutritional deficiencies.[3]

Mineral Deficiencies   The world-wide distribution of endemic goiter in the post-glacial world is well documented, and a good deal is known about the consequences of the chronic iodine deficiency that leads to this condition. There is increasing appreciation that iron deficiency anemia is widespread in human populations and that iron deficiency, even short of the severity nec-

---

2 George Beaton and Lance Taylor (eds.), "The Uses of Energy and Protein Requirement Estimates," in United Nations University, *Food and Nutrition Bulletin,* III (1981), 45–53.
3 Beaton and Earle W. McHenry (eds.), *Nutrition: A Comprehensive Treatise* (New York, 1964), II; Scrimshaw, "Nutritional Diseases," in James B. Wyngaarden and Lloyd H. Smith (eds.), *Cecil Textbook of Medicine* (Philadelphia, 1982; 16th ed.), 1354–1372. Historians will be interested in the review of the knowledge of beri-beri and hypovitaminosis A that took place at the Federation of American Societies for Experimental Biology Conference on Beri-Beri, Endemic Goiter, and Hypovitaminosis A. See *Proceedings,* XVII (1958), Pt. 2, 103–143. W. Leonard Braddon, *The Cause and Prevention of Beri-Beri* (London, 1907); Milton Terris (ed.), *Goldberger on Pellagra* (Baton Rouge, 1964).

essary to cause anemia, can have significant effects on physical capacity, cognitive performance, resistance to infection, and possibly even on adaptation to cold. Other mineral deficiencies are capable of producing clinical symptoms and more is constantly being learned about the role of trace minerals. However, there is no current basis for ascribing major population effects to them.[4]

Nutrition and Population Growth   The nutritional status of a population is a major factor and, as far as the global numbers of people in historical times is concerned, the major factor in the rate of change in population size. The effect on birth rate, although well documented in severe malnutrition and starvation, is quite secondary to the effects on mortality already emphasized.

Nutrition and Cognitive Behavior   The effects of iron deficiency on cognition have already been discussed. Even before these effects were known, extensive research provided evidence of the effects of chronic protein-energy deficiency in early childhood. Stunting is the best indication of the occurrence of malnutrition at the critical period when it can affect learning and behavior. There are many studies indicating that, when dietary factors limit the expression of genetic growth potential, performance on some behavioral tests is significantly affected by retardation in weight for age.[5]

Causes and Consequences of Famines   Famines are traditionally seen as the result of unforeseeable and uncontrollable vagaries of nature, but modern scholarship suggests that the cause is much

4 Conference on Beri-Beri; World Health Organization, *Endemic Goiter* (Geneva, 1960); John B. Stanbury and Basil S. Hetzel (eds.), *Endemic Goiter and Endemic Cretinism* (New York, 1980); Leif Hallberg and Scrimshaw (eds.), *Consequences of Iron Deficiency for Work Capacity and Performance,* forthcoming; Chandra and Newberne, *Nutrition, Immunity, and Infection*; Suskind (ed.) *Malnutrition and the Immune Response*; Ernesto Pollitt and Rudolf Leibel, *Iron Deficiency: Brain Biochemistry and Behavior* (New York, 1982). Chandra, "Iron, Immunity, and Infection: Is There a Causal Link?" in *Food and Nutrition Bulletin,* III (1981), 49–52. John Beard, Clement A. Finch, and Bruce Mackler, "Deleterious Effects of Iron Deficiency," in Alfred E. Harper and George K. Davis (eds.), *Nutrition in Health and Disease and International Development* (New York, 1981) 305–310.
5 Scrimshaw and John E. Gordon (eds.), *Malnutrition, Learning, and Behavior* (Cambridge, Mass., 1968); Josef Brozek (ed.), *Behavioral Effects of Energy and Protein Deficits* (Washington, D.C., 1979); Amartya Sen, "Famines," *World Development,* VIII (1980), 614–621.

more often social and political. Even the great Bengal famine in 1943 is now recognized to have been due to political decisions and not to an absolute shortage of food. With this perspective, examination of other famines, including the Irish famine so graphically portrayed in *The Great Hunger: Ireland 1945–1949*, indicates that food was readily available to those who could afford it. Even the frequent famines in various regional populations of Europe in past centuries were more the result of poverty and social inequity than an actual lack of available food. The consequences of brief periods of famine in otherwise well-nourished populations are minimal, but when superimposed on chronic undernutrition they can be devastating, as the Irish famine demonstrated. The demographic effects of famine must be viewed in this light rather than only on the basis of their acute biological effects.[6]

Interpretation of Clinical Symptoms in the Historical Record The same clinical signs and symptoms tend to be associated with many different types of nutrient deficiency. The older listings of the symptoms diagnostic of specific vitamin deficiencies cannot be relied upon except within a given epidemiological and dietary setting. Except in the less common circumstances of "classical" constellations of symptoms, modern diagnosis of nutritional deficiency relies on laboratory findings that are unavailable to historians. This situation is mentioned as a warning to historians not to make too much of the mention of isolated symptoms and as encouragement to them to examine the overall pattern of symptoms and multiple causes in populations for which these have been well described and verified by laboratory studies. If this approach is followed, historians will have more success in identifying the occurrence of malnutrition in past societies and in gauging its significance.

Non-Nutritional Food Factors   The adverse effects of food supply on human populations is by no means limited to the effects of nutritional deficiencies. Food contaminants and adulterants

6 *Ibid.*; Cecil Woodham-Smith, *The Great Hunger: Ireland 1945–49* (London, 1975); Zena Stein, Mervyn Susser, Gerhard Saenger, and Francis Marolla, *Famine and Human Development: The Dutch Hunger Winter of 1944/45* (New York, 1975).

have also played a significant role. For example, chronic lead poisoning from contaminated foods is well documented in eighteenth-century England and is suspected to have been a factor in the decline and fall of the Roman Empire because the use of lead vessels in wine-making and lead-lined cooking pots could have resulted in mental impairment of the aristocracy. Arsenic and other toxic adulterants have also long been used in foodstuffs. As another example, the heavy bacteriological contamination of the milk fed to young infants in nineteenth-century Europe is as well established as the role of contaminated weaning foods in the high infant mortality in many developing countries today.[7]

If, indeed, much that is obscure regarding the existence and effects of nutritional deficiencies in the past can be much better understood by knowledge of analogous contemporary situations, two conclusions can be drawn. One has already been emphasized: the need for historians to seek out contemporary nutrition literature relevant to their historical interests. The other is the potential value of collaboration between historians concerned with food and nutrition problems and those professional nutritionists who have a broad knowledge of the nature of malnutrition in contemporary populations. The publication of this issue should stimulate both these approaches.

7 George Baker, *An Essay Concerning the Cause of the Endemial Colic of Devonshire* (London, 1767); Jerome O. Nriagu, "Saturnine Gout Among Roman Aristocrats: Did Lead Poisoning Contribute to the Fall of the Empire?" *New England Journal of Medicine,* CCCVIII (1983), 660–663; Scrimshaw, "The Growing Child," in *Proceedings of the Borden Centennial Symposium on Nutrition* (New York, 1958), 27–37.